ArcView Market Research would like to make a few revisions to our 2013 and 2014 market estimates and projections. These changes are based on end-of-year survey data, business data and tax records. AMR bases its research on the best available data at the time and changes in regulations or public policy will result in changes to our projections.

For the latest updates and corrections to

The State of Legal Marijuana Markets – 2nd Edition

please visit: ArcViewMarketResearch.com/updates

ARCVIEW MARKET RESEARCH

The State of Legal Marijuana Markets

2nd Edition

Sponsors

NCIA

As the only national trade association for cannabis professionals, NCIA works to defend and advance the industry on the national stage. The mission of the National Cannabis Industry Association is to promote the growth of a responsible and legitimate cannabis industry and to work for a favorable social, economic and legal environment for that industry in the United States.

4Front

4Front provides a comprehensive model for opening world-class dispensaries by providing systems and support to clients, their staff and professional advisors. 4Front brings an unparalleled industry network, combined with a wealth of industry and professional experience to help you navigate the evolving medical cannabis landscape.

Cannasure

Cannasure specializes in providing insurance products and services to the legal cannabis industry. Cannasure was started with the singular purpose of helping the legal cannabis industry secure insurance products at a reasonable cost. Cannasure's management team includes some of the top insurance experts and cannabis industry experts to create the first insurance company by and for the cannabis industry.

Medicine Man Denver

Medicine Man Denver is the largest single dispensary in Colorado. We pride ourselves on extrodinary customer services and consistently offering our customers with marijuana products that are safe and high-quality at the best price in Colorado.

MJardin

MJardin is an integrated investment and management company focused exclusively on the cultivation and sale of premium cannabis, both as an investor in licensed cultivation and retail facilities and asa third-party professional operating company serving the emerging and rapidly expanding legal cannabis industry.

Sponsors

RODAWG™

Marijuana Policy Project
MPP
We Change Laws

Harborside
Health Center

GUARDIAN
DATA SYSTEMS

BioTrackTHC

DIXIE
ELIXIRS & EDIBLES

UPTOWN GROW
LAB

Credits

Publisher
The ArcView Group

Editor
Steve Berg

Lead Researcher
Kris Lotlikar

Layout Designer
Yoann Resmond

Project Manager
David Abernathy

Associate Researcher
Andrew Livingston

Technical Editor
Dave Wilton

Branding Consultant
Micah Daigle

Letter from the publisher

Dear Reader,

It is my pleasure to present to you the 2nd edition of the ArcView Market Research State of the Legal Marijuana Markets Report. By purchasing and reading this report, you can count yourself among a small group of people who really understand the most important, and often misunderstood, key actionable trends of this industry.

The ArcView Group acquired See Change Research earlier this year because we believe that well-researched market data and serious, nuanced analysis is vital for entrepreneurs and investors to navigate these fastest-growing emerging markets. As the market leader in researching and understanding the sale and distribution of cannabis, ArcView Market Research brings unparalleled expertise and insight to the task. Our 2011 market report set the industry standard and is still the most referenced resource on the size of legal marijuana markets.

As the leading national network of investors looking to capitalize on the legalization of marijuana, The ArcView Group believes the investment in high-level market data and analysis will pay dividends, not only for the investors and companies in our network, but also for the industry at large. By purchasing this report, you are not only gaining access to the thinking of some of the best business minds in the space, but you are also differentiating yourself in an industry where knowledge is power and a superior understanding of market dynamics can separate winners from losers.

On October 17, 2013, Gallup released a poll showing support for legalization at 58%, a ten-point jump in a year. This is just another sign that our industry is poised to explode, and our report shows marijuana markets will be growing faster than smart-phone markets. These are exciting times and new millionaires, and possibly billionaires, are about to be made while they simultaneously create a safer and freer society.

At ArcView, we believe that the development of a responsible, politically engaged, and profitable legal cannabis industry will hasten the day when not a single adult in the world is punished for this plant. I hope you use this report to take your business and our industry to the next level.

Regards,

Troy Dayton
CEO
The ArcView Group

THE ARCVIEW GROUP

Acknowledgments

By the Editor, Steve Berg

The State of Legal Marijuana Markets, 2nd Second Edition, represents substantial contributions from multiple parties who work on the front lines of the legal cannabis industry. Their first-hand knowledge of key industry dynamics, and willingness to share that information, was critical to the content and caliber of this report. Without their help, we could not have provided the most comprehensive and sophisticated research report on legal marijuana markets.

On behalf of ArcView Market Research, I would like to acknowledge and thank the following people in recognition of their vital contributions:

Marc Brandl, who provided the financing that made this report possible.

Steve DeAngelo, President of The ArcView Group, whose unparalleled knowledge, experience, and leadership in cannabis enterprise empowered him to literally define this industry more than any other individual has, including by the cofounding of The ArcView Group.

David Abernathy of The ArcView Group who had the herculean task of project managing this remarkable effort.

Kris Krane, 4Front Advisors, who is an industry sage who provides consultation to the new wave of business owners in new legal marijuana market states, and who has provided key insights about many facets of the markets.

Betty Aldworth and Aaron Smith of the National Cannabis Industry Association, who are collaborating with ArcView to pioneer the first-ever jobs-creation report in the legal marijuana markets.

Rob Kampia of the Marijuana Policy Project for his savant-like understanding of the political dynamics that drive the changing of laws and for sharing invaluable insights on when and how new legal marijuana laws are likely to pass throughout the country.

Gaynell Rogers for her public relations and media expertise and for helping to promote the report to a variety of media channels, including the Huffington Post, CNN, CNBC, and Fox News.

Yoann Resmond, our hero of a graphic designer who stepped in to create a superb layout and design of the report that meets our goal of creating the best looking and most professional report ever made for this industry.

Micah Daigle, for creating a great logo for the report.

Anne Holland and Chris Walsh of MMJ Business Daily, media trailblazers who provide industry participants with key information on business news (including both daily reports and the Marijuana Business Factbook), and with whom we are exchanging copy for our respective reports.

Mark Passerini, from the Om of Medicine in Michigan, who helped corroborate statistical and survey research data.

Gordon Katz, attorney, for his sage legal advice.

Jeff Dayton of The ArcView Group, for assisting with marketing the report and working with media.

Michael Blunk of The ArcView Group, for his industry insights and marketing the report.

Jessica Dugan of The ArcView Group, who is the backbone of business administration and tracking report sales.

Stacia Cosner, Students for Sensible Drug Policy, for finding great researchers who have a deep understanding of the legal marijuana industry.

Darrin Harris Frisby and Kim Sidwell for providing most of the photography for the report.

Alan Brochstein of 420 Investor and AB Analytical Services, for his review of public marijuana stocks and investment considerations.

P. Dave Wilton, proofreader and technical editor, for his copy editing expertise and grammatical consultations.

Jason Levin and Jessica Riley, of the Uptoke portable vaporizer company, for working the ArcView booth at the Marijuana Business Conference in November and for helping to sell the report.

Sam Chapman of the Marijuana Policy Report for his insights into the Oregon state market.

Matt Simon of the Marijuana Policy Report for his insights into the Vermont state market.

Becky DeKeuster from Wellness Connection of Maine for her insights into the Maine state market.

Keith Lambert of the Om of Medicine in Michigan, for his input on the Michigan state market.

Evan Nison, Jesse Peltz, Victoria Gates, Andrew Livingston of Vicente Sederberg, Amanda Muller of 4Front Advisors, and Scott Cecil of Students for Sensible Drug Policy, for their excellent research support

Rainier Copy & Print for the printing of the report's Executive Summary.

I'd also like to thank the following individuals for their willingness to be profiled as industry leaders in this report and for providing their insights, which informed a lot of the content.

Steve DeAngelo, The ArcView Group and Harborside Health Center

Tripp Keber, Dixie Elixirs & Edibles

Pat McManoman, Cannasure Insurance Services

Betty Yee, California Board of Equalization

Dan Williams, Canna Security America

Brendan Kennedy, Privateer Holdings

Jim Willett, Private Investor

Amy Poinsett, MJ Freeway

Jessica Billingsley, MJ Freeway

Kris Krane, 4Front Advisors

Aaron Smith, National Cannabis Industry Association

Dale Sky Jones, Oaksterdam University

Ralph Morgan, Organa Labs / O.penVape

Lance Ott, Guardian Data Systems

Khurshid Khoja, Greenbridge Corporate Counsel

Adam Cohen, Mjardin

This was truly a group effort that spanned months and represented an exceptional amount of work by an exceptional group of people aligned with a common goal. It has been a tremendous journey.

Disclaimers and Other Information

Marijuana is illegal under federal law. Under Federal Law, The Controlled Substances Act regulates, among other things, the cultivation, possession and distribution of certain controlled substances, including marijuana. This is true regardless of whether it is possessed for legitimate medical purposes, as provided for in certain state medical marijuana laws or if it is possessed within the few states that permit non-medicinal Adult Use. Marijuana is also illegal under the law of many states.

Determining how best to navigate this complex legal environment can be challenging. There is nothing in this report written to offer any legal advise or to suggest any actions or choices the reader may make regarding participation in this industry or in any of the businesses discussed.

This report is for information purposes only. It is not an offer to sell or the solicitation of an offer to buy any security or securities. It does not constitute an offer or solicitation with respect to the purchase of or sale of any investment. Further, it is not intended to form the basis of any investment decision and should not be considered a recommendation by The ArcView Group, Inc. ("ArcView") or any other person. Any material presented herein is intended as a basis for discussion. The sources of information relied upon by ArcView are believed to be reliable but ArcView makes no representation and gives no warranty that the information contained herein is accurate or complete.

Any opinions or estimates given may change. ArcView undertakes no obligation to provide recipients with any additional information or any update to or any correction of the information contained herein. ArcView, its owners, officers, employees, affiliates, and partners shall not be liable to any person in any way whatsoever for any losses, costs or claims howsoever arising from any information contained herein or any inaccuracies or omissions in the information contained herein or any reliance on that information.

Certain people involved in or related to the industry have been specifically profiled in this report. Any information in these pieces is based solely on information provided by the person profiled. Any opinions provided by the Profilee are solely the opinions of that person and do not reflect the opinions of ArcView. ArcView makes no representation and gives no warranty that the information or opinions contained in any of the pieces is or are accurate or complete.

Disclosures

ArcView is one of the most engaged companies in this market. It's actually hard to find many serious, credible, players in this small industry that do not already have some business relationship with ArcView or its principles. ArcView's knowledge of the industry borne out of having a bird's eye view of it via other core businesses, and ArcView's commitment to elevating the business conversation without neglecting the history and cultural roots of this movement/industry made it the ideal acquirers of See Change Strategy and perfectly situated to produce the most useful report about this exciting industry.

ArcView leadership does not have access to the raw data, only the aggregate data, that comes from the research. The interpretation of that data to come up with ArcView Market Research's market numbers is entirely the domain of our lead researcher, Kris Lotlikar -- who is unique in that he does not have business relationships with anybody in the cannabis industry, yet he has superior knowledge of it and how new expanding markets are evaluated in other industries.

Below is a list of everyone who is written about in the report who also has a business relationship with ArcView or Steve Berg's consultancy, Berg Risk Capital.

The following people/companies mentioned in this report are members of the ArcView Investor Network either as investors or companies.

Ralph Morgan - Organa Labs/O.penVape
Brendan Kennedy - Privateer Holdings
Khurshid Khoja - Greenbridge Corporate Council
Steve Berg - Berg Risk Capital
Adam Denmark Cohen - Mjardin
Kris Krane - 4Front Advisors
Jessica Billingsley - MJ Freeway
Amy Poinsett - MJ Freeway
Steve DeAngelo - Harborside Health Center
Tripp Keber - Dixie Elixirs
Dan Williams - Canna Security America
Jason Levin - Uptoke
Andy Williams - Medicine Man Denver
Jim Willet - private investor
Isaac Dietrich - Mass Roots
Patrick McManamon - Cannasure
Andy Joseph - Apeks Fabrication
Ross Kirsch - Quark Distribution

Also, Steve DeAngelo is the President of The ArcView Group and also serves on the board of the National Cannabis Industry Association, Emerald Growers Association and Steep Hill Labs. ArcView's CEO, Troy Dayton serves on the board of the Marijuana Policy Project and the National Cannabis Industry Association. ArcView is a part owner of Cannasure Insurance Services and Steve DeAngelo and Troy Dayton serve on the board. ArcView is a major advertiser with MJ Business Daily and Steve DeAngelo and Troy Dayton often speak at their events.

Report editor Steve Berg is a major shareholder of The ArcView Group and also runs his own business consultancy called Berg Risk Capital. Some of his clients at the time of writing include:

Canna Security America
Dixie Elixirs & Edibles
Organa Labs / O.penVape

David Abernathy, who is the production manager for the report is also a teacher at Oaksterdam University which is headed by Dale Sky Jones.

As you can see, the ArcView team is deeply engaged in this industry. We've learned a few things in the process. We hope you find these insights valuable.

TABLE OF CONTENTS

EXECUTIVE SUMMARY

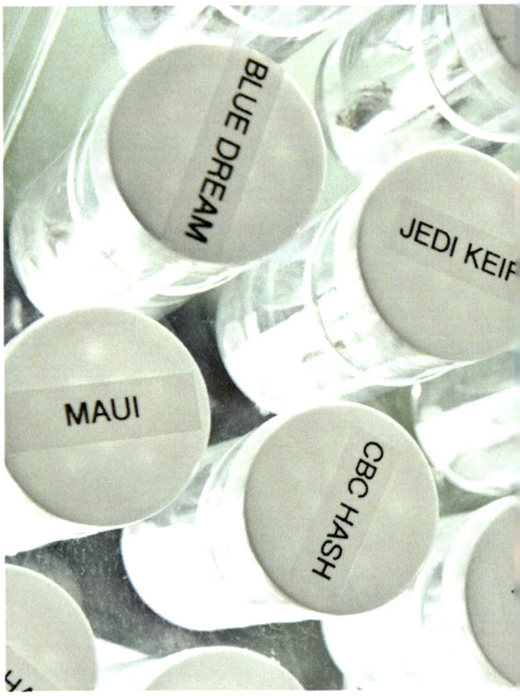

The state of legal marijuana markets is strong for many, yet daunting for others. The watershed implementation of full retail marijuana legalization for adults in Colorado and Washington State, coupled with the adoption of medical marijuana regulations by new states, are fueling industry growth. Yet, even as the broadening definition of legal marijuana expands the addressable market, enforcement actions that target dispensaries, cultivators, and regulators in some states have actually contracted the overall market since the last edition of this report was published in 2011. Phases of growth and retrenchment in legal marijuana markets have been more rule than exception.

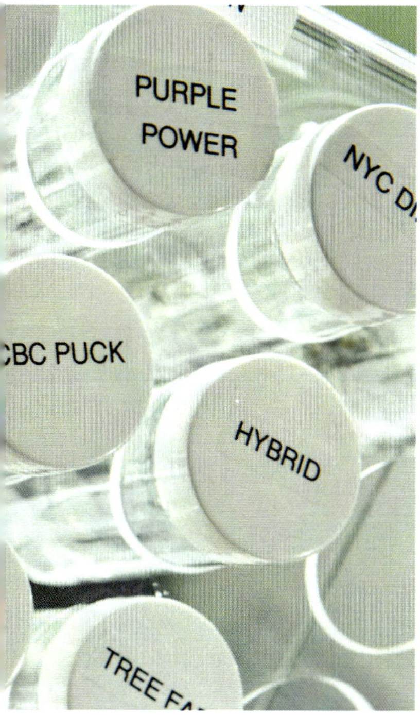

Beneath big news headlines, such as the US Justice Department indicating that it will respect Colorado's and Washington State's legalizations of adult retail sales, more subtle but powerful changes are transforming the legal marijuana industry. The crosscurrents of politics, regulatory shifts, advocate initiatives, entrepreneurship, investor activity, technology, and federal intervention create a complex landscape of economic microclimates representing both opportunity and risk.

ArcView Market Research has undertaken the most extensive industry examination to date. The full State of Legal Marijuana Markets report is available for purchase at LegalMarijuanaMarkets.com, and provides solid data points and analysis needed for a deep understanding of the quickly evolving legal marijuana industry. The goals are to remove the mystery of legal marijuana markets and to help investors and entrepreneurs navigate a growing yet uncertain terrain.

ARCVIEW MARKET RESEARCH

What Exactly Are Legal Marijuana Markets?

The markets are composed of individuals who legally consume marijuana as allowed by state laws, together with the businesses that constitute the supply chain to serve those consumers.

Presently, 20 states and the District of Columbia have some form of marijuana legalization. Not all of these states allow for the sale of cannabis. This report details those states that do in terms of market size, regulatory framework, and key dynamics.

Consumers:

In all legal marijuana states, the consumption of cannabis is permitted for patients who have obtained recommendations from medical physicians for qualifying medical conditions (referred to as "Medical Use" in this report). Colorado and Washington State additionally allow for all adults (21 years and older) to purchase and consume cannabis within certain limitations (referred to as "Adult Use"). Some also refer to Adult Use as "recreational" or "retail" marijuana.

Businesses:

Businesses serving Medical Use patients and Adult Use consumers include companies that directly handle legal marijuana, such as producers, processors, and distributors of cannabis. These businesses range from marijuana cultivators and processing operations, to medical dispensaries and retail store distributors.

Another category of businesses in the industry are companies that don't directly handle the plant, but cater to those who do, as well as to consumers. These "ancillary" businesses cover a wide range of companies in segments such as consumption devices, product packaging, information technology, production equipment, insurance services and many more.

Industry Transformation

The legal cannabis industry has seen transformative change since the first edition of this report in 2011. Massive shifts in the business environment have altered the industry landscape in expected and unexpected ways.

Groundswell Support for Full Legalization:

A substantial majority of Americans now think marijuana should be legal, according to a Gallup poll released in October 2013. Support surged to 58 percent in favor, a ten-point increase since 2012. This record level of support reflects accelerating momentum in favor of legalization, as further evidenced by the passage of new marijuana regulations in some states and by multiple law reform initiatives underway in others.

Dawn of Adult Use:

Full state legalization, in the form of both Medical Use and Adult Use state laws, has been an elusive goal of marijuana proponents for many years. Now, the landmark implementation of Adult Use regulations, whereby all adults 21 and older can legally purchase cannabis from licensed retailers in the states of Washington and Colorado, will become a reality in 2014 and will change the industry forever. Seven new states are likely to seek Adult Use regulations by 2017.

New Medical Use States Growth:

Six new states plus the District of Columbia have approved medical marijuana sales regulations including Massachusetts, Illinois, Connecticut, Vermont, Delaware and New Hampshire - thus bringing the total number of states permitting Medical Use to 20, in addition to Washington DC. ArcView Market Research predicts two more states – New York and Minnesota - will approve Medical Use laws by 2016.

Federal Enforcement Whiplash:

Contrary to federal indications of medical cannabis enforcement disengagement early in the Obama Administration, there have been sporadic, and occasionally severe, IRS and DEA crackdowns on some dispensary and cultivation operations. The most recent US Department of Justice memo on marijuana policy, however, signals deference to laws in states that enforce tight regulatory systems. Experts anticipate federal interference in state legal marijuana businesses to cease or decrease for the remainder of the Administration's tenure.

Cannabusiness 2.0:

Legal marijuana business practices are quickly professionalizing, adapting to new state regulations, and employing increasingly sophisticated business models and investor strategies to raise capital, increase scales, and access new markets.

Rise of Ancillary Business:

Whole industry sectors are rising around businesses engaged in the legal marijuana supply chain. Ranging from security to insurance, advertising to professional services, and ecommerce to horticulture products, the companies catering to the businesses that make and sell marijuana products are some of the most dynamic ventures in the industry.

Proliferation of concentrates:

Marijuana concentrates are the fastest growing category of cannabis products. Produced by manufacturing processes that condense marijuana cannabinoid content into concentrated forms, these products are meeting greater demand for alternatives to consuming cannabis by smoking the plant's flowers and leaves.

Key Findings

Having conducted a multidimensional study of markets, key trends, and industry dynamics in 2013, ArcView Market Research concludes the following:

The US national legal marijuana market value is now assessed at $1.43 billion, comprising all states that have active and open sales of cannabis to people legally allowed to possess it under state law. The national market is projected to grow 64 percent from current levels to $2.34 billion by 2014.

The five-year national market potential is $10.2 billion, which is more than a 700 percent increase above the current national market value. Gains will come in the form of increased demand in existing state markets, as well as from new state markets coming online within a five-year horizon.

Adult Use in Washington and Colorado is projected to add $208 million and $359 million to their respective markets in 2014. In addition to forecasting how these markets will grow in coming years, this report examines implementation dynamics of new regulations and how Adult Use sales will impact the Medical Use market segment.

ArcView Market Research predicts 14 states will adopt Adult Use regulations within five years. Those states are: Alaska, Oregon, Rhode Island, New Hampshire, Vermont, Maryland, Hawaii, Maine, Missouri, Massachusetts, Nevada, Arizona, California and Delaware.

California remains the largest state market at $980 million, even without Adult Use regulations. As detailed later in this report, once Adult Use is adopted—which is likely by 2017—the total California market is projected to increase dramatically and to secure an even more dominant portion of the national market.

Many new promising markets are opening around the country. Massachusetts, Illinois, Vermont, and Connecticut will open brand new markets and reach $61 million collectively in 2014 alone, with significant room for growth. Oregon and Nevada will move from loosely regulated markets to state licensed dispensaries and together hit $46 million in 2014.

The retail legal marijuana price has been under downward pressure from increased competition between retailers and from falling production costs as cultivators improve their processes and take advantage of economies of scale. Although prices vary greatly between state markets, Colorado has seen the retail price fall almost 30 percent in the last two years. A price rebound, however, could soon be in store for Colorado as Adult Use implementation in 2014 may greatly increases demand in excess of near-term supply growth.

Some dispensaries have come under fire, primarily in states without any formal statewide licensing provisions. Forfeiture letters sent by U.S. Attorneys to dispensary landlords have proven to be a powerful weapon against distribution operations. Since 2010, at least 150 dispensaries have been shut down in California alone because of federal enforcement actions. Approximately 70 percent of all Los Angeles dispensaries have recently been targeted for closure by popular vote. Attorney Khurshid Khoja of Greenbridge Corporate Counsel explains how to mitigate some of the critical enforcement risk exposures in the

Managing Business Legal Risk section of this report.

Ancillary company market sectors, which include companies that don't directly handle the cannabis plant or related byproducts but that serve those that do, is a fast growing area for investment. CEOs of leading ancillary companies, such as Amy Poinsett of inventory management and point-of-sale software company MJ Freeway, Pat McManamon of Insurance provider Cannasure Insurance Services, and others talk about opportunities in these key markets in the Ancillary Businesses section.

The precursors of true national cannabis companies have emerged in the form of multistate licensors and are leveraging strong branding and scalable business models. In the Multistate Expansion section of this report, Dixie Elixir's Tripp Keber describes how his infused products company is employing a national branding and licensing strategy. These companies will be prime candidates for acquisition or public listing, especially upon federal legalization.

ArcView co-founders Steve DeAngelo and Troy Dayton

Alternative ingestion methods that offer consumers cannabinoid delivery formats other than smoking are one of the fastest growing segments of the cannabis industry. Applications of nonsmoking technologies, such as vaporization, as well as infused products such as edible, oral mucosal, and capsule formats, are increasing. Beyond some consumer preferences for not smoking, popularization of these ingestion methods is also based on more precise cannabinoid dosage and effect delivery.

The rise in popularity of alternative ingestion methods is fueling a boom in cannabis oil extraction. Oil extracted from raw cannabis "trim" is often used in alternative ingestion method product formulations. It improves dosing calibration and benefits from the convenience of portability. As demand for oil increases, the price of trim will continue to trend higher and can be worth more per pound to cultivators than are the plant's flowers. Demand for oil extraction equipment is also accelerating. Organa Labs CEO Ralph Morgan speaks to the market expansion in extraction products in the Extraction Products section of this report and identifies where he sees key developments for the future.

Interest in Cannabidiol (CBD)–based products is soaring. CBD is a non-psychoactive compound found in the marijuana plant that has demonstrated significant medicinal benefits. Promising CBD research and beneficial patient experience has caused demand to rise sharply. CBD supplies are limited because of legal and technological constraints, which keep prices elevated. Some companies see an enormous opportunity in attempting to solve the CBD sourcing puzzle.

Vertical integration, whereby marijuana cultivation and distribution operations are tied together (a.k.a. "seed-to-sale") as pioneered by Colorado regulators, now shapes how some new marijuana state regulations are being cast. This trend makes the cannabis industry unlike almost any other industry, and it has large impacts on what makes a successful cannabis business in those states. Obtaining maximum efficiency gains through production and distribution integration will be increasingly vital to the success of licensed marijuana businesses in those states.

The international legal marijuana market is expanding. Uruguay, Canada and Israel are leading the way, and a number of countries in Europe and Central and South America are not far behind. Opportunities are on the rise outside of the United States for experienced US consultants and ancillary companies. Because US scientific research remains constrained, much of the most advanced pharmacological research in cannabinoid science is being conducted abroad.

PROJECTED GROWTH

In Millions $

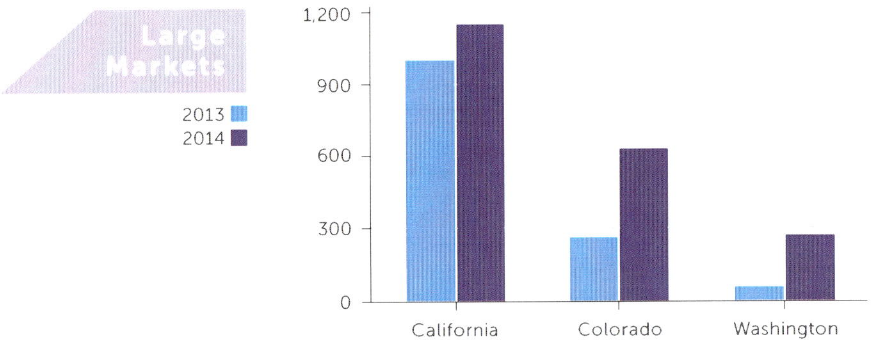

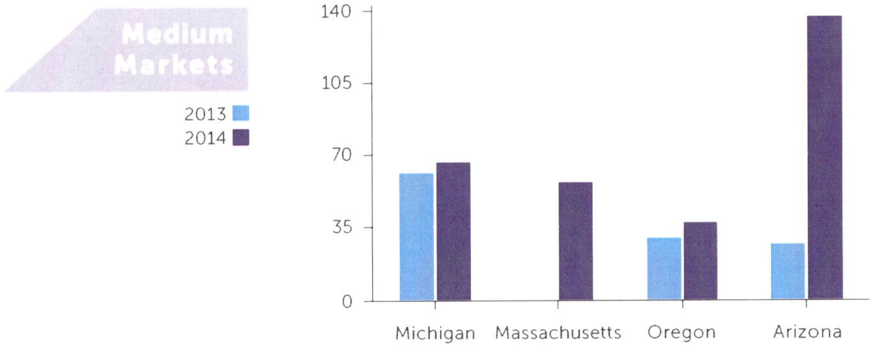

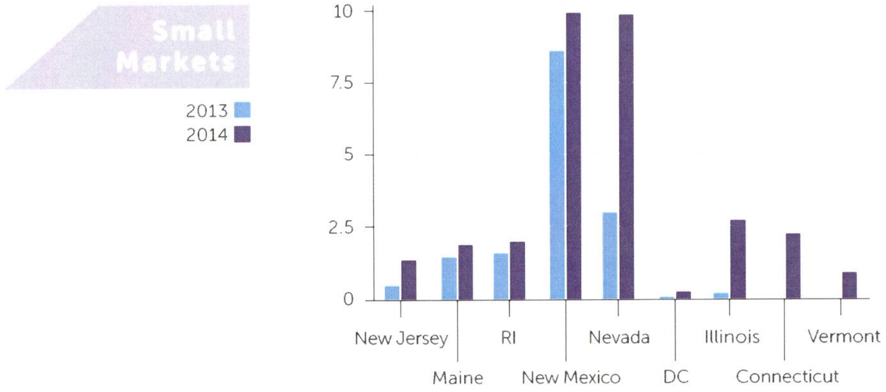

ArcView Investor Network Meeting, NYC June 2013

Ross Kirsh of Quark Distribution pitches investors on his cannabis packaging company

Framework

The context for the ArcView Market Research State of the Legal Marijuana Markets report is framed by the regulatory environment governing the legal state markets.

ArcView Market Research is focused primarily on the US legal marijuana markets, which are defined in this report as those states that have allowed some form of cultivation, processing, sale and consumption of cannabis. Marijuana remains illegal according to federal law, so the phrase "legal marijuana" is a relative term. In spite of federal prohibition, businesses are paying taxes, raising capital, being licensed by state governments, and hiring employees. In addition to Washington DC, 20 states have passed bills that have legalized medical marijuana to some degree, most recently New Hampshire and Illinois.

Most of these states have enacted or will enact regulatory systems that govern the cannabis supply chain to allow for the legal purchase of marijuana by Medical Use patients, and in some cases, by Adult Use consumers. Since California became the first state to adopt medical marijuana laws in 1996, the rate of new states adopting cannabis laws has accelerated: Seven new legal medical marijuana states and DC have come online since 2010.

The first states to approve cannabis laws tended to be market-led, meaning entrepreneurs began operating businesses prior to the adoption of state regulations in response to market conditions. More recent states have been regulation-led, with regulators working to define and control the legal framework prior to businesses setting up shop.

Another distinction of regulation-led states is how policies are modeled. Regulators in newer legal marijuana states have learned from the policy successes and failures of states that have preceded them. California, for example, was the first state to adopt medical marijuana regulations, but to this day has failed to establish a common statewide regulatory agency or a comprehensive set of rules. The resulting patchwork of city and county policies lacks uniformity and strong

Blazing a trail
isn't easy.
But you don't
have to go at
it alone.

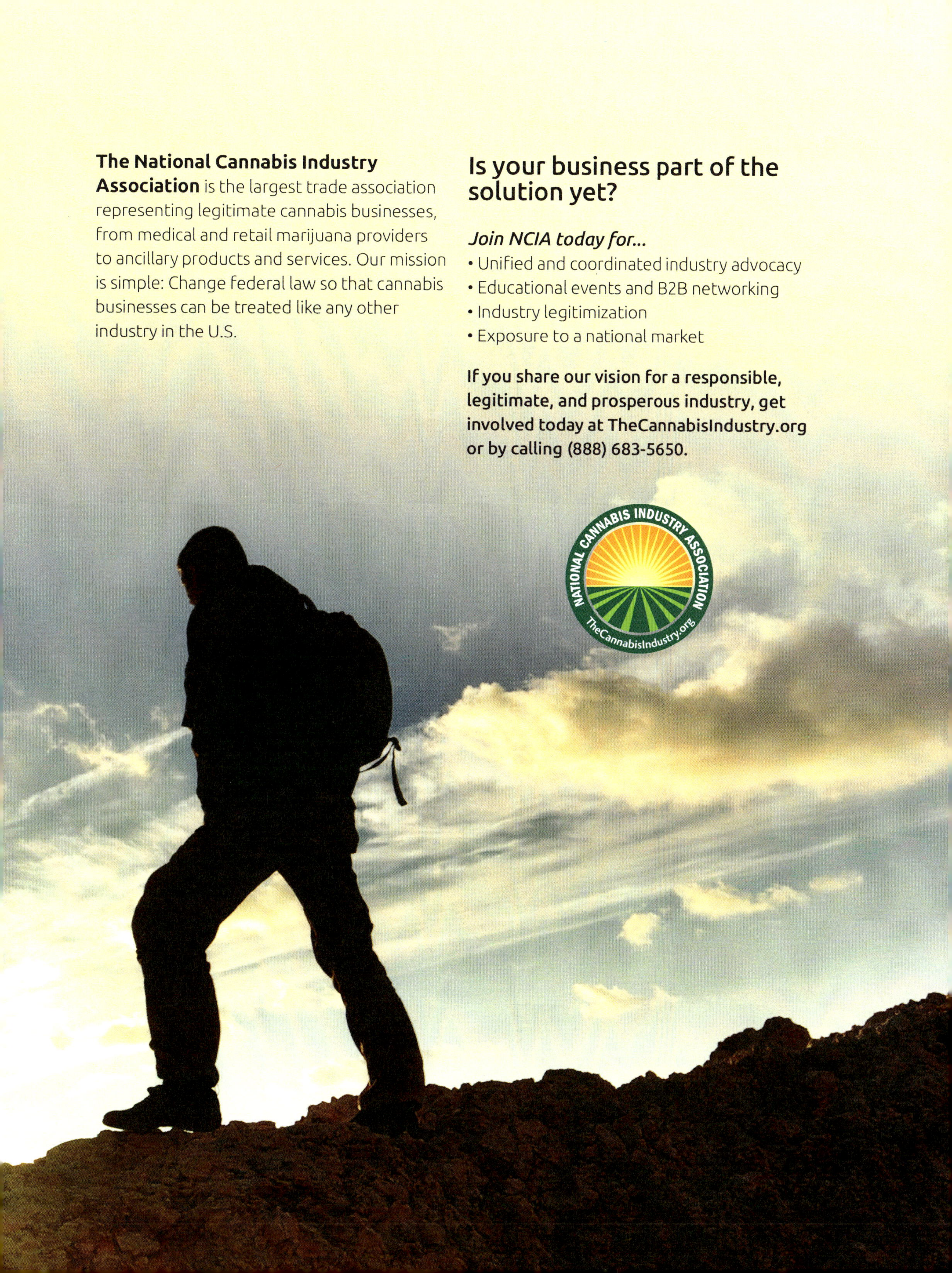
The National Cannabis Industry Association is the largest trade association representing legitimate cannabis businesses, from medical and retail marijuana providers to ancillary products and services. Our mission is simple: Change federal law so that cannabis businesses can be treated like any other industry in the U.S.
Is your business part of the solution yet?
Join NCIA today for...
• Unified and coordinated industry advocacy
• Educational events and B2B networking
• Industry legitimization
• Exposure to a national market
If you share our vision for a responsible, legitimate, and prosperous industry, get involved today at TheCannabisIndustry.org or by calling (888) 683-5650.
NATIONAL CANNABIS INDUSTRY ASSOCIATION
TheCannabisIndustry.org

O.penVape afterparty at The Four Seasons Denver after an ArcView Investor Network Meeting

controls. Colorado, in contrast, has tightly controlled regulatory oversight by the Department of Revenue's Marijuana Enforcement Division. Policy makers in newer states have modeled aspects of their regulatory framework after Colorado's system, which includes statewide licensing of legal marijuana businesses.

Some of the motivation for state regulation is to reduce or eliminate the illicit market for marijuana, for which there are neither safety standards nor opportunities for tax revenue generation. ArcView Market Research estimates that around $500 million was shifted back to the illicit market from legal channels following federal enforcement actions against certain operators in legal marijuana states in 2011 and 2012. In spite of the growing number of states permitting the sale of legal cannabis, the US illicit market for marijuana is estimated to be $18 to $30 billion, which far exceeds the legal market, now seen at $1.43 billion.

Opportunities and Risks:

Opportunities for investors and businesses are accelerating as more state medical markets come online, the scope of legal consumption increases to include Adult Use, and technological advances give rise to new products and services. ArcView Market Research expects two new states to implement

medical cannabis regulations within five years, and foresees at least fourteen states also adopting Adult Use laws over the same timeframe.

The fastest opportunity for profitability in some states centers on wholesale cultivation, whereas in other states vertically integrated cultivation and dispensary operations take the lead. However, these businesses often have the most restrictions on investors and carry the greatest risk of federal enforcement actions. Ancillary businesses, which are at least once removed from the cannabis plant, carry less criminal risk, but have longer ROI horizons, and some are still exposed to the risk of customer attrition resulting from enforcement actions.

In addition to federal enforcement risk, businesses in the cannabis industry also face a host of other specialized risks and challenges, including pushback from local politicians, lack of access to banking services, constrained capital -raising channels, tax accounting restrictions, and competition with the illicit market. Businesses also face greater competition within the legal market as more participants are attracted to the industry.

Risks and opportunities of these market sectors and the individual states are analyzed in the pages that follow.

METHODOLOGY

State of the Legal Marijuana Markets 2nd Edition was written based on original research, reporting and analysis by ArcView Market Research (AMR) to provide market data and financial analysis of the U.S. medical marijuana markets and the new Adult Use marijuana markets in the states of Colorado and Washington.

This analysis estimates the size of marijuana markets, market growth and market saturation in the U.S. based upon publicly available data, expert interviews and surveys of market participants. Estimating market size in marijuana markets is difficult, however, due to the nascent stages of market development, lack of publicly available data and confidentiality of individual business owners' data. In most states, tax and sales records of marijuana markets are not recorded separately or not reported.

In order to acquire the most current information on the performance of existing marijuana markets, AMR conducted an industry-wide survey of active market participants from June 2013 to October 2013. This survey focused largely on medical marijuana dispensaries in key states, but also included ancillary business operators and independent cultivators.

AMR identified medical marijuana dispensaries in states with medical marijuana regulations based on public and proprietary listings. A survey and informational packet was sent to these companies and AMR followed up with voice verification of operational status and interviews with business owners/proprietors.

Over the course of the research, more than 2000 surveys were sent out both electronically and through U.S. mail and AMR Research collected 322 complete and partial responses. The survey results provided data regarding the number of operational dispensaries in each state, average customer numbers, purchase size, price points and volumes for each state. AMR used this data to model preliminary estimates of market size in each state.

While AMR attempted to complete as many participant interviews as possible, data acquired through participant interviews may or may not be representative of the full universe of operational dispensaries in each state. To overcome data limitations and further inform its market size estimates, AMR compiled relevant information from state agencies, nonprofit organizations and private companies in the marijuana industry. AMR entered into agreements with multiple businesses in the marijuana markets in order to acquire financial and operational data to inform assumptions on volume, sales, prices, cost structures and investment activity. AMR used this data to adjust its estimates of market size in each state, as it deemed necessary.

AMR's estimate of the size of marijuana markets also includes wholesale sales. Estimates of wholesale sales were developed using wholesale pricing and gross margin data. This data was supplied by survey participants and individual companies under confidentiality agreements. Wholesale sales are largely affected by specific provisions in state marijuana regulations. For example, Colorado requires that retailers grow 70% of the product they sell at their dispensaries. Such provisions reduce wholesale market activity. AMR adjusted the wholesale market sizes to reflect the role that wholesale markets play in each state.

The analysis also provides a market projection (AMR's best estimate of the size of the marijuana market in 2014 based upon growth in existing and new markets) and an estimate of market potential (AMR's best estimate of maximum potential market size if new states pass medical or Adult Use marijuana regulations in the future).

In estimating the market size for 2014 in existing and new medical marijuana markets, AMR analyzed the relationships between policy implementation, patient access and market performance. AMR considered the potential customer populations (percentage of general population with a qualifying condition) in these states and also potential saturation rates (percentage of this population that would in fact use legal cannabis). Much of the data used in the estimates of market projections and potential market size was produced by extrapolating the best available epidemiological data. Extrapolated data carries certain limitations and potentially large margins of error. Some of the extrapolated data for this report utilized national incidence and prevalence rates adjusted for statewide population figures.

AMR created individual models for each state based on its 2013 market size or comparable market. These models were informed by data collected through AMR's 2013 surveys, proprietary data collected by AMR in 2011 and historic data from government sources. In each state, AMR conducted a detailed analysis of policy implementation and adjusted retail activity and consumer adoption based on the regulatory hurdles and implementation timelines. In many new markets, retails sales are assumed to only be occurring for a fraction of the year.

To project Adult Use of marijuana sales in 2014, AMR took into account three drivers of demand: current illicit market use that may transition to the legal Adult Use market, new adult users who were not illicit market consumers and out-of-state consumers (tourist demand). After aggregating the total potential demand in the Adult Use market, AMR adjusted the total by subtracting the demand being met by the existing medical markets. Not all illicit demand will move to the legal Adult Use market in year one. AMR's model makes adjustments to factor in increased taxes' effect on price (without including the tax in the final market number), operational limitation on meeting demand, geographical constraints driven by local ordinances and regulatory limits on implementation. While it is difficult to accurately estimate each of these demand drivers because of severe data limitations, AMR believes that our working knowledge of the existing marijuana markets and access to proprietary business intelligence positions us to provide the most accurate estimate available.

AMR's estimate of potential market size assumes the passage of medical marijuana and Adult Use policy in additional states through legislation and ballot initiatives. AMR consulted with the best and most experienced political and policy experts and utilized the latest polling data. AMR assumes only two additional states will establish medical marijuana markets, New York in 2014 and Minnesota in 2015. AMR assumes 14 more states will legalize Adult Use. In 2014, AMR assumes that Alaska and Oregon will legalize Adult Use. In 2015, AMR assumes that Rhode Island, New Hampshire and Vermont will follow suit. AMR's model assumes that Maryland, Hawaii, Maine, Missouri, Massachusetts, Nevada, Arizona and California will legalize in 2016, followed by Delaware in 2017. As described above, AMR then considered the potential impacts of policy implementation on the universe of potential customers. Based on our detailed models of existing Adult Use markets, AMR derived market potential estimates for 2018 based on the maturity of the markets and size of the states. Finally, saturation rate estimates and assumptions regarding retail sales were applied to estimate a potential market size.

sparkling peach
T H C
INFUSED
40
MG
E L I X I R S
ELIXIRS
E L I X I R S
E L I X I R S
MANDARIN
E L I X I R S

THE INTERSECTION OF ADVOCACY & ENTREPRENEURSHIP

Legal marijuana markets are forged from the intersection of advocacy and entrepreneurship. Understanding these twin dynamics is essential to gauging market growth and opportunity prospects.

As unique drivers of this industry, advocacy and entrepreneurship spur the political and economic forces which create legal marijuana markets. These markets exist in the U.S. as a result of the repeal of cannabis prohibitions at the state level coupled with the creation of businesses that comprise the supply chain to serve consumers. Federal marijuana prohibition was in large measure a political agenda enacted via an economic policy in the form of the Marijuana Tax Act of 1937. More than five decades later, undoing prohibition at the state level and facilitating consumer access required both political and entrepreneurial initiatives.

Enter the marijuana advocate/entrepreneur. Some of the most notable early champions of the marijuana rights movement recognized the need to concurrently change laws and establish the supply chain for consumer access. Civil rights activist Dennis Peron fought for marijuana law reform via authorship of initiatives including Proposition 215, the passage of which in

1996 made California the first Medical Use state. He also opened the first cannabis buyers clubs in San Francisco even in the absence of clear regulatory guidelines (and at considerable personal risk), thereby establishing the first collectives-based dispensary model.

Today, advocates and entrepreneurs combine in many forms to both expand legal marijuana markets and augment the business environment for companies in the industry.

Donors from across all levels of social strata contribute to policy reform organizations such as the Marijuana Policy Project and the Drug Policy Alliance. These groups are instrumental in creating reformed marijuana laws in an increasing number of states where businesses can operate. The National Cannabis Industry Association is the industry's first trade association, and works on multiple fronts to advance legal marijuana business interests (see Aaron Smith profile in the National Market section). Locally, business owners often engage political communities and help organize participation in marijuana advocacy.

INDUSTRY LEADER PROFILES

Steve DeAngelo / Harborside Health Center

Considering his four decade career, Steve DeAngelo might be described as the embodiment of marijuana advocacy and entrepreneurship. His early work as an antiwar protestor evolved to organizing and fund raising for marijuana law reform initiatives. As he emerged as a business leader, his entrepreneurial work resulted in the creation of several of the legal cannabis industry's preeminent companies, including the first model professional dispensary (Harborside Health Center), the first commercial cannabis testing laboratory (Steep Hill Laboratory), and the first investment company focused exclusively on the cannabis industry (The ArcView Group).

As DeAngelo puts it: "Cannabis entrepreneurship has been an essential part of my activism since my earliest days as a young Yippie in the mid-1970s". Funding his activism work through marijuana distribution freed him from dependence on big donors. This independence allowed him to chart his own strategies, which he considers key to his success.

In the early 1990s, DeAngelo mobilized networks to launch activist and business projects, including Hempilation I and II, which were releases of cannabis-related CDs under the Capricorn Records label. The proceeds raised several hundred thousand dollars in vital funding for the nonprofit National Organization for the Reform of Marijuana Laws. He also launched Ecolution, Inc., in the 1990s, a leading hemp company that produced over 100 products distributed through stores in 21 different countries (and by extension taught the benefits of the cannabis plant). In the 2000s, he continued to build businesses, including co-founding the Harborside dispensaries (where he serves as Executive Director) and Steep Hill Laboratory, the first cannabis testing lab, which sparked a whole new industry segment composed of laboratory testing services companies. He also co-founded and is President of The ArcView Group, which operates an investor network that matches investors with cannabis entrepreneurs seeking capital.

DeAngelo describes Harborside dispensary operations in Northern California as "an almost seamless integration of business and activism." In establishing Harborside, he sought to build an exemplar of responsible cannabis distribution, bringing benefits to the community at a time when some dispensary operators were going in a different direction. He saw the image of medical cannabis moving from one of compassion to one of exploitation. Operating under a weak California regulatory structure, certain dispensary operators were clearly playing fast and loose with medical marijuana laws. In some cases, they were releasing rap videos featuring piles of cash, "half-naked babes," and generally not promoting a positive image of cannabis distribution. Harborside, in contrast, has been recognized by local and state regulators as a model dispensary and community business.

Building what DeAngelo characterizes as a best practices distribution model has led to great commercial success. Harborside's two dispensaries together have over 125,000 patients and generated more than $32 million in sales in 2012. This success and community support has proven to be its best defense against federal enforcement actions targeting the dispensary. In addition to a $2.4 million lawsuit by the IRS, the U.S. Department of Justice brought forfeiture proceedings against Harborside's landlord in 2012. The dispensary has successfully pursued law suits against both federal agencies, and garnered support from many quarters, including local elected officials and a counter-suit against the DOJ by the City of Oakland. According to DeAngelo,"the activist stance of Harborside has been the single most important factor to our survival, and helped advance the movement simultaneously."

Does marijuana advocacy ever impede legal markets development? Yes, in DeAngelo's view. As an example, he cites some activists' support of not-for-profit requirements for cannabis distribution in many Medical Use states. Activists supported these provisions in the belief they were protecting patients. "What they failed to realize," he said, "is that without the ability to take in investment capital, dispensaries and growers have been largely unable to create truly professional operations, which led to poor service, low quality, and substandard facilities."

On the topic of federal legalization, DeAngelo views this as happening in increments, not instantaneously. He sees key early steps as the codification of the Obama Administration's position of not targeting state regulated cannabis distribution, as well as tax equity for licensed cannabis businesses on par with other legal businesses. Longer term steps will include rescheduling or descheduling cannabis from the Controlled Substances Act, allowing for interstate commerce, and insuring all states enact reform. He cautions, however, that history rarely moves in a straight line, and overcoming deeply rooted superstitions will take time.

In terms of the outlook for advocacy and entrepreneurship, DeAngelo is optimistic. He sees the development and growth of the legal cannabis industry as having changed the face of advocacy, and he expects business influence to further increase. As board member of the National Cannabis Industry Association and the Emerald Growers Association cannabis industry groups, he points to how involvement of entrepreneurs and businesses are expanding the scope of marijuana advocacy to include commercial interests. He views these organizations, along with The ArcView Group, as having become both the focus and source of media coverage that challenges and dissipates prevailing negative stereotypes. These groups have brought a new set of high net worth donors to advocacy organizations such as Students for Sensible Drug Policy, Marijuana Policy Project and Law Enforcement Against Prohibition. These donations in turn have enabled the advocacy organizations to pass more laws, which create more opportunities for entrepreneurs and legal marijuana businesses.

DeAngelo believes that "a fortuitous cycle of mutually reinforcing success has been created; and that cycle will power a mighty engine of change—an engine of change that will not stop until every marijuana market on the planet has been opened." He adds that advocates will remain dedicated to reforming cannabis laws until "the very last prisoner walks out of the very last cell and nobody ever goes to prison for cannabis again." It's worth noting that over 750,000 people were arrested for marijuana in 2011, according to the FBI.

What's next for DeAngelo's business endeavors? Opportunities for leveraging the Harborside brand are increasing as new state markets open. Having withstood federal attempts to immediately close Harborside dispensaries, DeAngelo has moved from defense to offense. He is actively pursuing licenses in several states with strong legal systems for cannabis distribution. "In five years," he says, "I expect Harborside to be a well-established national brand, poised for international expansion in countries that adopt legal cannabis regulations."

Past is prologue. DeAngelo's vision for a multinational Harborside cannabis company, like the domestic counterpart, would again be created from the intersection of advocacy and entrepreneurship.

NATIONAL MARKET

Overview

Although the growth outlook is strong, the national legal marijuana market has suffered a period of contraction since 2011. Federal and state enforcement actions against some cultivators and dispensaries reduced the market size by nearly 16% (i.e., $268 million) over the past two years. With federal intervention appearing likely to diminish, and the impending activation of new state markets, a significant national market turnaround is now underway.

The original State of Legal Medical Marijuana Markets report projected the market to be $1.7 billion in 2011. The report was published in March of that year and came right before a significant shift in federal enforcement policy. Not only did U.S. Attorneys pursue more aggressive enforcement against dispensaries in California, Colorado, Washington and Michigan, but such action also raised the possibility of prosecution in other states with medical marijuana laws. This aggressive enforcement caused projections for some states, such as Rhode Island, Arizona and New Jersey, to be pushed back. Additionally, as a result of the policy shift and local reactions, Montana's legal market was almost completely shut down. These changes resulted in a downward revision of the 2011 market size estimate from $1.7 billion to $1.25 billion. All ArcView Market Research market estimates and projections are based on the current policy and outlook at the time of publication. Since these markets are shaped by regulations and enforcement, a change to either can significantly shift the numbers.

ArcView Market Research currently assesses the 2013 US national legal market to be valued at $1.43 billion. The projected national value for 2014 is $2.34 billion, an annual increase of 64%. This increase represents the fastest growth rate of any US industry ArcView Market Research could find. Primary growth drivers include new Adult Use markets in Colorado and Washington State, as well as the addition of four new Medical Use state markets coming online (Massachusetts, Illinois, Connecticut, and Vermont—collectively projected to add $61 million in market value in 2014).

On a five-year horizon, ArcView Market Research sees the national annual market value potential at $10.2 billion by 2018. This long-term outlook assumes the following key growth factors:

- 14 new state Adult Use markets
- Two new state Medical Use markets
- Organic growth in current legal marijuana states as a result of growing populations
- Continued migration of illicit market purchases to legal market purchases

The national market value figures reflect the aggregate value of all states with active legal marijuana markets, current and projected. Market values comprise all legal wholesale and retail commercial purchases (see Methodology), and do not include the value of medical marijuana transfers from caregiver to patients, nor home personal use cultivation.

Annual Retail Sales by Industry

US Beer (2012)	$246 billion[1]
US Wine (2012)	$34.6 billion[2]
Vodka (2012)	$5.5 billion[3]
Legal MJ (2013)	$1.43 billion
E-Cigarettes (2012)	$500 million[4]

The national legal marijuana market is comparatively small, compared with the markets for beer, wine, and vodka. However, at a projected 64% annual growth rate, legal marijuana is growing over 30 times more quickly than the mature beer market, which domestically is increasing at around two percent. Some estimates of the illicit marijuana markets have been in the $18 billion to $30 billion range. In terms of the value of national legalization of marijuana, Bloomberg Industries estimates the US market potential at $35 billion to $45 billion, which would eclipse the US market for wine.

1. http://www.beerinstitute.org/assets/uploads/BeerInstitute_AnnualReport2012-2013_FinalWeb1.pdf
2. Includes table, sparkling, and dessert. This source has historical data from 1993 - http://www.wineinstitute.org/resources/statistics/article697
3. http://www.marketwatch.com/story/us-vodka-revenue-stream-continues-surging-2013-10-07
4. (projected to more than double in 2013) -http://www.statisticbrain.com/electronic-cigarette-statistics/
http://www.forbes.com/sites/marijkevroomendurning/2013/08/06/what-are-electronic-cigarettes-and-do-they-actually-work/2/

Current National Market

More than one in three Americans live in a state that has legalized some form of marijuana consumption. In addition to Washington DC, there are presently 20 states with legal marijuana regulations. Not all of the states, however, have active markets, which ArcView Market Research defines as those state markets in which marijuana can be legally purchased at a storefront location (i.e., Medical Use dispensary or Adult Use retailer). ArcView Market Research finds that more than 590,000 consumers legally purchased cannabis from a storefront in 2013. As part of our market estimates, ArcView Market Research also does not count grow-your-own consumers or consumers who purchase from caregivers.

Active markets presently include 11 states and DC, and this number will expand by another four states in 2014. To illustrate the difference between active and inactive legal state markets, consider Colorado and Hawaii. Colorado, with its hundreds of licensed dispensaries, represents an active market with many thousands of market transactions occurring annually. Hawaii, in contrast, has medical marijuana laws that don't allow for dispensaries, and is therefore not considered to be an active market. A Medical Use patient in Hawaii may be able to grow marijuana for personal use or may receive it from a caregiver, but those sources are not viewed as active legal market transactions.

The following map shows which of the legal state markets represent active and inactive markets (as of December 2013):

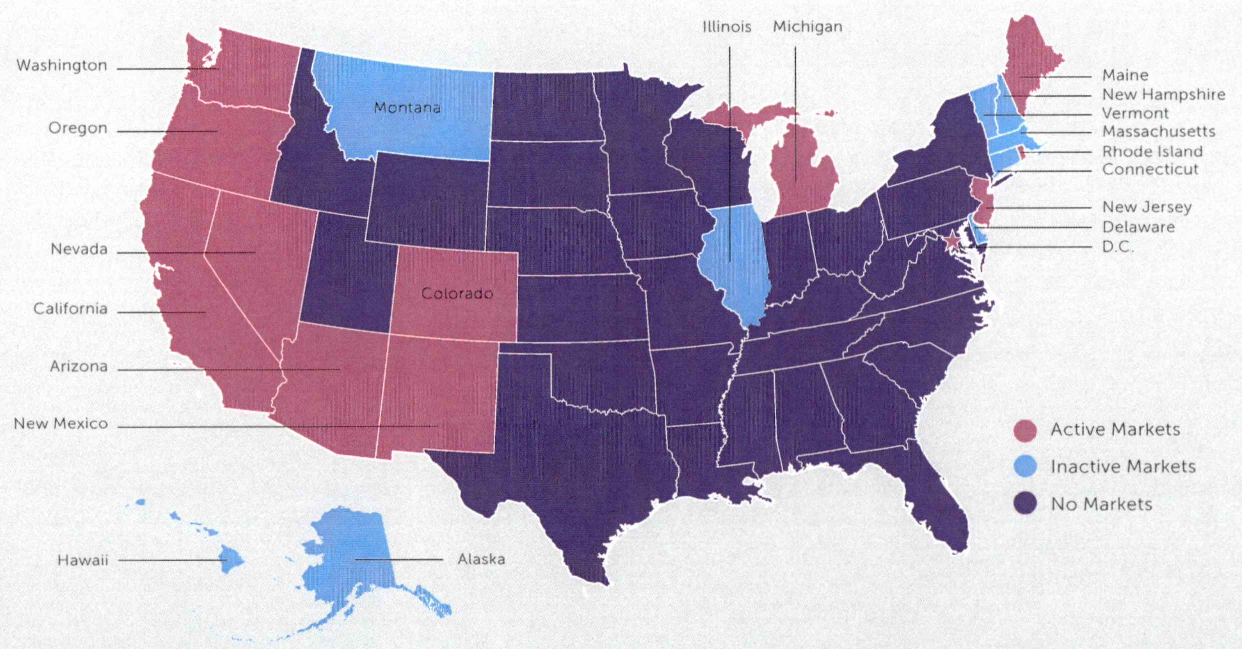

More than 590,000 consumers legally purchased cannabis from a storefront in 2013

While the majority of states do not have Medical Use or Adult Use laws, the rate of new states adopting those laws is accelerating: seven states and DC have adopted Medical Use regulations since 2010 (New Jersey, Massachusetts, Illinois, Delaware, New Hampshire, Arizona, and Connecticut), and two have adopted Adult Use (Colorado and Washington). For most marijuana companies catering to the industry, these are insular markets, given prohibitions on interstate commerce. However, ancillary companies, which do not handle the plant, usually serve customers throughout the country. Some companies have also been able to access multiple states through licensing agreements (see Multistate Expansion section).

As defined earlier in this report, all legal marijuana states have Medical Use laws, and two also have Adult Use laws.

The following map identifies the distribution of these states:

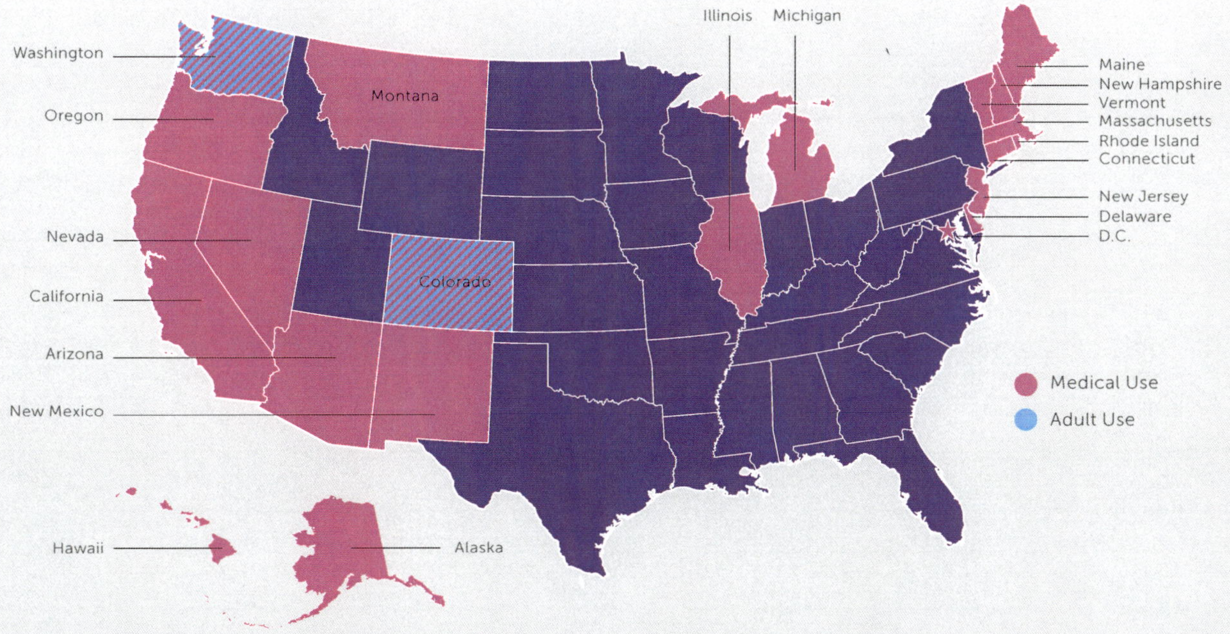

Potential National Market

ArcView Market Research anticipates that the national market potential in five years to be $10.2 billion, over seven times the size of the current market.

Much of the national market growth will be a function of new state marijuana laws and of the expectation that federal authorities will respect these laws. This expectation is based on the most recent Department of Justice memo (see Cole Memo in the appendix).

On a five-year horizon, 14 new Adult Use States are anticipated, and two new Medical Use states are anticipated.

The following map details ArcView's prediction of new state laws passing.

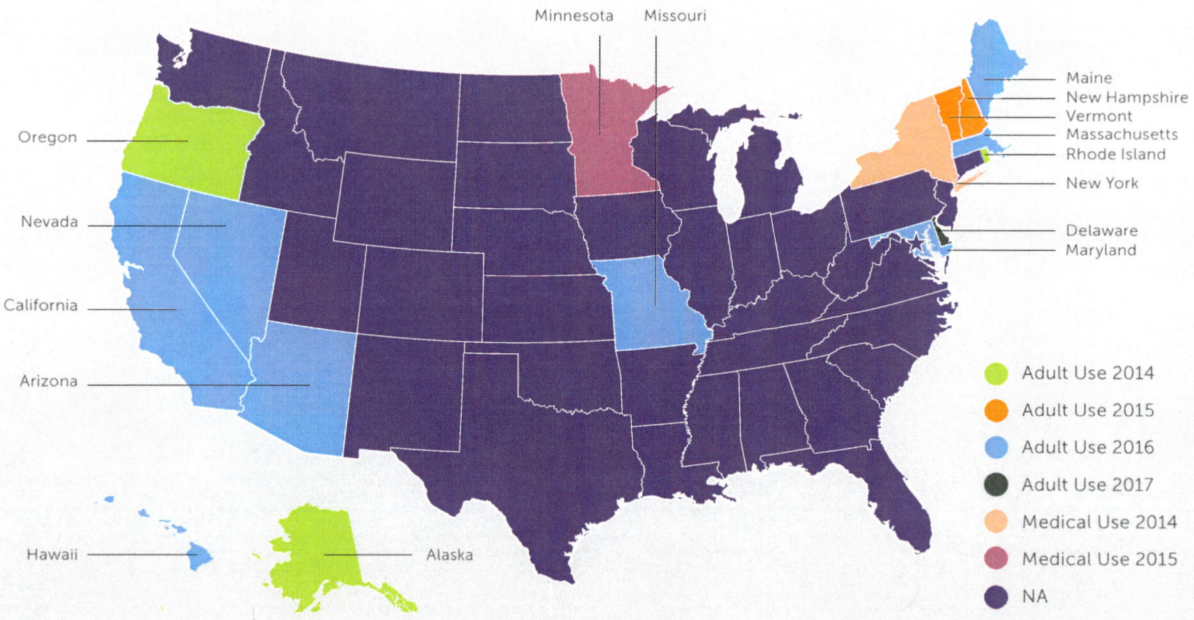

National Market Growth Risk Factors

Primary risks to the outlook for the national market potential include the following factors:

- Federal Opposition – Although the US Department of Justice has signaled a policy of noninterference in legal marijuana states, enforcement action may persist. There have been instances of federal crackdowns in spite of indications of federal disengagement. A DOJ memo issued early in the Obama Administration (see Ogden memo in the appendix) had suggested noninterference with medical marijuana markets; however this was followed in 2011 and 2012 by severe DEA and IRS actions against some operators, which caused the closure of hundreds of dispensaries. ArcView Market Research finds that around $500 million in market value was moved back to the illicit market as a result of these actions.

- Poor Adult Use Implementation – Colorado and Washington State are effectively modeling Adult Use for the rest of the country. If successfully implemented with tight regulatory controls, new state efforts for Adult Use will gain momentum. Alternatively, if implementation goes poorly and there are substantial violations of federal enforcement priorities (e.g., distribution to minors, diversion to other states), other states may be resistant to adopt new Adult Use regulation.

- Local Pushback – Although states may adopt legal marijuana laws, some local cities and counties have limited implementation. For example, more than 100 Colorado municipalities have chosen to ban or have provided moratoria on Adult Use within their localities.

- Capital Constraints – Legal marijuana businesses in need of funding often are limited by constraints on raising capital. These constraints include lack of access to bank loans, reticence by investors to provide capital to businesses that operate in violation of federal law, and state restrictions on nonresident investors. In spite of these constraints, there has been improvement in funding channels for legal marijuana companies (see Investment & Finance section).

- Lack of Political Donations – Growth in the legal markets is largely dependent on the passage of expensive ballot initiatives and on raising sums of money that have never before been raised for this cause. The public already feels that there is a sense of inevitability to legalization, but the reality is that winning will likely cost a lot of money and will require the political ingenuity of many people. That false sense of inevitability could lead people to stop donating. Also, although donations from industry players are on the rise,

most donations come from wealthy individuals who want, on principle, to see cannabis made legal, not because of any business interest. If too many of these donors see the rise of the industry as the new driving force behind political donations and therefore decide not to donate, and the industry doesn't pick up the slack, there could be a funding shortfall. Also, the movement is overly reliant on a few billionaires who could change their minds or could die. In fact, the largest donor to marijuana legalization efforts in history, Peter Lewis, recently died at the age of 80, and whether his estate will continue to donate millions of dollars per year to legalization causes is unclear.

Addressable Market

The addressable market for legal marijuana in the US includes Medical Use patients with qualifying conditions and Adult Use consumers residing in, or visiting, Colorado and Washington State.

Medical Use

Three key concepts in terms of customer markets in the Medical Use states are the potential customer population, customer population, and saturation rates.

ArcView Market Research finds there is a total US population of 25.9 million **potential customers** in 2013, and distributed amongst the states as shown in the following chart.

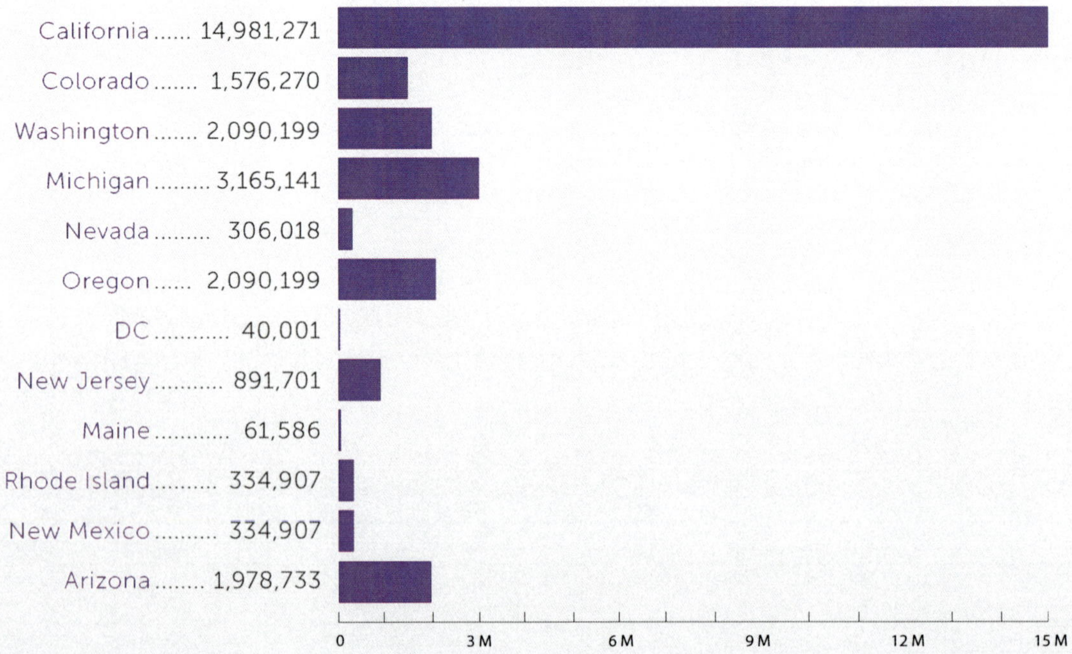

More than 592,000 customers purchased cannabis from a legal marijuana business in 2013.

- Potential Customer Population – This is defined as the total number of residents with medical conditions which qualify them use of medical marijuana under state laws. Each state has a list of qualifying conditions for which a physician can recommend cannabis. These lists vary from state to state, and dictate which residents represent potential patients in each state. Some states have relative narrow qualifying condition, limited to severe illnesses like cancer or HIV. Other states also allow for broader conditions like chronic pain, which greatly increases the potential patient population.

- Customer Population – The Medical Use customer population includes those individuals within the potential patient population that purchase cannabis at a retail medical marijuana center (i.e., dispensary). A person with a qualifying condition who obtains the requisite state Medical Use certification in a legal marijuana state and who cultivates cannabis for his or her own use, or who receives cannabis from a caregiver instead of purchasing from a dispensary, is not included in the customer population. These patients do not contribute to the marijuana market value as measured in this report. ArcView Market Research finds that more than 592,000 customers purchased cannabis from a legal marijuana business in 2013.

The 2013 **actual customer** population by state is shown in the following table:

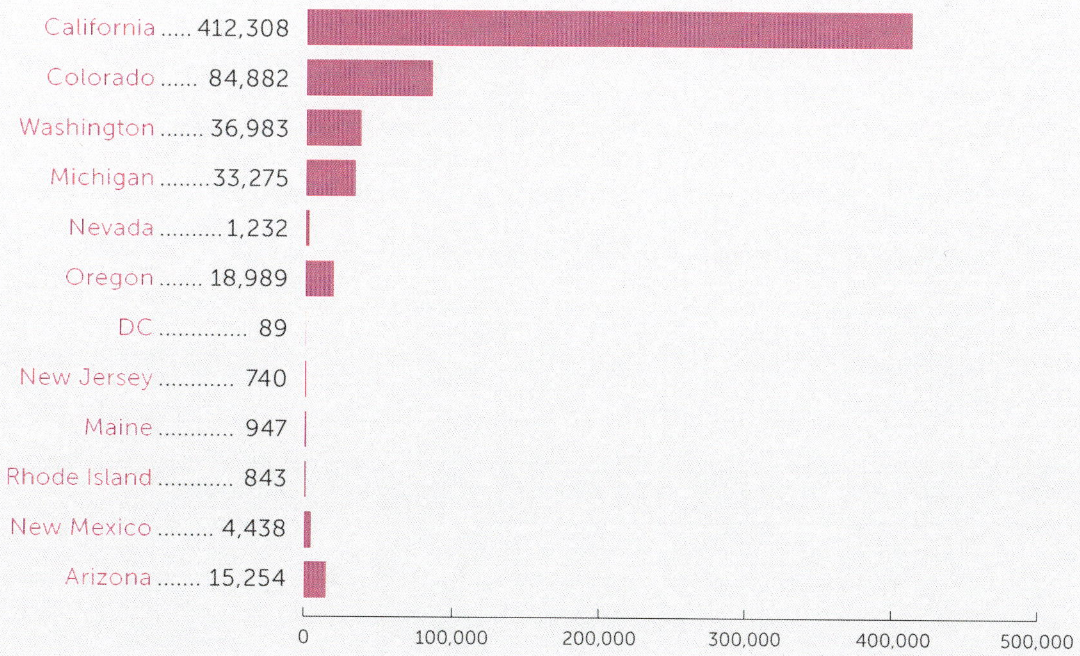

- Saturation Rate – As a measure of customer growth potential, the saturation rate represents the percentage of the customer population who are actively purchasing Medical Use cannabis, relative to the potential patient population who qualify to make those purchases. On that basis, a 54 percent saturation rate for Colorado implies a smaller growth potential relative to Arizona's, which—as a newer and emerging Medical Use state—has a seven percent saturation rate. The relatively low saturation rates in many state markets indicate strong growth potential for Medical Use markets.

The individual state saturation rates are shown in the following table:

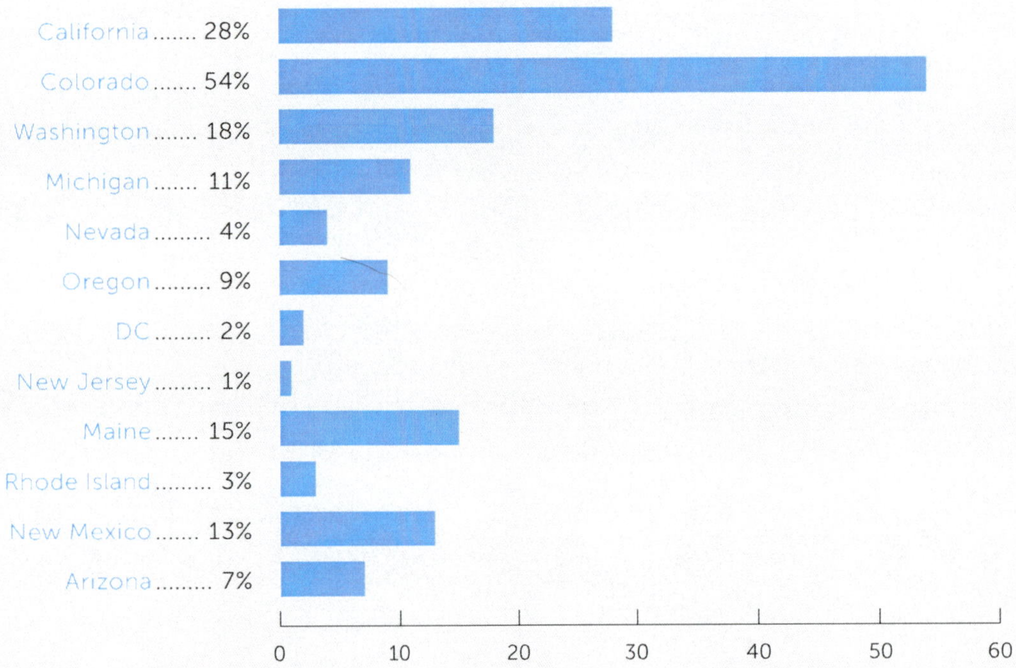

Growth in the Medical Use addressable market will be a function of new medical marijuana states coming online, as well as of growth within existing Medical Use states. However, in the states of Washington and Colorado, the Adult Use stores will likely cannibalize Medical Use sales to some degree. Some individuals may not elect to renew their Medical Use registration cards to purchase cannabis when they can do so legally from full-legalization retailers. However, Adult Use marijuana in these states is taxed at higher rates than Medical Use marijuana. The extent of this migration is difficult to estimate at this early stage and will depend on factors such as the individuals' geographic proximity to Adult Use retail stores and product cost differentials between dispensaries and retail stores as a result of differing sales tax treatment.

Adult Use

In 2014, the first Adult Use addressable markets will emerge in Colorado and Washington State. These markets represent all adults residing in these states who may legally buy cannabis, as well as nonresidents who visit. Estimation of these populations includes the following elements:

- State Resident Medical Use Migration to Adult Use – some medical marijuana patients will become legal marijuana retail market customers as retail stores open. Gauging how big this migration will be is difficult at this early stage. Some limiting factors include bans and moratoria by certain cities in the Adult Use states. For example, more than 100 localities in Colorado have banned Adult Use sales, including Colorado Springs, a city that has a substantial number of dispensaries. Some residents won't be willing to drive to cities where Adult Use shops are open, and instead will patronize dispensaries or illicit market sources. The higher taxes applied to Adult Use sales also implies more expensive retail costs, compared with Medical Use purchases (even after the cost of maintaining a medical marijuana patient registration is included).

- Tourists – ArcView Market Research anticipates that a significant number of nonresident visitors to Colorado and Washington State will purchase marijuana at Adult Use stores. Some tourists will travel to these states specifically to experience the first Adult Use marijuana in the US; some companies already offer canna-tourism packages that feature visits to cultivation centers and retail shops. Tourists are likely to add significantly to the value of Adult Use markets in the near-term. In later years, however, as more Adult Use states come online, tourist purchases will become less significant for the individual Adult Use state markets because national consumer access will have increased.

- Illicit Market Migration to Adult Use – a number of individuals in the illicit market are expected to become customers of legal marijuana businesses. In addition to access, these new customers may be attracted to the variety of products offered and quality standards that are required of legal businesses (e.g., testing, packaging) and that don't exist in the black market. The safety of a licensed storefront, as opposed to buying "on the street," may be another compelling reason for illicit market migration. However, pricing may not favor illicit market migration. The imposition of taxes, particularly in the state of Washington, may cause a legal market premium that limits migration.

- New Adult Users – some individuals who have not used marijuana before or who were cannabis consumers years ago will become Adult Use customers.

These new consumers may be attracted by the sense of freedom that comes from legality, by access to the plant without having to go through patient registration, and by simpler and more appealing ingestion methods.

Although there may be a significant number of new users, they will likely be the lightest of users and thus may not make much of an impact on these markets.

National Market Sentiment

A dramatic shift in attitudes toward marijuana use has occurred recently, particularly toward Adult Use. For several years a strong majority of Americans have been in favor of Medical Use; a 2010 ABC News/Washington Post poll showed 81 percent of Americans favoring medical marijuana use. More recently, a 2013 Gallup poll showed that 58 percent of Americans support full legalization, which is a 10-point increase in one year (see chart).

Americans' Views on Legalizing Marijuana:

Do you think the use of marijuana should be made legal, or not?

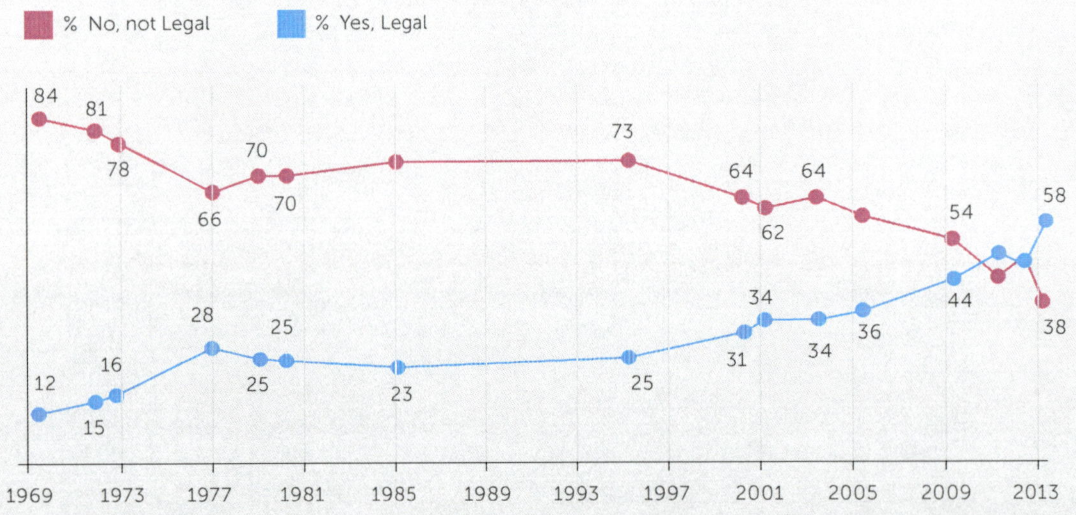

Source: Gallup

Shifts in support for marijuana are also evident in the media, including from those who were previously strongly against cannabis. Dr. Sanjay Gupta, CNN's chief medical correspondent, produced a documentary about marijuana that included highlighting the efficacy of medical marijuana for the treatment of children who suffer from chronic seizures.

In a complete reversal of his previous stance and reporting on marijuana, Gupta apologized for helping to "mislead" the American public about cannabis.

He also wrote an op-ed titled "Why I Changed My Mind on Weed." The media has also had an increasing focus on legal marijuana businesses. In a cover story titled "Marijuana Inc.," Fortune magazine published an in-depth report on the legal marijuana industry. Seattle Business Magazine, Venture Capital Journal, and Reason Magazine have followed suit with cover stories of their own.

The increase in new marijuana state laws, many by ballot initiatives, also evidences increased national support for legal cannabis. Of the twenty legal marijuana states and DC, seven adopted legal marijuana regulations since 2010.

Support for marijuana legalization has also come from other nontraditional population segments, such as seniors and parents of children with serious illnesses, with both groups seeking access to cannabis for treatment of medical conditions. Conservative Utah state Representative Gage Froerer (R-Huntsville) is backing Hope 4 Children with Epilepsy, an advocacy group composed of Mormon mothers who are fighting for safe access to Cannabidiol oil to treat epileptic children.

National Advocacy

As highlighted towards the beginning of this report, advocacy and entrepreneurship are the twin engines that power the creation of legal marijuana markets. Advocacy aimed at political systems and constituents has proven successful at opening markets by reforming marijuana laws at the state level, and is also causing some shifts in federal policy. Initial advocacy gains were to decriminalize possession of small amounts of cannabis in some states in the 1970s. Medical marijuana advocacy, much of it stemming from the AIDS epidemic, prompted the adoption of Medical Use state laws beginning in the mid-1990s. More recently, advocacy for full marijuana legalization produced the first Adult Use regulations in Colorado and Washington State.

Cannabis advocacy takes many forms, from well-funded national organizations to small grass roots groups of various shapes and sizes. Some advocacy efforts entail major campaigns focused on changing state laws, while smaller scale efforts include appeals to city council members to accept marijuana businesses within the municipality based on laws approved at the state level. In addition to social advocacy, business advocacy in the form of trade associations has also emerged as a powerful force in recent years.

National Policy & Industry Groups

At the national level, there are both policy organizations working to reform drug laws and industry associations focused on advancing commercial interests. Policy organizations are funded primarily by donations from individuals and groups seeking to advance drug policy reform. The primary national policy organizations include the following groups:

The National Organization for the Reform of Marijuana Laws was founded over 40 years ago and is focused on changing public opinion about cannabis to hasten the end of prohibition.

The Drug Policy Alliance was formed in 2000 and seeks to decriminalize responsible drug use, including cannabis.

The Marijuana Policy Project was formed in 1995 and is focused on two primary areas: 1) advocacy to reform state and federal marijuana laws and 2) public education about cannabis. The Marijuana Policy Project and the campaign committees it funded have succeeded in passing eight of the 12 most recent state medical marijuana laws, and played a lead role in drafting the successful Amendment 64 full legalization initiative in Colorado.

You see an empty warehouse.

The American Civil Liberties Union has been active in state cannabis law reform initiatives, as well as providing legal support to cases involving marijuana laws. It also generates research reports and information for the public on a host of issues such as marijuana enforcement statistics and scientific research of cannabis.

The Coalition for Cannabis Policy Reform was formed in 2011 and is dedicated to marijuana social rights issues and promotion of sound regulations of marijuana use and commerce.

Americans for Safe Access is focused on ensuring safe and legal access to cannabis for therapeutic uses and research. With over 50,000 members, Americans for Safe access provides information and training services to patients and health care professionals, as well as legal support for cases involving patients' rights.

Students for Sensible Drug Policy is an international, grass roots student-led organization working to end drug prohibition. The group was formed in 1998 and includes more than 200 student chapters. It provides advocacy and educational resources and promotes student and teacher activism for drug policy reform.

Law Enforcement Against Prohibition is an educational organization comprising former and current police officers, government officials, and law enforcement agents who oppose prohibition policies as embodied by the "War on Drugs."

Marijuana Majority is an organization advocating reform of marijuana criminalization laws, as well as the establishment of regulation of marijuana sales. Its supporters include celebrities and thought leaders ranging from those with conservative to liberal backgrounds.

The ability of these organizations to continue to raise funds is essential to the work they do, including continuation of the opening of new legal marijuana markets.

A sign of the legal marijuana industry's maturation is the 2010 founding of the National Cannabis Industry Association (NCIA), the first trade association for commercial interests (see Aaron Smith profile). It is composed of legal marijuana professionals and organizations. The NCIA lobbies for the advancement of commercial interests and cannabis law reforms. The association is funded primarily by membership fees, and recently designated a full-time industry lobbyist based in DC. Two state-level affiliates of the NCIA emerged in 2013, including the California Cannabis Industry Association and the Nevada Cannabis Industry Association. Both focus on state and local level political issues governing legal marijuana businesses.

INDUSTRY LEADER PROFILES

Aaron Smith / NCIA

"The future of the cannabis reform movement is in harnessing the entrepreneurial spirit," according to Aaron Smith. "That's a force stronger than any prohibition law." As co-founder and Executive Director of the National Cannabis Industry Association (NCIA), Smith's assertion is strengthened by the rapid increase in membership of the only national marijuana industry trade association.

Legal marijuana businesses face enormous challenges that would devastate most mainstream companies. NCIA meets the critical needs for education and for changing onerous laws, such as those that prevent cannabis companies' access to financial services and equitable taxation.

NCIA works to promote the growth of a responsible and legitimate cannabis industry, and to hasten a favorable social, economic, and legal environment for the industry. While there are several well-established policy organizations focused on consumer rights and changing social laws, NCIA provides representation specifically to cannabis industry professionals and businesses.

The association's membership is diverse; it includes the largest of dispensaries and mom-and-pop operators, as well as cannabis companies and ancillary businesses. In addition to supporting favorable changes in the laws affecting cannabis businesses, members derive value from networking within an industry peer group for which business communication and information sharing has historically been very limited.

Smith previously worked at the Marijuana Policy Project, where he witnessed the emergence of a cannabis industry with increasingly sophisticated business operators striving to be treated like any other businesses. "There were huge challenges to the industry, such as Section 280E of the Tax Code and lack of banking access," he noted, "yet there was no voice in Washington DC representing cannabis businesses." There were industry image problems, too. In spite of many business owners trying to do things the right way, the media tended to focus on less savory actors, Smith observed. "A professional trade association was dearly needed to put the industry's best face forward."

In 2010, Smith and veteran marijuana policy reformer Steve Fox cofounded NCIA by assembling what he describes as "the best and brightest" marijuana entrepreneurs from across the industry spectrum. "Before we founded NCIA, the general public wasn't looking at cannabis as an industry, they just saw it as a fringe issue related to social justice and personal rights," Smith said. Establishing a trade association would integrate the social agenda with the strength of enterprise and help the public understand that an important legitimate industry was emerging.

Growth in NCIA membership reflects trends in the industry at large. Upon formation, there were about 20 members. But soon after, the industry was hit hard by enforcement actions in 2011 and much of 2012, which hampered membership growth. However, the November 2012 election cycle, which ushered in new medical cannabis states and the first Adult Use states, resulted in a dramatic change for NCIA. Enrollment has more than tripled in the last year and now stands at around 375 members.

New members are often recruited by existing members. NCIA events are held around the country, and these also serve to attract new members who often seek opportunities to learn from seasoned industry veterans. An NCIA newsletter also serves to keep members informed of the organization's work and to bring in new members.

Smith is generally optimistic about the prospects for changes to laws that impede the growth of the legal marijuana industry. "Improvement on the banking front is right around the corner," he said, adding "within four to six months we should see relief in the form of financial institutions providing services to legal marijuana companies in states with strong regulatory systems." Smith sees the Department of Justice's admission during the recent Senate Judiciary Committee that the banking issue needs to be resolved as key to impending changes. "The Justice Department has given their blessing to a change in banking regulations that would favor the industry, and now it's time for the Department of Treasury to make those changes, which it can do without an act of Congress," he observed.

Reforming 280E is a bigger challenge, as it requires an act of Congress to change the tax law. Smith points to one encouraging development in the form of a bipartisan coalition that includes liberal Oregon Democrat Earl Blumenauer (D-Oregon), conservative Dana Rohrabacher (R-California), and Grover Norquist (president of Americans for Tax Reform). Blumenauer and Rohrabacher are pushing legislation that would exempt state-legal marijuana businesses from the provisions of 280E. Americans for Tax Reform produced a white paper titled "Legal Cannabis Dispensary Taxation: A Textbook Case of Punishing Law-Abiding Businesses Through the Tax Code," which strongly supports 280E reform.

What's on the horizon for NCIA? Smith points to increased political resources. "We've hired a full time Director of Government Relations in DC." He notes that this is the first time the cannabis industry has had a full-time, dedicated staff lobbyist who is able to meet with federal policy makers in support of the industry's agenda. NCIA is also focused on increasing resources for the Political Action Committee it formed last year, which supports federal candidates who take a favorable stance toward the industry. State-level NCIA affiliates have also emerged, including the California Cannabis Industry Association and the Nevada Cannabis Industry Association. These affiliates increase the depth of NCIA's membership reach and strengthen efforts to advance cannabis business interests specific to individual states, according to Smith.

Smith notes that NCIA is also spearheading an educational campaign within the industry to ensure that "legal cannabis businesses maintains unique values predominantly rooted in corporate responsibility, advocacy, and community engagement."

"With increased momentum and resources," Smith said, "NCIA is going to make sure that policy makers and the public fully understand the contributions our industry provides to the economy and to society and that federal law reform is needed to grant the freedom and equality the industry rightly deserves."

Regulatory & Legal Framework

Federal

In spite of recent important shifts by the Department of Justice regarding state marijuana laws, cannabis remains illegal at the federal level. Despite a growing body of evidence about the potential therapeutic qualities of marijuana, it is classified as a Schedule 1 drug under the Controlled Substances Act. This designation means the federal government (in the form of the Drug Enforcement Agency and the Food and Drug Administration) has determined cannabis may not be prescribed because it is deemed to have a high potential for abuse, has no accepted medical use in treatment, and has a lack of accepted safety of use. The Schedule 1 classification is at odds with Medical Use laws currently on the books in 20 states plus DC. Some of the state and municipal challenges to the enactment of medical marijuana laws specifically cite the Schedule 1 designation as the basis for blocking adoption of Medical Use regulations.

Evidence of the federal government's shifts on marijuana laws is captured in memoranda released by the Department of Justice (see Appendices). Following the 2008 election of Barak Obama, who pledged to respect medical marijuana laws, there appeared to be a significant policy change regarding cannabis laws. The Ogden Memo of 2009 seemed to convey that the Obama Administration would not use federal resources to override state legal marijuana laws. Under this apparent cover, many new medical marijuana businesses emerged in states with Medical Use laws, a dynamic that was sometimes referred to as the "Green Rush". Following the issuance of the Ogden Memo, however, there were sporadic, and occasionally severe federal enforcement actions against dispensaries and commercial cultivators. A subsequent Justice Department communiqué, in the form of the 2011 Cole Memo, seemed to backtrack on some of the assertions of the Ogden Memo. The raids and the 2011 Cole Memo sounded a cautionary alarm in the legal marijuana markets, causing dozens of businesses to exit the landscape and significantly shrinking the national legal market value.

Most recently, the 2013 Cole Memo, issued in response to the passage of Adult Use regulations in Colorado and Washington State, has been the strongest statement to date regarding federal deference to states legal marijuana regulations. The memorandum indicated that states with tightly regulated marijuana laws and oversight would be allowed enforce their own laws. Absent evidence of violations of eight top federal enforcement priorities, the Department of Justice indicated is would not use enforcement resources to go after legal marijuana businesses. Those enforcement priorities include preventing the following:

- the distribution of marijuana to minors;
- revenue from the sale of marijuana from going to criminal enterprises, gangs and cartels;
- the diversion of marijuana from states where it is legal under state law in some form to other states;
- state-authorized marijuana activity from being used as a cover or pretext for the trafficking of other illegal drugs or other illegal activity;
- violence and the use of firearms in the cultivation and distribution of marijuana
- drugged driving and the exacerbation of other adverse public health consequences associated with marijuana use;
- growing of marijuana on public lands and the attendant public safety and environmental dangers posed by marijuana production on public lands;
- marijuana possession or use on federal property.

Following the release of the 2013 Cole Memo, Department of Justice officials met with the governors of Colorado and Washington State and provided further assurances of federal deference to implementation of the new Adult Use laws. It is notable that there have been federal raids on Colorado businesses since the release of the 2013 Cole Memo. Disclosures have been limited, but there are indications that these actions followed the discovery of evidence that some of the eight enforcement priorities had been violated by one or more of the raided businesses. ArcView Market Research anticipates that there will inevitably be some intrusions upon federal enforcement priorities following implementation of the new Adult Use market rules in 2014 and beyond. Periodic responses by enforcement officials to these violations will cull marginal operators from the landscape, but may also dampen some of the enthusiasm for these emerging markets. For investors in Adult Use-related businesses, backing strong management teams with tight controls is essential to managing risk and realizing the full potential upside in these new markets.

Another significant Department of Justice pronouncement following the 2013 Cole Memo release was testimony by Deputy Attorney General James Cole to the Senate Judiciary Committee hearing on Washington State and Colorado Adult Use legalization. He conceded that the Justice Department does not have a solid legal basis on which to challenge those state laws on federalism grounds. He cited that the Adult Use laws do not create a "positive conflict" with the Controlled Substances Act, inviting federal preemption of those laws. Cole also indicated that work is underway with federal regulators to address money laundering laws and commercial banks' resulting fears of dealing with legal marijuana businesses. Normalizing access to banking services for cannabis-related businesses has the potential to increase the volume of commercial transactions and the values of state markets. Congressional representatives from the Adult Use states - Ed Perlmutter (CO), and Danny Heck (WA) – backed by bipartisan support, have introduced new legislation to allow marijuana businesses acting in compliance with state laws to access banking services.

Another key regulatory challenge for legal cannabis businesses relates to federal tax law in the form of Internal Revenue Code Section 280E, which prevents businesses from taking ordinary expense deductions for income tax purposes. While cannabis businesses are allowed to deduct cost of goods materials (for example, a dispensary can deduct the cost of cannabis inventory), any costs associated with selling cannabis cannot be expensed. The result can be exceedingly high effective tax rates and liabilities, which some regard as a federal tool to limit or eliminate the viability of marijuana businesses. Repeal of Section 280E is a major focus of the NCIA trade association, as well as for 280E Reform, a multistate partnership of cannabis patients and providers.

Interstate commerce in cannabis products is illegal, in large measure limiting businesses to serving consumers in their home states. Some businesses have been able to transcend borders via licensing agreements with local partners (see Multistate Expansion section). Several states also have patient reciprocity laws, enabling limited interstate access for some patients to possess and consume marijuana within multiple states based on correspondent states' laws.

State

20 US states and the District of Columbia have adopted some form of marijuana legalization. With each state operating under a unique regulatory regime, the state regulatory landscape is quite complex. The ArcView Market Research State Regulatory Matrix Guide, as a special feature fold-out poster contained in this report, summarizes the individual state laws according to 15 key regulatory criteria. When evaluating the individual states, the history and trends of state regulations provide important context to understanding industry dynamics and the outlook for each state.

Beginning with California, the first state cannabis regulations were concentrated on the west coast and later spread through much of the country via ballot initiatives or legislative bills. No southern state has adopted marijuana laws, although an Arkansas ballot initiative permitting medical marijuana came very close to victory during the November 2012 elections.

Each state's regulatory structure is unique. An individual state's regulations dictate the market characteristics and define the business opportunities, limitations, and risks within that state. Understanding individual state markets requires accounting for multiple regulatory factors, from who may legally purchase cannabis to how it may be sourced, processed, and distributed.

Knowing this regulatory landscape is critical—that which is permitted in Colorado could be a jailable offense in New Jersey.

Investors may be allowed to own marijuana business interests in some states, but be forbidden from ownership in others. Interstate commerce prohibitions that prevent the free movement of trade goods serve to further segregate each state into its own unique and insular market. The resulting patchwork of regulations presents barriers to some market participants and opportunities for others on a state-by-state basis.

State regulations have varied widely in the past, though newer state marijuana legal initiatives are starting to share similar patterns. Having been informed by the successes and failures of past state initiatives, newer state initiatives are eschewing the likes of California's regulatory model and favoring Colorado's laws.

Although California was the first legal marijuana state to adopt elemental regulations in 1996, seventeen years later there is still no state regulatory agency commissioned with overseeing the industry, defining market standards, or licensing businesses. The lack of a strong statewide regulatory system exposes the California market to periodic turmoil from law enforcement actions and changes in individual city and county policies. Absent any true unified industry oversight, the California marijuana industry demonstrates a wide range in the quality of market practices and operators. Some California cities have established local regulatory oversight, and the California Board of Equalization has created standards for statewide sales permitting and taxation of dispensaries (see Betty Yee profile).

Colorado adopted a stronger regulatory system, and commissioned the state Department of Revenue's Medical Marijuana Enforcement Division with regulatory oversight of businesses. It became the first state to tie production and distribution together to create a "closed-loop" system between the plant source and market distribution channels (known as "seed-to-sale" tracking). Colorado dispensaries and retail outlets are presently required to grow at least 70% of marijuana products that they sell, and this requirement is thought to facilitate tight regulatory oversight and to reduce diversion risk. There are provisions allowing for the decoupling of cultivation and retail operations in the future for the Colorado Adult Use market, but Medical Use must preserve the closed loop between marijuana production and distribution.

Newer state regulations have been structured with the benefit of hindsight from the strengths and weaknesses of earlier regulatory regimes. All newer states now commission agencies to oversee the market (Department of Health, Department of Revenue, Liquor Control Board, etc.) and many follow Colorado's precedent of tying dispensaries to cultivation operations.

As a result, some degree of coalescence in state regulatory schemes has developed, and this dynamic is likely to persist as new state markets come online. The 2013 Cole Memo reinforces the importance of implementing tight state regulatory structures patterned after elements featured in Colorado's legal marijuana market. It seems likely that California will introduce Adult Use regulations by 2016 and will emulate the best features of more-developed programs in Colorado and Washington State. By 2018, ArcView Market Research expects substantial homogenization of regulations among the legal marijuana states.

Betty Yee

State regulators have to blaze new policy trails in their oversight of legal marijuana businesses. Betty Yee is a pioneering government leader who was the first to stand up for the legal cannabis industry through the exercise of statewide tax authority to benefit California's economy.

As an elected Member of the California Board of Equalization, Yee saw something startling in the legal cannabis industry, even after serving decades in public finance. It wasn't the fact that dispensaries were redefining how marijuana was being distributed; it was the fact that businesses were pleading to be regulated.

"Responsible dispensary owners were actually crying out for regulations," Yee said, adding, "No other industry does that!"

The 1996 passage of Proposition 215 in California was auspicious for being the first medical marijuana ballot measure to succeed. Although it pioneered state legalization of Medical Use, it didn't adequately address the commercial supply chain to facilitate practical patient access to cannabis, nor did it establish statewide business tax policy.

"The Prop 215 experience demonstrated the kinds of problems that crop up when key questions concerning statewide medical marijuana regulations aren't answered as early as possible," observed Yee. These problems include a lack of statewide dispensary standards, constrained patient access in some cities, unchecked proliferation in the numbers of dispensaries in other cities, such as Los Angeles, and missed opportunities for tax and permitting revenue. To address these problems, Yee saw the beginnings of a solution: "Start with the tax issue."

It was an appeals matter before the Board of Equalization, involving The Hemp Center dispensary in San Francisco, that raised the state sales tax issue. The Hemp Center had been paying sales tax on merchandise, but not on cannabis sales. The dispensary asserted that marijuana as a medicine should not be subject to sales tax. The BOE ruled that cannabis sales were not exempt from tax because such sales were not pursuant to a prescription by a physician, dispensing by a pharmacist, and wide recognition and approval of cannabis in treating states of disease.

Beyond clarifying sales tax policy for Medical Use cannabis, the Hemp case showed a potential avenue toward statewide regulation of California legal marijuana businesses via the issuance of sellers' permits. With many dispensaries operating largely underground, however, getting them to apply for permits would be a challenge.

To encourage permit application, the BOE issued special notices to dispensaries informing them that they must each obtain a seller's permit, but that the permit did not require them to specify the merchandise sold. This "General Merchandise" disclosure was intended to help allay dispensary fears that incriminating information could be acquired by enforcement authorities. Any back-taxes owed could be paid on an installment plan. These measures constituted the first statewide agency efforts for oversight of California's legal cannabis industry.

"This effort created an opportunity for dispensaries to comply with state tax regulations by applying for sellers' permits and opening their books," according to Yee. BOE reviews revealed that large dispensaries applying for permits were great employers and community members. "These operations had good employee wages and diversity, were generating good sales taxes, and were concerned with public safety."

Regarding California's adoption of Adult Use regulations, Yee is optimistic about the prospects, because she assumes that any new ballot or legislative measure will include a Colorado-style statewide tax policy. Before it failed in 2010 by a 53.5% "no" vote, she was pessimistic about some of the merits of Proposition 19. The Adult Use ballot measure lacked a specific sales tax proposal, which left legislators and local governments to determine levies and licensing fees. While a BOE analysis of a previous Assembly Bill estimated potential state legal marijuana revenues of $1.4 billion, Yee stated that Prop 19 left "too many unknown variables to develop a credible statewide revenue estimate."

With the benefit of hindsight and past regulatory problems, the prospect for full legalization under comprehensive statewide regulations in California appears to be positive. An October 2013 poll by San Francisco–based Tulchin Research found that 65% of likely voters in the state support legalization under a thorough regulation and taxation system, which emulates gains in the most recent national Gallup opinion poll. Lieutenant Governor Newsom (D), along with the ACLU and a research panel, are undertaking a two-year effort to research legalization proposals. Given this effort, strengthened public support, and Adult Use precedents in Colorado and Washington

State, ArcView Market Research projects that California will likely adopt full legalization in the 2016 election cycle and will cure many of the problems that are present in the fragmented market created by the nation's first, but now archaic, set of legal marijuana laws.

"It's only a matter of time now, " Yee observed, "when California will enact a comprehensive regulatory framework for cannabis to ensure benefits to patients, the safety of communities, and tax revenue to states and localities." Yee's work exemplifies how state regulations can work, and has helped to guide the furtherance of statewide regulatory oversight of the legal cannabis industry.

Managing Business Legal Risk

The complexity of legal marijuana business regulations, coupled with the potential severity of consequences for not adhering to laws, makes managing business legal risk essential to the viability of business operators. In all states, violations of federal marijuana enforcement priorities can mean inviting raids by the Drug Enforcement Agency, the Internal Revenue Service, and local agencies. Operators in states with strong regulatory systems and adhering to those requirements are likely exposed to less legal risk than operators in states with weaker systems. But as industry regulations evolve, businesses are well-advised to have a strong familiarity with applicable legal nuances, and to work with attorneys who are skilled at legal interpretation and navigating what can be a patchwork of regulatory requirements (see Khurshid Khoja profile).

INDUSTRY LEADER PROFILES

Khurshid Khoja

As founder and principal of Greenbridge Corporate Counsel, attorney Khurshid Khoja taps both his legal expertise in sophisticated commercial transactions and his history of activism on human rights, the environment, and the rule of law, to guide businesses working toward environmentally conscious and politically progressive goals. This includes advising renewable energy companies as well as those working in the legal cannabis industry.

"My mission is to help build professional cannabis enterprises that comply with applicable laws, and help dismantle cannabis prohibition in the process" says Khoja, explaining how business and capital have been used to accelerate revolutionary social and political change. "Take the anti-Apartheid movement," cites Khoja. Change in South Africa was aided by activists through international boycott and divestment campaigns. "This successfully mobilized consumer capital and multinational businesses against Apartheid."

Khoja characterizes prohibition as "unjust and misguided, but it's federal law," noting that it creates problems such as "keeping medical cannabis away from patients, enriching drug cartels, and producing mass incarceration."

He believes the infusion of capital into legal cannabis companies is helping to assure lasting policy and legal reforms.

When it comes to legal issues for cannabis companies, general matters of legal compliance are important. Additionally, navigating the complex legal landscape of marijuana markets requires specialized counsel particular to the industry. Most law firms lack this kind of experience, and many refuse to deal in legal cannabis markets based on perceived reputational risk. Greenbridge has emerged as one of a small group of law firms providing legal counsel to marijuana, hemp, and ancillary companies. These attorneys help businesses understand the relevant federal, state, and local laws, and adhere to the unique regulatory environments in which they operate.

In terms of managing cannabis business legal risk, "the first query is whether the company is handling marijuana directly, or catering to those who do," according to

Khoja. For cultivators, processors, distributors, and retailers, the main legal exposure is prosecution under the federal Controlled Substances Act (CSA). All such companies are at risk of enforcement actions such as raids, asset forfeiture, and criminal prosecution based on the CSA. Those companies operating in compliance with state laws, though less exposed than illicit market operators, are still exposed to these potential enforcement actions. Harborside Health Center in California, for example, is regarded as a model dispensary by some state and local officials, yet has been targeted by federal prosecutors. Khoja notes that the August 2013 Department of Justice Cole memo (see Appendicies) may appear to protect companies in states with strong regulatory systems, but it's yet unknown what that means in practice.

"People need to understand the Cole memo relates to policy...it's not law," Khoja cited.

Internal Revenue Code Section 280E is a key federal law that cannabis companies need to abide, but that most entrepreneurs don't anticipate based on Khoja's experience. Section 280E prevents cannabis companies from taking ordinary business deductions when computing income tax. As a result, the effective tax rates can be far in excess of 50%.

Cannabis companies, and financial institutions providing them services, are also exposed to liability through anti-money laundering laws under the Bank Secrecy Act. Consequently, it is very difficult for most businesses to open a bank account and acquire payment processing services (see Investment and Finance section). In addition to the legal risk, the necessity of cash transactions also limits business opportunities and increases security risks.

For ancillary companies, the risk exposures depend on what business operations entail and the relationship of products and services to the plant, explains Khoja. For consumption devices, an important part of the overall market, businesses are exposed to federal drug paraphernalia laws under the CSA. While there is no federal ban on consumers possessing paraphernalia, the CSA makes it illegal to sell, offer for sale, transport, import, or export, devices used for production or consumption of cannabis. However, the CSA also expressly exempts the application of federal law in instances where state law authorizes the manufacture, possession, or distribution of cannabis paraphernalia, as in Washington and Colorado. This includes pipes, vaporizers, cultivation and processing equipment, and related products. Accordingly, companies selling consumption devices have attempted to manage this legal risk by avoiding explicit references to cannabis in packaging and marketing materials, choosing instead to highlight other legitimate product uses. Cultivation equipment manufacturers and retailers have for years featured tomatoes on product packing. While there haven't been any recent high profile drug paraphernalia prosecutions, actor Tommy Chong served nine months in federal prison beginning in October 2003 and lost all the merchandise seized during the raid of his business, since "paraphernalia" businesses are also subject to federal asset forfeiture.

Testing labs are an interesting case in terms of legal exposure, notes Khoja. They are neither producers nor distributors of cannabis, and some view them as being ancillary companies while others disagree since testing companies often handle cannabis samples. Part of the legal exposure for testing companies is the actual transporting of samples. To manage risk, some testing companies require their clients to transport the samples. Another approach to mitigating transportation legal risk, are testing systems using Near-Infrared Spectroscopy. This technology entails the scanning of samples by testing units located onsite at the cannabis business, with the scan then transmitted electronically to the lab for analysis.

In the course of his work with startups, Khoja has seen entrepreneurs rush into new state markets without understanding whether laws allow for-profit marijuana business models. Assuming they'll operate as for-profit businesses, entrepreneurs may have already taken in capital, spent substantial sums on assets and services, and then been hit with the realization that state laws require marijuana companies to be formed as not-for-profit entities. In these cases, not only are they not allowed to take in equity investment, there are strict limitations that apply in other areas like employee compensation, and return of capital upon dissolution.

Investment in marijuana companies has been rapidly accelerating, and securities laws apply to those soliciting funds from investors. "It's important for people to understand, that filings need to be made with the Securities and Exchange Commission even for exempt private offerings." He added, "and notwithstanding the fact that a company is not selling on the public markets, there are still key disclosures that must be made to investors to comply with state and federal laws." He also highlights that there are varying legal barriers to investment amongst the legal marijuana states. Some only allow state residents to own equity in businesses; others permit nonresident stakeholders or don't have explicit regulations. Investors and companies need to adhere to these investment rules (often nestled in licensing regulations, as opposed to state statutes), and carefully weigh the risks where there are ambiguities.

Contract enforceability is another big issue, according to Khoja. Parties to a contract can't bring contract disputes to federal court for resolution, because the underlying transaction may be federally illegal. In terms of other resolution channels, the subject matter and geography are of key importance. An ancillary company versus a company which handles cannabis face very different legal issues, as detailed above. And contract disputes in states which don't have legal marijuana laws will not be heard in their state courts. He points out that even in states with cannabis regulations, it may be difficult or impossible to get cases to court because of earlier precedents. More often there are legal ambiguities and little to no precedents for reference. As alternatives to courts, Khoja employs alternative dispute resolution provisions in industry contracts, including: 1) informal discussions, perhaps including trusted industry peers; 2) mediation; and 3) binding arbitration. "U.S. Supreme Court precedents in the last ten years have affirmed that private arbitrators can resolve disputes involving contracts that while illegal, contain an otherwise enforceable arbitration provision. The awards given by arbitrators are binding and enforceable in court, irrespective of the underlying illegality of the contract." He acknowledges with a lack of legal precedents given the early stage of cannabis industry, this dynamic complicates successful dispute resolution irrespective of the format of appeal.

Regarding the impact of the August 2013 Department of Justice Cole memo, Khoja sees it as a major development, but still leaves businesses and investors exposed to plenty of risk. He points out that the memo appears to be an important policy shift to allow for state enforcement of tightly regulated cannabis laws, assuming federal enforcement priories are not violated. However, he cautions that it takes an act of Congress to establish this new stance as law. He believes the Justice Department's delineation that the size of a marijuana business alone should not be the basis for federal enforcement action was a very significant development for the industry (albeit one which contradicts actions by US Attorneys in California). This is particularly notable, given that some states such as Massachusetts are poised to have large cannabis facilities to accommodate restrictions on the number of businesses that will be serving a large addressable market.

Although much remains to be seen, "the latest Cole memo should provide investors more stability in the legal markets like Washington State and Colorado," according to Khoja. "But not so in California," he added. "In markets with weak regulations, the Cole memo may not translate into any legal risk improvement until laws change and strong regulatory systems are enacted."

Attorney Disclosure: This is Not Legal Advice. *The content herein is presented for informational purposes only and not for the purpose of providing legal advice.*

Product Regulation and Standards

There is no national set of standards governing safety requirements for legal marijuana products, though efforts for quality controls have evolved substantially in recent years. Depending on strains and growing conditions, the cannabinoid content of marijuana produced can vary greatly in terms of strength and composition of therapeutic compounds. Without testing for cannabinoid content, consumers don't know what intensity and overall effects of the marijuana product will be.

Cannabis safety can be compromised during cultivation and processing from the presence of mold, powdery mildew, pesticides, residual chemicals left by soils and nutrients, and other potential contaminants. Food safety issues also apply to infused products manufacturing. Together with potency content, these are important elements that affect the consumer experience and safety.

Provisions for ensuring the safety of cannabis products are evolving. Quality controls for legal marijuana occur both via self-regulatory efforts of some industry operators as well as mandated testing and disclosures in some states. Initially, product quality controls were conducted by a handful of dispensaries. In addition to careful visual inspection of cannabis, laboratory testing services were used to check for the presences of molds and evaluate cannabinoid content. Steep Hill Laboratories in California was the first lab to test cannabis samples, and there are now dozens of testing service companies in the industry. In states such as California, where there is no regulatory mandate for product testing, marijuana testing occurs on a voluntary basis by some producers and distributors. In states with more evolved regulatory systems, such as Colorado and Washington State Adult Use markets, testing is mandatory. Newer regulatory programs are also requiring packaging standards such as tamper-evident and child-resistant packaging, as well as prohibition of the use of aesthetics that are highly appealing to children (i.e., cartoonish, candy appearance, etc).

Patient advocacy organization Americans for Safe Access has recently introduced the Patients First Certification program for Medical Use products. This entails a third-party verification program to ensure product safety and is based on quality standards issued by the American Herbal Products Association. A set of recommendations for regulators has been developed in four areas: 1) manufacturing, packaging and labeling; 2) analytics; 3) dispensary operations; and 4) cultivation. ArcView Market Research anticipates cannabis product safety and packaging regulations will continue to evolve via both state mandates and self-regulatory initiatives like Patients First Certification.

STATE MARKETS

Twenty U.S. states and the District of Columbia have adopted some form of marijuana legalization. When evaluating the individual states, the history and trends of state regulations provide important context to understanding industry dynamics and the outlook for each state.

Overview

Beginning with California, the first state cannabis regulations were concentrated on the west coast and later spread through much of the country via ballot initiatives or legislative bills. No southern state has adopted marijuana laws, though an Arkansas ballot initiative permitting medical marijuana earned strong support during the November 2012 elections.

Each state's legal marijuana market is unique. An individual state's regulations dictate the market characteristics and define the business opportunities, limitations, and risks within that state. Understanding individual state markets requires accounting for multiple regulatory factors, from who may legally purchase cannabis to how it may be sourced, processed, and distributed. Knowing this regulatory landscape is critical—that which is permitted in Colorado could be a jailable offense in New Jersey. Investors may be allowed to own marijuana business interests in some states, but be forbidden from ownership in others. Interstate commerce prohibitions that prevent the free movement of trade goods serve to further segregate each state into its own unique and insular market. The resulting patchwork of regulations presents barriers to some market participants and opportunities for others on a state-by-state basis.

Although state regulations have varied widely in the past, newer state marijuana legal initiatives are starting to share similar patterns. Having been informed by the

successes and failures of past state initiatives, newer state initiatives are eschewing the likes of California's regulatory model and favoring Colorado's laws.

California was the first legal marijuana state to adopt rudimentary regulations in 1996, yet seventeen years later there is still no state regulatory agency commissioned with overseeing the industry, defining market standards, or licensing businesses. Consequently, the California market suffers from periodic turmoil as a result of enforcement actions and from upheaval caused by changes in individual county policies. Absent any true industry oversight, the California marijuana industry demonstrates a wide range in the quality of market practices and operators.

Colorado adopted a stronger regulatory system in 2010, under the auspices of the Department of Revenue's Medical Marijuana Enforcement Division, and was the first state to tie production and distribution together to create a "closed-loop" system between the plant source and market distribution channels (aka "seed-to-sale"). Colorado dispensaries and retail outlets are presently required to grow at least 70% of marijuana products that they sell, and this requirement is thought to facilitate tight regulatory oversight and to reduce diversion risk. There are provisions allowing for the decoupling of cultivation and retail operations in the future for the Colorado Adult Use market, but Medical Use must preserve the closed loop between marijuana sourcing and distribution.

Newer state regulations have been structured with the benefit of hindsight from the strengths and weaknesses of earlier regulatory regimes. All newer states now commission agencies to oversee the market (Department of Revenue, Liquor Control Board, etc.) and many follow Colorado's precedent of tying dispensaries to cultivation operations.

As a result, some degree of coalescence in state regulatory schemes has developed, and this dynamic is likely to persist as new state markets come online. The Justice Department's August 2013 memo reinforces the importance of implementing tight state regulatory structures patterned after elements featured in Colorado's legal marijuana market. It seems likely that California will revamp regulations by 2016 and will emulate the best features of more-developed programs in Colorado and Washington State. By 2018, See Change expects substantial homogenization of regulations among the legal marijuana states.

California

California was the first legal state marijuana market, and it represents a commanding 68% of the national total. Yet the California addressable market remains largely untapped. Shortcomings of the current regulatory environment will limit near-term growth. However, with deep roots in marijuana culture and advocacy, coupled with a tradition of entrepreneurship, the state market is poised to greatly expand slightly next year and to drastically expand after the Adult Use regulations are projected to be implemented in 2017.

		Rank
2013 Market Size	$ 980 milion	# 1
Customers	412,308	# 1
Saturation Rate	28%	# 2
2013 vs. 2014 Growth Rate	15%	# 8 (tied)

Overview: Strong

The California state market suffers from archaic Medical Use marijuana regulations, which have exposed business operators to some of the most severe federal and local enforcement crackdowns experienced in any of the legal states. Though the result has been a 30% decline in California market value from what our report projected two years ago, the sheer size of the state still affords it the top position, with close to a billion dollar market value. Market fundamentals and potential also rank at the top which is largely driven by the sheer size of California compared to the other states with legal markets.

California and cannabis have been closely associated for decades. Marijuana culture is deeply ingrained in the state, dating back to the counter-culture movement of the 1960s and '70s. California cannabis production is unmatched. The famed Emerald Triangle region in the north, composed of the premier marijuana growing counties of Humboldt, Mendocino, and Trinity, supplies a large share of both state and national markets (the latter through black market channels). Cannabis buyers' clubs—predecessors of modern dispensaries—originated in Northern California.

Recent contraction aside, ArcView Market Research foresees state market growth of 15% in 2014 to $1.1 billion, based on organic factors (i.e., higher state population) under the current regulatory regime. The multiyear growth outlook is much higher and is attributed to the potential for higher saturation rates and the premise of Colorado-type changes to existing state marijuana laws. California bifurcated market would benefit from more regulatory certainty and a clearer delineation between legal and grey market business activity.

While no official count of patient totals exist, ArcView Market Research believes that the 412,000 customers are likely a fraction of the patients who have received recommendations from their doctors and are legally purchasing in the state. The state has a robust number of caregivers and delivery services that sit outside our model for the legal market.

Regulatory Status: Weak

Proposition 215, passed by California voters in 1996, was the watershed Medical Use initiative that created the first state legal market and established precedent for other states to follow. It allowed for patients with a doctor's recommendation to cultivate, possess and consume cannabis for personal medical use. It also allowed designation of a caregiver to supply the marijuana, which became the basis of the nonprofit collective distribution system practiced by dispensaries. Senate Bill 420, passed in 2003, clarified application of Prop 215 by including a voluntary patient state ID card system and possession limits of six mature (or 12 immature) marijuana plants or 8 ounces of usable medical marijuana. However, that limit was subsequently ruled unconstitutional by the Second District of California Court of Appeals in 2008.

Absent in these laws was any provision for appointing a state agency to oversee the Medical Use system, and for licensing of businesses in the supply chain to provide patient access. Individual counties were left to determine whether to allow medical marijuana businesses, and if so, to weigh other considerations such as taxation and zoning. In May 2013, the State Supreme Court affirmed that cities have the right to prohibit storefront dispensaries, and around 200 cities have enacted bans. Other cities have imposed moratoria. Several cities have allowed medical marijuana, and Oakland became the first U.S. city in 2009 to tax Medical Use sales. The tax rate has been raised several times, and the City of Oakland sales tax rate currently stands at a maximum of 6.8%. In 2005, the California State Board of Equalization also began requiring medical marijuana retailers to hold sales permits and to pay sales taxes.

Lacking solid guidelines from a statewide regulatory body, many California cities and counties struggled to establish medical marijuana policies. Los Angeles notoriously strained for years to determine policy amid a failed 2007 moratorium and competing ballot measures. Unchecked, the number of LA dispensaries proliferated to over 1,000 storefronts and outnumbered the number of Starbucks in the city. The May 2013 passage of Measure D called for restricting the number of dispensaries to the 135 in operation before a 2007 requirement for city registration. In addition to the practical challenges of enforcing that limit, several lawsuits challenging Measure D have emerged. Although some LA dispensaries have closed, others have simply reformatted as delivery services and operate below the radar. The quality of operators varies widely.

In 2010, California Proposition 19, a ballot initiative for Adult Use regulations, was defeated by voters. Many had warned against attempting to pass the initiative in an off-year election, given reduced younger voter participation. Younger populations consistently poll more favorable to marijuana legalization. Some added that had it been on the 2012 ballot, it probably would have passed. These same cautions extend to new initiatives now under way.

Though rejected, Prop 19 still garnered 46.5% "Yes" votes, and is credited with spurring successful 2012 Adult Use initiatives, such as Initiative 502 in Washington State and Amendment 64 in Colorado. As is the case in some other states, there are now efforts underway for another legalization ballot initiative in the 2014 California election. The Secretary of State granted clearance in September 2013 for a petition to circulate a full legalization measure during the November 2014 election. However, many are now concerned that an initiative put forth in another off-year election risks a repeat of the 2010 failure for similar reasons. The lack of any major donor currently for a 2014 initiative is another important hurdle.

Perhaps more promising is a 2016 initiative also now underway. In addition to the prospect of being on the ballot during a Presidential election year when young voter turnout is stronger, it is also backed by political heavy weights: the American Civil Liberties Union, state Lieutenant Governor Gavin Newsom, the Drug Policy Alliance, Californians for Cannabis Policy Reform, and the Marijuana Policy Project (the latter was instrumental in the successful 2012 Colorado Adult Use legalization measure). Many big donors are said to be lining up to back the 2016 initiative, which will likely cost between $10 million and $20 million dollars. ArcView Market research expects passage of a ballot initiative will most likely bring Adult Use legalization to California in 2016.

Although the longer-term California regulatory outlook is constructive based on the introduction of Adult Use state laws, the near-term regulatory outlook is uncertain. Variables include how effectively the City of Los Angeles will implement Proposition D dispensary limits. It also remains to be seen how operators will navigate a state system lacking a strong centralized industry oversight agency, and the express protections such an agency would otherwise seem to afford under the new Department of Justice stance regarding federal enforcement.

Patient Access: Strong

California doctors may recommend Medical Use marijuana for patients diagnosed with any debilitating illness. The implied bar for obtaining a medical marijuana doctor's recommendation is very low, which enables virtually anyone to obtain a Medical Use recommendation at a relatively low annual cost. Some services advertise new patient recommendations for $39, and annual renewals for $29, and obtaining a recommendation may take less than 20 minutes.

Medical Use possession limits vary among counties, although the state default guidelines under Senate Bill 420 allow for up to 8 ounces of useable marijuana or 6 mature (or 12 immature plants). The ability to grow, to designate a caregiver, and to acquire medical marijuana from a dispensary provides patients with relatively strong access to cannabis. However, since many cities have enacted bans or don't otherwise have dispensaries, access is stronger for some California patients than for others, depending on where they live.

Competition: Strong

California includes numerous operators competing in a seasoned market. Many hundreds of commercial indoor and outdoor cultivators serve both the state and national markets (the latter illicitly). Grower competition peaks in the mid summer and fall months as marijuana grown outdoors comes to market, though national demand limits any substantial softening of prices.

Vendor competition in the California market varies by city and county, depending on where distribution is permitted and how effectively cities are able to enforce regulations.

In Los Angeles, despite recently sanctioned limits on dispensaries, many hundreds remain in operation and aggressively compete for patient sales. In other locales, such as Oakland, where cities are able to enforce dispensary limits, competition is more limited. Still, Oakland's proximity to other medical marijuana cities such as Berkeley, San Francisco, and San Jose means overall competition remains quite strong.

Trends & Analysis

- Retrenchment – Federal and county enforcement actions against dispensaries and cultivators caused the California market to contract by around 80,000 patients over the two years ending in 2013, and resulted in about $400 million being moved back to the illicit markets. ArcView Market Research sees the California 2013 market value at just under one billion dollars, versus our estimate $1.3 billion in 2011 before the federal crackdown.
- Dispensary Numbers Decline – For the reasons cited above, ArcView Market Research estimates that 100 fewer dispensaries now exist in the Los Angeles area, though those businesses may now be operating under different formats. Dozens of dispensaries in other regions also closed on the heels of federal crackdowns in 2012.
- Dispensary to Delivery Shift – Crackdowns have caused the number of California dispensaries to shrink, though many have likely been recast as delivery services. Delivery services are more difficult to detect, compared with store fronts, and enable some marijuana distribution businesses to operate below the radar. Given this cover, some delivery services may simply be fronts for black market

distribution. During the course of ArcView Market Research Research market surveys, many listed delivery services had disconnected phone lines, or simply did not answer calls. This "grey" market for delivery services leaves room for questionable business operators and complicates efforts for market measurement. On that basis, ArcView Market Research recognizes that there may be some underestimation of the actual size of the California legal market. However, once tighter marijuana regulations are implemented, delivery services will not represent a very significant share nor the best growth opportunities in the state.

- Elevated Prices – Cultivators are generally able to command relatively high pricing in California. Wholesale prices remain elevated, as many growers can opt for selling their product into the legal state market or to the illicit market where out-of-state buyers are willing to pay a substantial premium for California cannabis. California also lacks vertical integration, whereby dispensaries produce their own marijuana for sale, and which can lower the cost of sourcing inventories. California wholesale prices range from $2,500–$3,500 per pound, compared with $1,500–$2,000 per pound in Colorado. Seasonal fluctuations allow for some price compression for marijuana grown outdoors, when supplies peak in the midsummer and fall months. Premium marijuana grown indoors, however, is largely insulated from this seasonal price compression.

- Moderate Near-Term Market Growth – For 2014, ArcView Market Research estimates the California market will grow to $1.1 billion, 15% above the California 2013 $980 million market value. This will stem from organic growth factors—meaning growth coming from a higher state population and a small increase in the saturate rate—rather than from a significant increase in the number of dispensaries.

- Strong Long-Term Growth Potential – Likely after the 2016 elections, assuming passage of strengthened Medical Use and new Adult Use state laws, the California market is positioned for robust growth. Saturation rates for Medical Use are expected to rise under stronger medical marijuana regulations, and Adult Use laws are foreseen to draw in many consumers from the black market.

- Sizeable Storefronts – the average California dispensary is slightly larger than dispensaries in other states. This is in part a result of certain cities imposing restrictions on the number of dispensaries allowed, which increases the average patient traffic per dispensary. Harborside Health Center in populous Oakland, for example, is one of 6 dispensaries, and does over $25 million in annual revenue.

Survey Responses

1 Regulations

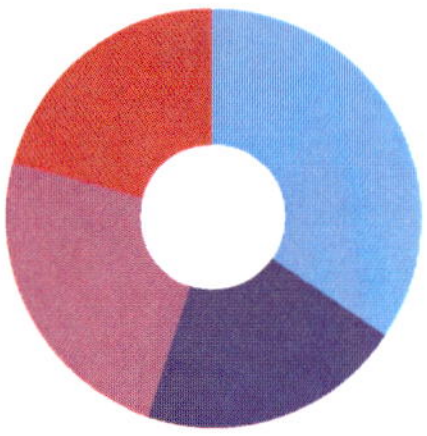

As a business operator, how do you feel about the medical marijuana **regulations** in your state?

- 34.5% Too complex
- 20.7% Too lenient
- 24.1% About right
- 20.7% Are harmful

2 Patient Access

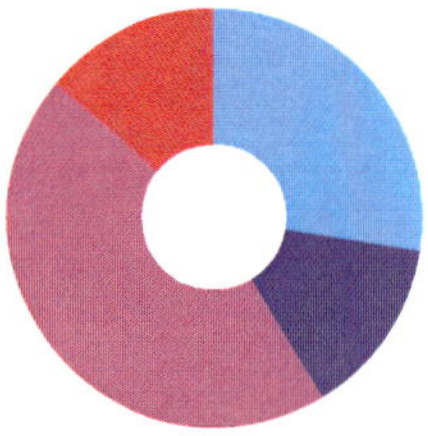

How do you feel about the **patient access** in your state?

- 27.6% It is too hard for patients
- 13.8% It is too easy for patients
- 44.8% It is about right
- 13.8% There should be no patient restrictions

3 Local Competition

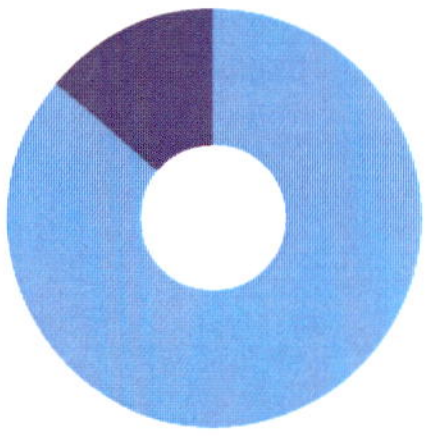

How would you describe your **local competition**?

- 86.2% Very competitive
- 13.8% Not competitive

4 Competitive Environment

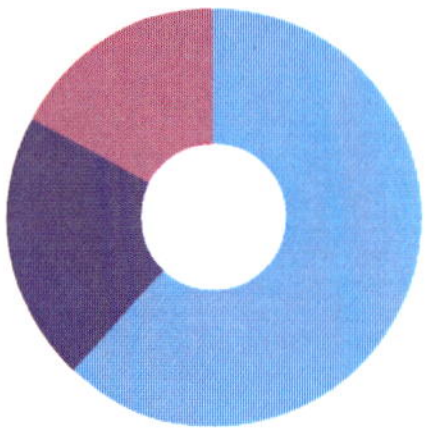

Over the past year, how would you describe your **competitive environment**?

- 62.1% Competition has gotten stiffer
- 20.7% Competition has reduced
- 17.2% No change in competition

5 Local Law Enforcement

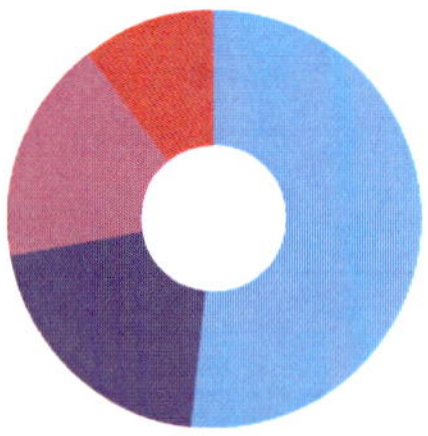

How concerned are you about state or **local law enforcement being a threat** to your business?

- 51.7% Very Concerned
- 20.7% Somewhat concerned
- 17.2% Not concerned
- 10.3% Local law enforcement is helpful to my business

6 Federal Law Enforcement

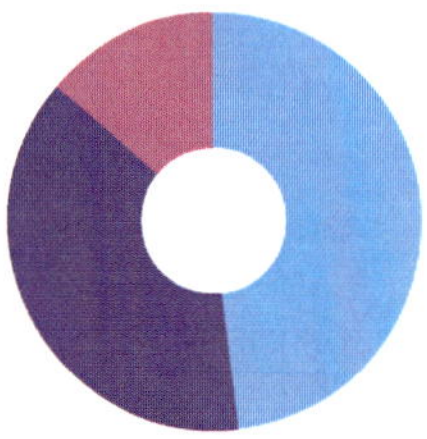

How concerned are you about **Federal law enforcement being a threat** to your business?

- 48.3% Very Concerned
- 37.9% Somewhat concerned
- 13.8% Not concerned
- 0.0% Federal law enforcement is helpful to my business

8

Product Sales Percentage

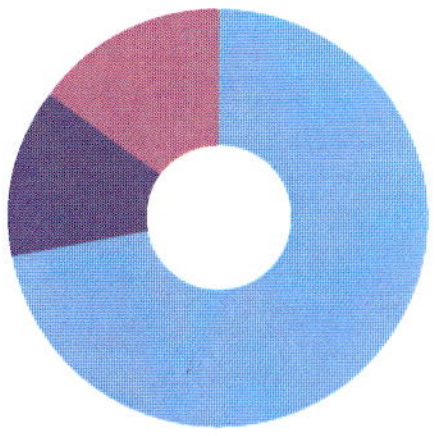

Please estimate what is the **percentage of total sales** for the following products?

- 72.0% Cannabis flowers
- 13.0% Concentrate
- 15.0% Infused Product

9

Retail Price Changes

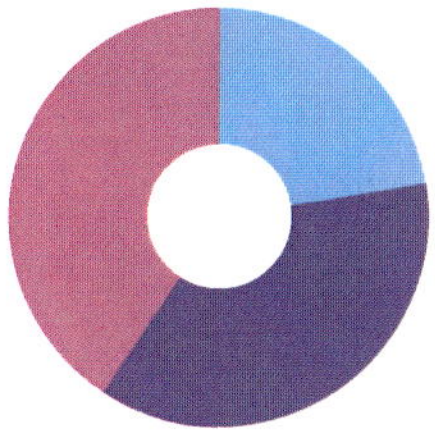

Over the past year, what changes have you seen in **retail prices** for customers?

- 22.2% Prices have gone up
- 37.0% Prices have done down
- 40.7% Prices have stayed the same

10

Previous Retail Experience

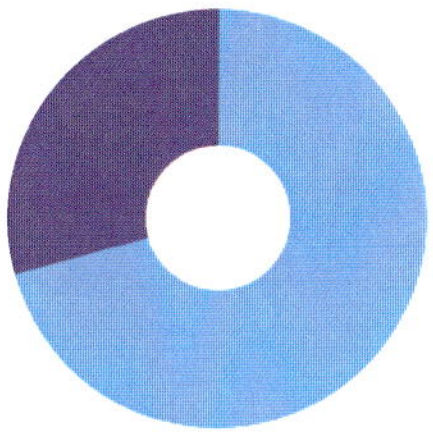

Have you had **previous experience** in the retail industry?

- 70.8% Yes
- 29.2% No

11

Previous Entrepreneurial Experience

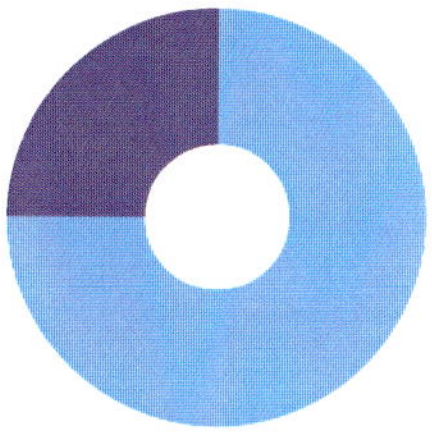

Have you had previous **entrepreneurial experience**?

- 75.0% Yes
- 25.0% No

12

Initial Start-up Costs

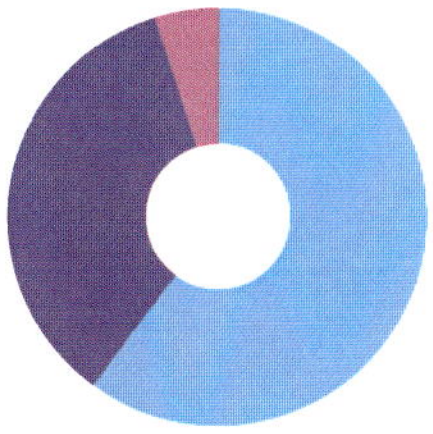

How did you fund your businesses **initial start-up costs**?

- 60.0% Self-financed
- 35.0% Family and friends investment
- 5.0% Angel investment
- 0.0% Institutional investment
- 0.0% Bank loan

Colorado

Though currently only about one quarter the market size of California, the Colorado market value is poised to more than double in 2014 under Adult Use and will equate to about 60% of the projected California market. The state also leads the national scene in terms of market development, in large measure due to a strong regulatory and competitive environment. The implementation process of new Adult Use laws will benefit from the experience of Medical Use regulations that have been in place for years. As one of the two first states to adopt Adult Use, all eyes are on Colorado to see how it will fare under full legalization. Successful implementation of the new laws will accelerate market value creation, as well as the number of new states seeking to adopt Adult Use. Conversely, any shortcomings could set legal marijuana markets back at both state and national levels.

		Rank
2013 Market Size	$ 260 million	# 2
Customers	84,882	# 2
Saturation Rate	54%	# 1
2013 vs. 2014 Growth Rate	138%	# 6

Overview: Strong

Colorado is a seasoned legal marijuana state, with plenty of experienced operators that have honed for-profit businesses under a tight regulatory system. A favorable state political environment, which paved the way for Adult Use laws, also puts Colorado at the forefront of legal marijuana markets. Therefore, it should come as no surprise that some of the most sophisticated U.S. legal marijuana businesses are based in Colorado (see Multistate Expansion section).

Implementation of Adult Use laws aside, the Colorado market is not without limitations. Nonresidents of the state cannot own marijuana businesses, and many municipalities have opted for bans and moratoria. Current vertical integration requirements for cultivation and dispensing are also limiting factors. In terms of Medical Use, the Colorado saturation rate is the highest of any legal state market, leaving relatively modest room for medical marijuana growth.

In spite of these constraints, the enactment of Adult Use regulations means that the Colorado market is about to take a quantum leap forward in 2014. Adult Use laws greatly expand the Colorado addressable market by adding adult consumers from both resident and tourist populations. How significant will canna-tourism add to the Colorado market? Though this is unchartered territory in the U.S., an inference from the popularity of canna-tourism in Amsterdam, Holland, is that tourists will likely add substantially to Colorado market value. Denver alone attracts over 13 million out-of-state visitors annually. Overall, See Change projects that the Colorado market will grow by 138% in 2014 to $619 million as Adult Use comes online.

Regulatory Status: Strong

Colorado voters passed Amendment 20 in 2000, thereby permitting Medical Use for approved patients with written medical consent and in possession of an identification card registered with the Colorado Department of Health. Patients are allowed to possess up to two ounces of usable marijuana and to cultivate no more than six marijuana plants (subject to maximum of three flowering plants). It also allows for designation of a caregiver, although a state health department ruling limited each caregiver to five patients. This caregiver limit was subsequently removed in 2009, and along with a favorable Department of Justice memo issued that year, caused the number of Medical Use patients and legal marijuana businesses to expand quickly.

The passage of House Bill 1284 in 2010 assigned medical marijuana regulatory oversight to the Department of Revenue, which implements Medical Use regulations through its Medical Marijuana Enforcement Division. It also created specific types of medical marijuana business licenses:

- Medical Marijuana Center License ("MMC") – for businesses selling medical marijuana and medical marijuana infused products (see Alternative Ingestion Methods).

- Optional Premises Cultivation License ("OPC") – for MMCs growing medical marijuana at another location.

- Medical Marijuana Infused Products Manufacturing License ("MIPs") – for businesses manufacturing marijuana-infused products.

HB 1284 also imposed certain limitations on businesses, including the prohibition of ownership for non-state residents, as well as vertical integration rules mandating that licensed marijuana businesses purchase no more than 30% of total on-hand inventory from other MMCs. As a result, MMCs must produce at least 70% of the medical marijuana they sell to patients. It is not uncommon to see medical marijuana production facilities in the same buildings that house dispensaries.

The landmark November 2012 passage of Amendment 64, with 55% of the vote, opened the door for the Colorado Adult Use market. Adult Use is regulated by the Marijuana Enforcement Division of the Department of Revenue. This effort was led by law firm Vicente Sederberg and the nonprofit organization SAFER. It was funded largely by The Marijuana Policy Project. As of January 1, 2014, licensed retail centers will begin to sell marijuana to adults 21 years and older. More than 100 municipalities have opted-out of allowing Adult Use retail centers via bans or moratoria. This includes large cities like Colorado Springs, which has allowed Medical Use dispensaries for years.

Colorado residents are limited to possessing and purchasing one ounce of marijuana at a retail store, while nonresidents may purchase a maximum of one quarter ounce per retail store transaction (although they may possess up to one ounce). It remains illegal to transport any cannabis across state lines.

Adult Use marijuana products must conform to testing and labeling requirements, indicating potency (THC), instructions on product use, and a list of nonorganic pesticides, fungicides, and herbicides used during cultivation. Warning statements must also be part of product labeling.

Adult retail store licenses will remain limited to applicants who are current MMC license holders until July of 2014, after which other state residents (with a minimum of 2 years residency) may apply for retail store licenses. In November 2013 voters passed Proposition AA which subjects retail sales to a 15% excise tax and 10% sales tax. These tax revenues will fund industry regulation and oversight, as well as contributions to school programs. All retail stores must identify and track marijuana inventories from cultivation to the point of sales via the state sanctioned Marijuana Inventory Tracking Solution system.

As with Medical Use distribution, 70% vertical integration requirements apply to Adult Use retail businesses. However, in contrast to Medical Use laws, Adult Use vertical integration rules will only apply for a limited time. Vertical integration requirements expire on September 30, 2014. From October 1, 2014, forward, retail stores can elect to decouple from cultivation facilities, and new Adult Use business licensees at that point can choose to enter the market solely as retail stores or as cultivation facilities.

Consumer Access: Strong

Even before the availability of Adult Use marijuana, the high ranking of market size and saturation rate in Colorado implies strong Medical Use patient access. Patients may obtain medical recommendations for a fairly broad list of qualifying conditions. The annual state application fee for a patient card is $15, in addition to the cost of the doctor recommendation.

With the implementation of Adult Use regulations, patients and adult consumers will have increased access to legal marijuana. Access to MMCs or Adult Use retail stores for individuals varies in terms of geography, given the dispersion of cities that have opted out of allowing those distribution centers.

Competition: Strong

The for-profit business model in Colorado strengthens competitive forces among businesses in the Medical Use Colorado market. The number of Medical Use businesses grew rapidly during the 2009–2010 period, which was followed by a consolidation. There were over one thousand medical marijuana businesses at the end of 2010. The number fell to 675 by early

2013. Some of the decline resulted from federal enforcement actions, although declining product prices amid stiff competition squeezed profit margins and forced some small scale operators to exit or to merge with other businesses to improve cost efficiencies.

The overall level of competition will also increase with the introduction of Adult Use retail stores. While the number of retail stores will be limited initially because of regulatory constraints on who may apply for retail licenses, more stores will likely open as the pool of potential applicants increases in late 2014. Retail stores will compete in some measure with MMCs for Colorado resident sales, since residents with qualifying medical conditions may acquire cannabis through both of those distribution channels.

Trends & Analysis

- Modest 2013 Growth – Given the high saturation rate in the Medical Use market and limited growth in the number of dispensaries, the Colorado market will grow modestly in 2013 to $268 million. This market value does not include the "grow-your-own" and caregiver markets, whereby cannabis is cultivated by individuals for personal use.
- Pricing Declines – Larger production capacity, lower cost of goods, and active competition among dispensaries is squeezing retail prices. Medical Use retail marijuana prices declined 20% in the past year, and are some of the lowest prices in the nation. Lower wholesale prices are a function of increases in the size and efficiencies of growing operations. Dispensaries have the incentive to grow as much of their inventory as possible given the cost advantages, and thereby to limit the need for wholesale purchases from other parties. Dispensaries with efficient cultivation operations are able to produce

marijuana at a cost of around $1,000 per pound, while the cost to purchase marijuana from other producers is approximately $1,500 per pound.

- Stable Total Sales – Dispensaries have been able to maintain stable total revenue levels in spite of retail-product price compression. This price stability is due to increased average package sizes, which help to offset the impact of the trend toward lower prices.

- Product Mix Shift – Sales of marijuana extraction and infused products is increasing relative to the sale of flowers. Dispensaries are reporting 70% of sales are for marijuana flowers, and 30% for nonflower products such as edibles, elixirs, tinctures, and extracts.

- Strong 2014 Growth – The total Colorado market value is poised to increase by 138% to $619 million in 2014 as Adult Use retail stores come online, which will add to Medical Use sales. Adult Use sales are generated from both resident and tourist populations.

- Raids Continue – The DEA and IRS, together with local law enforcement agencies, conducted raids on some Colorado dispensaries and grow sites in November 2013 (just as Adult Use laws are about to be implemented). Initially, these actions caused alarm throughout the industry. However, it appears the raids targeted businesses that may be in violation of some of the federal marijuana enforcement priorities enumerated by the Department of Justice (see Cole Memo – August 29 in the Appendices). Some now feel that these latest enforcement actions are actually strengthening the industry by removing "bad actors" that are not operating within the rules.

Colorado

Survey Responses

1
Regulations

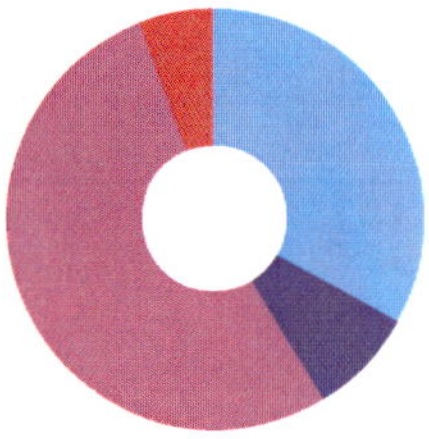

As a business operator, how do you feel about the medical marijuana **regulations** in your state?

- 33.3% Too complex
- 8.3% Too lenient
- 52.8% About right
- 5.6% Are harmful

2
Patient Access

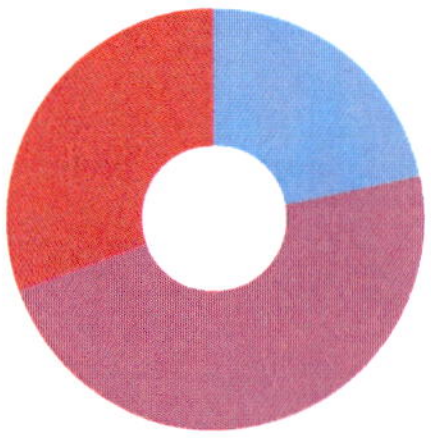

How do you feel about the **patient access** in your state?

- 19.4% It is too hard for patients
- 11.1% It is too easy for patients
- 50.0% It is about right
- 19.4% There should be no patient restrictions

3
Local Competition

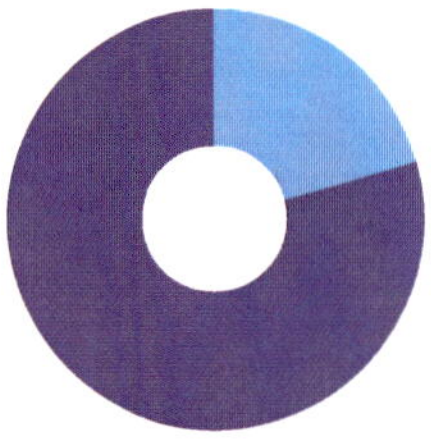

How would you describe your **local competition**?

- 79.4% Very competitive
- 20.6% Not competitive

4
Competitive Environment

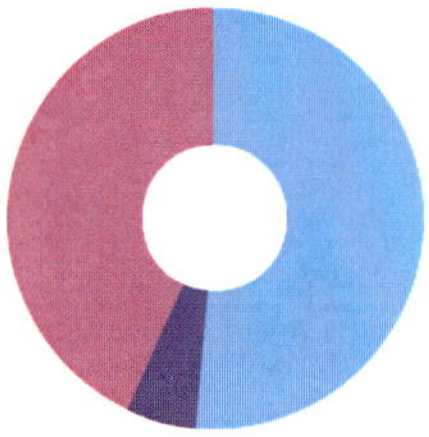

Over the past year, how would you describe your **competitive environment**?

- 51.4% Competition has gotten stiffer
- 5.7% Competition has reduced
- 42.9% No change in competition

5
Local Law Enforcement

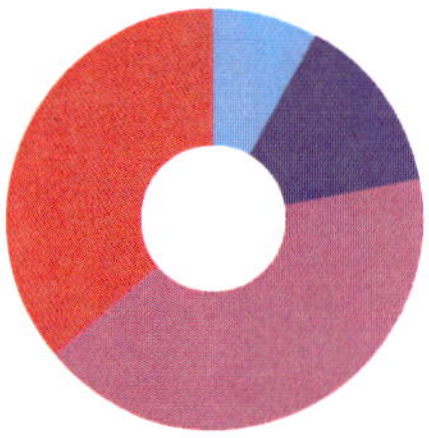

How concerned are you about state or **local law enforcement being a threat** to your business?

- 8.3% Very Concerned
- 13.9% Somewhat concerned
- 41.7% Not concerned
- 36.1% Local law enforcement is helpful to my business

6
Federal Law Enforcement

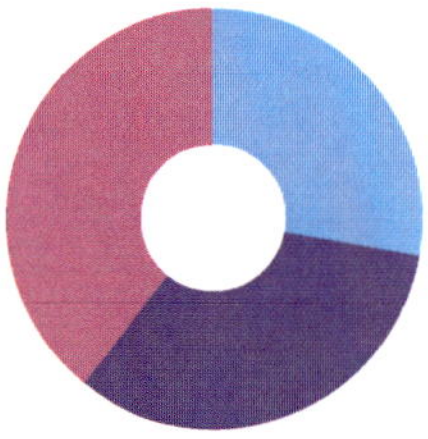

How concerned are you about **Federal law enforcement being a threat** to your business?

- 27.8% Very Concerned
- 33.3% Somewhat concerned
- 38.9% Not concerned
- 0.0% Federal law enforcement is helpful to my business

7
Adult-Use

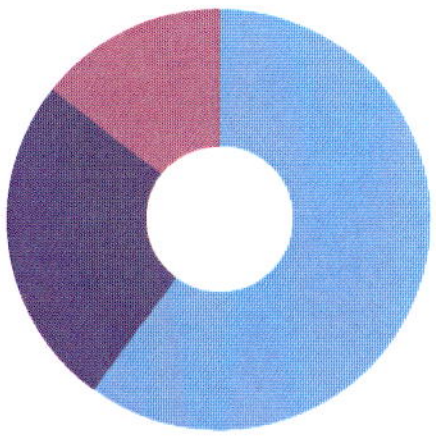

If located in Washington or Colorado, how do you feel about how the legalization of adult-use in your state will affect your business?

- 60.0% Too complex
- 25.7% Too lenient
- 14.3% About right

8
Product Sales Percentage

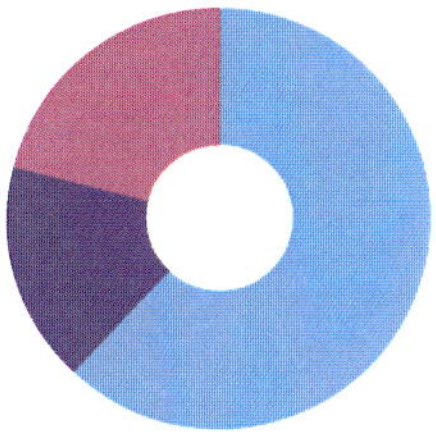

Please estimate what is the **percentage of total sales** for the following products?

- 62.0% Cannabis flowers
- 17.0% Concentrate
- 21.0% Infused Product

9
Retail Price Changes

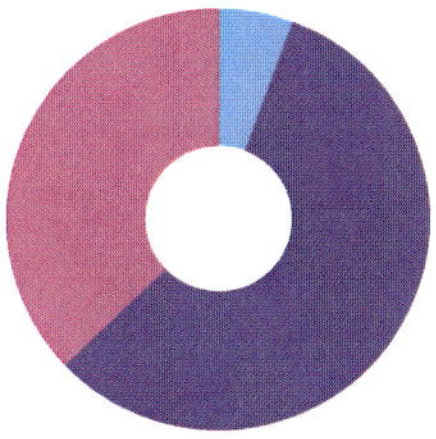

Over the past year, what changes have you seen in **retail prices** for customers?

- 5.7% Prices have gone up
- 57.1% Prices have done down
- 37.1% Prices have stayed the same

10
Previous Retail Experience

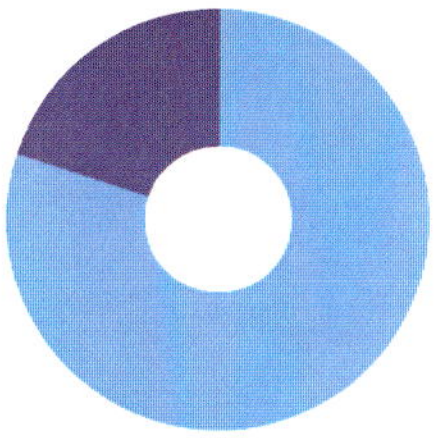

Have you had **previous experience** in the retail industry?

- 80.0% Yes
- 20.0% No

11
Previous Entrepreneurial Experience

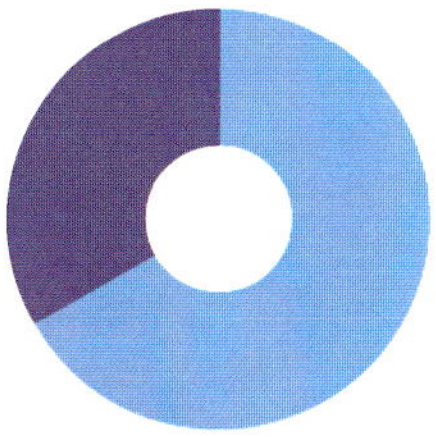

Have you had previous **entrepreneurial experience**?

- 66.7% Yes
- 33.3% No

12
Initial Start-up Costs

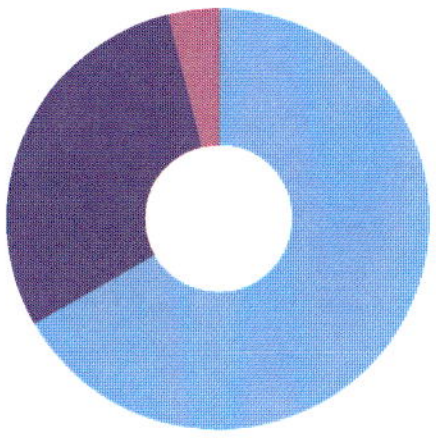

How did you fund your businesses **initial start-up costs**?

- 66.7% Self-financed
- 29.6% Family and friends investment
- 3.7% Angel investment
- 0.0% Institutional investment
- 0.0% Bank loan

Washington

Washington was one of the first states to pass Medical Use laws but has suffered from a virtually nonexistent regulatory system. Yet the state is now positioned to grow at the highest annual rate of any legal marijuana state in 2014 with respect to market value following implementation of strong Adult Use laws.

Although there are similarities to Colorado's Adult Use laws and market potential, there are also several key differences. Unlike the Colorado market, the Washington market has been limited by the absence of a strong regulatory system for Medical Use cannabis. As a result, the 2014 Washington Adult Use market is projected to be several times larger than the state's Medical Use market, whereas Colorado Adult Use is projected to eclipse Medical Use by only about 35%.

Washington Adult Use laws also differ from Colorado's by eschewing vertical integration and by placing much higher taxes on the cannabis supply chain. The fate of the Washington medical cannabis system is very much up in the air, as the state debates reforming Medical Use laws, potentially in ways that may force many current medical operators out of the market. The overall legal state market, however, is projected to become the third largest in the US in 2014.

		Rank
2013 Market Size	$ 63 million	# 3
Customers	36,983	# 3
Saturation Rate	18%	# 3
2013 vs. 2014 Growth Rate	329%	# 2

Overview: Strong

The Washington State market is currently assessed at a value of $25 million, on the basis of the prevailing Medical Use status. ArcView Market Research projects the market to surge nearly 10 times, to over $250 million in 2014 as Adult Use comes online. Minimal residency requirements invite participation by others, including experienced operators who are eager to set up shop or to invest in Washington businesses.

Washington Medical Use business operators—particularly dispensaries—have also been subjected to significant DEA crackdowns as recently as July 2013. Tactics similar to those used in California, which also has weak Medical Use regulations, exposed some Washington business operators to federal enforcement actions. The Medical Use market faces an uncertain future as new legal reforms are being debated. Nonetheless, dramatic overall market growth in 2014 is foreseen as a result of implementation of Adult Use regulations, which are expected to make Washington the third-largest legal marijuana market in the country.

Regulatory Status: Moderate

Washington State is in the unusual position of having both weak Medical Use laws and strong Adult Use laws. This paradox will not last. Adult Use laws are already influencing efforts to draft reforms of Medical Use laws.

Medical Use

Washington arguably has the weakest Medical Use laws of any legal marijuana state. There is no state licensing, patient registry, or taxation. Like those of other states that were part of the first wave to enact medical marijuana laws, (e.g., California and Oregon), the Washington Medical Use regulations that were adopted did not establish a state agency to oversee the industry. Initiative 692, passed in 1998, received 59% yes votes compared with 41% no votes. It legalized the use, possession, and cultivation of marijuana for patients with a medical recommendation. I 692 was seen as being quite liberal in that it allowed medical use for a broad set of qualifying conditions and allowed a patient to possess up to 24 ounces of useable marijuana and up to 15 plants—far more in aggregate than the amount allowed in any other legal state.

In the Washington Medical Use market, cultivation operations are unregulated, and medicinal cannabis may be grown either in individuals' homes or under a collective garden model whereby growers cultivate on behalf of a group of patients. Under current draft reforms, legal home growing and collective gardens would no longer exist. Medical sales will likely occur primarily through dispensaries, although again, there is no specific regulatory allowance for this form of distribution. The lack of regulations for production and distribution of Medical Use has exposed business operators to local and federal enforcement actions
The state legislature passed extensive regulatory reform measures on Medical Use in 2011. These measures were vetoed by Governor Chris Gregoire on the basis that state regulatory workers could be prosecuted under federal law.

In the wake of new Adult Use regulations, Medical Use reform efforts are once again underway in Washington. A working group consisting of three state agencies—the Department of Health, the Department of Revenue, and the Liquor Control Board—has put forth draft recommendations for new medical marijuana regulations. The group is calling for several changes:

- Elimination of collective gardens, home growing, and dispensaries
- Medical Use sales under the
- Adult Use regulatory system
- Establishment of a state patient registry
- Prohibition of personal-use home cultivation
- Tax exemption for Medical Use sales (although not for excise taxes)
- Labeling, testing, and safety requirements

After completion, the recommendations will go to the legislature in January 2014. If adopted, dispensaries would have to comply with the standards that are required of Adult

Use retail stores. The Liquor Control Board may cap the number of permitted dispensaries, as it did with Adult Use stores (see below). The costs and other practical challenges associated with these new rules could effectively put most dispensary operators out of business. Medicinal marijuana cultivators may also have to adhere to Adult Use standards, which could severely curtail their numbers too.

Adult Use

Washington Adult Use laws were approved in November 2012 via Initiative 502, which passed by a margin of 56 to 44. The measure provides for regulatory oversight by the LCB, which finalized the new laws on October 16, 2013, and the measure became effective the following month.

Adult Use regulations allow for a maximum of 334 retail stores statewide, allocated by population and accessibility. Businesses may operate under a for-profit enterprise model. An annual production cap of 80 metric tons is imposed (40 tons of usable marijuana and 40 tons for other marijuana products). The production limit is intended to minimize diversion risk, although some express concern that the cap also supports illicit market cultivation to meet overall demand. Personal-use cultivation is prohibited, and all cultivation must be indoors. As with Colorado Adult Use laws, there are requirements for lab testing and seed-to-sale inventory tracking, as well as for package labeling, child-proof packaging, the disclosure of test results, and safety warnings. Stores may sell to adults 21 years and older, with individual purchase transactions and possession limited to one ounce.

In contrast to Colorado, vertical integration is prohibited on the basis of the LCB's goal of avoiding monopolies that could keep retail prices artificially high and thus could risk favoring the illicit market. Prospective business owners may file applications for only one type of business operation per party (i.e., cultivation, processor, and retailer), beginning on November 18, 2013.

Adult Use retailers are expected to open for business in late spring or summer 2014.

The Washington Adult Use legislation entails a three-tier tax scheme: a 25% excise tax on cultivator-to-processor transactions, a 25% excise tax on processor-to-retailer transactions, and a 25% sales tax on retailer-to-consumer transactions. The state estimates $300 million in tax revenues in 2014, rising to $2 billion by 2017.

Investors and business owners must be residents of Washington State; however the residency requirement may be established in three months.

Consumer Access: Moderate

Prior to implementation of the I 502 Adult Use market in 2014, access to legal marijuana will be limited for patients, primarily through dispensaries, caregivers, and home cultivation. Weak regulatory controls, such as the lack of a patient registry and dispensary oversight, bolstering access. The broad list of qualifying patient conditions, such as the "chronic pain" catch-all category, also supports patient access.

Once Adult Use stores open by the summer of 2014, overall consumer access will be stronger. Production limits are offset by access to retail stores, as well as by the ability of both state residents and nonresidents to purchase up to an ounce of cannabis per transaction.

Competition: Moderate

Presently, a moderate level of competition exists among Medical Use cultivators and dispensaries under the currently unregulated market regime.

Once the Adult Use market comes online in 2014, competition will strengthen substantially, especially given the potential for out-of-state parties to satisfy the low residency requirement barrier and to compete with long-time residents. Increased product offerings will provide consumers with much greater selections of strains and products. It remains to be seen what the net effect will be on pricing, particularly given the new tax scheme. Medical Use products are not taxed, whereas the three-tier Adult Use taxation system may augment retail pricing above that of illicit market alternatives, even with more legal operators competing in the market.

Trends & Analysis

- 2014 Market Surge – the introduction of the Adult Use market in 2014 is projected to increase the Washington market by almost 1000% to $250 million.
- 2013 Market Retrenchment – Crackdowns by federal enforcement agencies and by local police have contracted the number of dispensaries and shifted some Medical Use patients to the illicit market.
- Grey Market Mystery – A majority of Medical Use patients are likely accessing marijuana through grey- or illicit-market channels. Out of an estimated 120,000 patients, only 30,000 are thought to be buying cannabis at dispensaries.
- Higher Dispensary Sales per Transaction – Washington dispensaries report that average package sizes are trending higher, although prices are stable. The larger transaction value, coupled with increased patient counts, have driven increases in state market value.
- Private-Sector Adult Use Consultation – in an elaborate RFP bidding process, the LCB accepted over 100 bids from independent consultants to advise on I 502 rules and implementation. The winning firm, Botec Analysis Corp, is headed by UCLA professor of public policy Mark Kleinman and has advised the state in four areas: product and industry knowledge, product quality standards and testing, product usage and consumption validation, and product regulation.

Survey Responses

1
Regulations

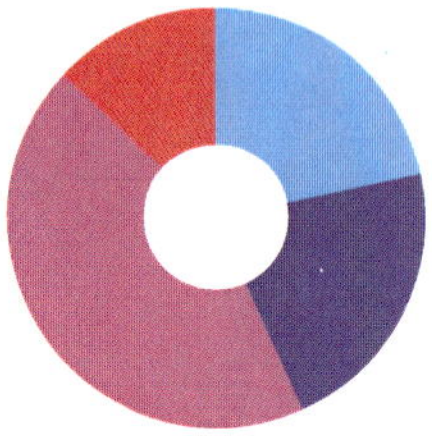

As a business operator, how do you feel about the medical marijuana **regulations** in your state?

- 21.7% Too complex
- 21.7% Too lenient
- 43.5% About right
- 13.0% Are harmful

2
Patient Access

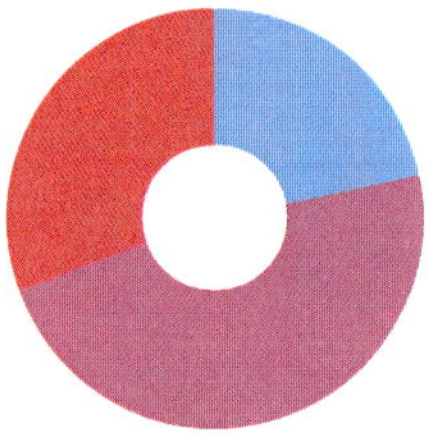

How do you feel about the **patient access** in your state?

- 21.7% It is too hard for patients
- 0.0% It is too easy for patients
- 47.8% It is about right
- 30.4% There should be no patient restrictions

3
Local Competition

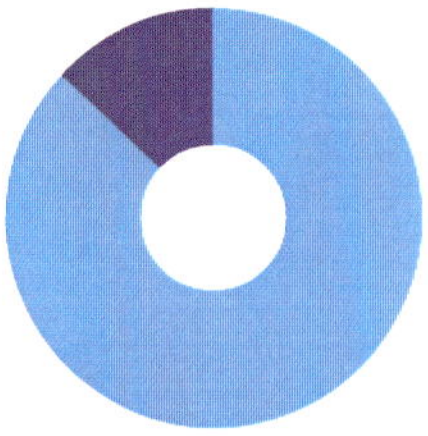

How would you describe your **local competition**?

- 87.0% Very competitive
- 13.0% Not competitive

4
Competitive Environment

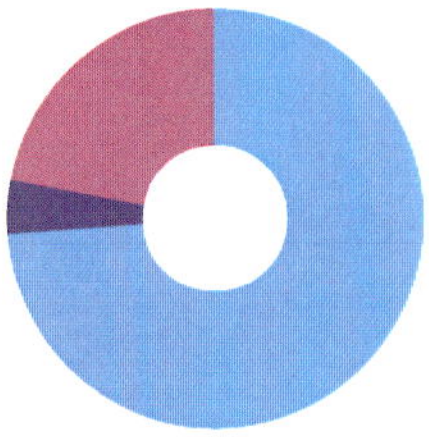

Over the past year, how would you describe your **competitive environment**?

- 73.9% Competition has gotten stiffer
- 4.3% Competition has reduced
- 21.7% No change in competition

5
Local Law Enforcement

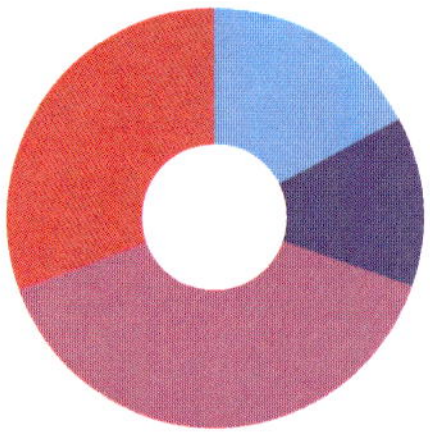

How concerned are you about state or **local law enforcement being a threat** to your business?

- 17.4% Very Concerned
- 13.0% Somewhat concerned
- 39.1% Not concerned
- 30.4% Local law enforcement is helpful to my business

6
Federal Law Enforcement

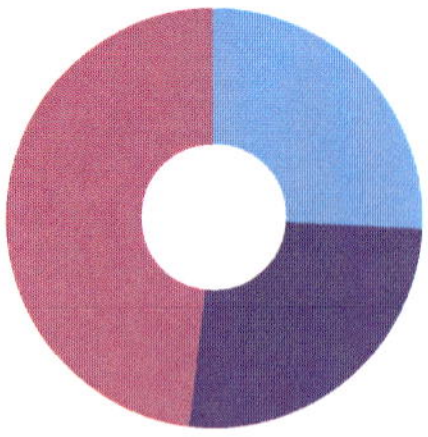

How concerned are you about **Federal law enforcement being a threat** to your business?

- 26.1% Very Concerned
- 26.1% Somewhat concerned
- 47.8% Not concerned
- 0.0% Federal law enforcement is helpful to my business

WELCOME TO
Washington
THE EVERGREEN STATE

7

Adult-Use

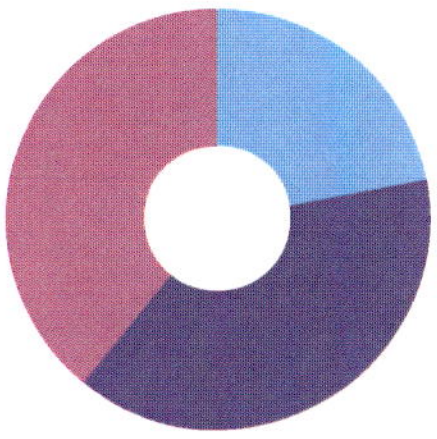

If located in Washington or Colorado, how do you feel about how the legalization of adult-use in your state will affect your business?

- 22.0% Too complex
- 39.0% Too lenient
- 39.0% About right

8

Product Sales Percentage

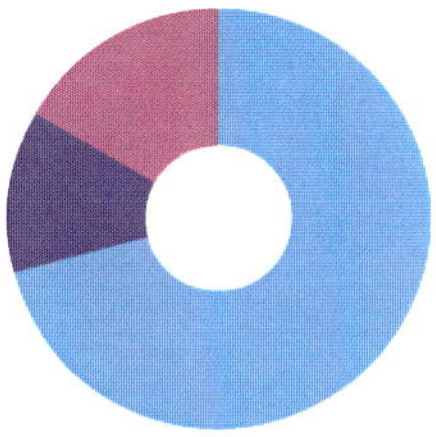

Please estimate what is the **percentage of total sales** for the following products?

- 71.0% Cannabis flowers
- 12.5% Concentrate
- 16.5% Infused Product

9

Retail Price Changes

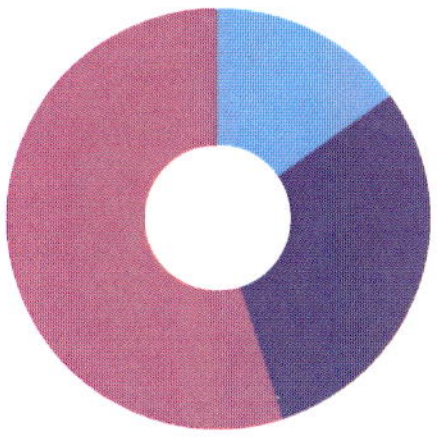

Over the past year, what changes have you seen in **retail prices** for customers?

- 15.0% Prices have gone up
- 30.0% Prices have done down
- 55.0% Prices have stayed the same

10

Previous Retail Experience

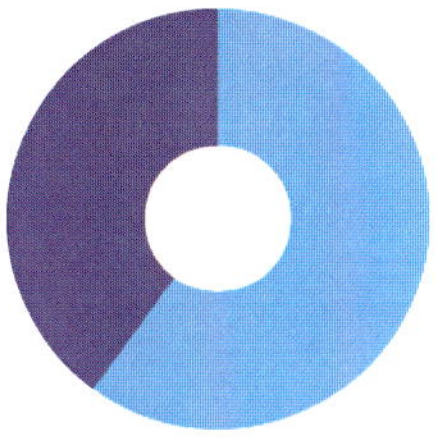

Have you had **previous experience** in the retail industry?

- 60.0% Yes
- 40.0% No

11

Previous Entrepreneurial Experience

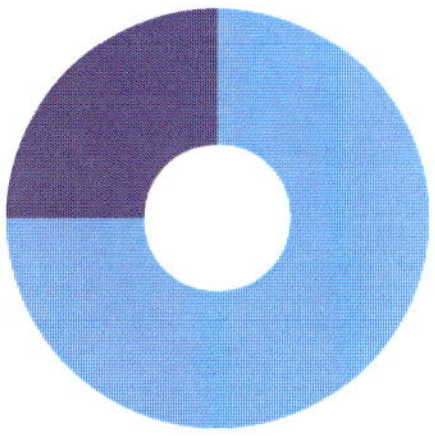

Have you had previous **entrepreneurial experience**?

- 75.0% Yes
- 25.0% No

12

Initial Start-up Costs

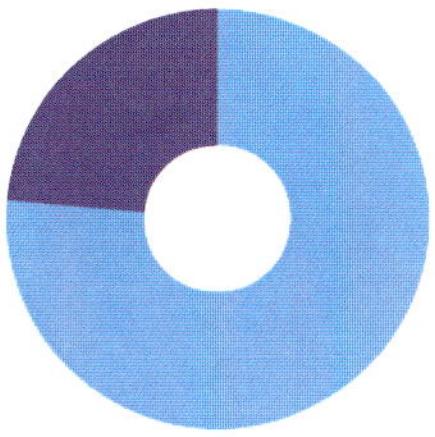

How did you fund your businesses **initial start-up costs**?

- 76.5% Self-financed
- 23.5% Family and friends investment
- 0.0% Angel investment
- 0.0% Institutional investment
- 0.0% Bank loan

Michigan

Michigan is the fourth-largest legal marijuana state in terms of both market value and the number of customers, even though it has faced strong pushback in some cities. A recent State Supreme Court case challenging state law will have significant impact on whether Michigan cities can restrict medical cannabis. This case has key implications for near term market growth potential.

		Rank
2013 Market Size	$ 60 million	# 4
Customers	33,275	# 4
Saturation Rate	11%	# 6
2013 vs. 2014 Growth Rate	10%	# 9

Overview: Moderate

In 2008, Michigan voters approved a Medical Use law funded and managed by the Marijuana Policy Project via ballot initiative, which won by a substantial majority. Even though no provision was made for dispensaries, up to 100 retail centers opened for business.

The state's substantial number of patients, coupled with a low saturation rate, implies that many purchase their cannabis from illicit sources or from the large pool of caregivers. With over 120,000 registered patients, but only 27% of which are dispensary customers, customer transactions represent a small fraction of the potential state market. These fundamentals also imply Michigan could become a fast-growing market, but only if some daunting legal hurdles on the horizon are overcome.

Regulatory Status: Weak

Proposal 1, the Michigan Medical Marihuana Act, was approved with 63% voting yes in November 2008. It allows Medical Use for patients diagnosed by a physician as having a debilitating illness under a fairly broad set of medical conditions, including chronic pain. The law calls for a state registry for patients (Michigan Medical Marijuana Program), although issuance of a registry card can take months after application. This delay is mitigated by the fact that a patient can legally purchase medical marijuana with the application alone. Patients are allowed to possess up to 2.5 ounces of medical cannabis.

Proposal 1 did not set provisions for cultivation or distribution businesses. Patients may grow up to 12 plants of their own medical cannabis or may designate a caregiver to cultivate on their behalf. Caregivers are each limited to serving five patients, and may receive compensation for costs, which approaches the nonprofit business model seen in other states. Outdoor cultivation is permitted in a locked area that is not visible to the unaided eye and that is within a structure enclosed on all sides. Considering Michigan's weather pattern, however, most cannabis is likely cultivated indoors.

Absent provisions for retail distribution, Michigan dispensaries exist in a state of limbo. Although the Michigan Supreme Court ruled that dispensaries are illegal in 2013, dozens of these businesses operate within the state. Some cities, such as Ypsilanti, have licensed and regulated marijuana distribution centers. Other cities, including Wyoming and Livonia, have taken action to institute bans within their municipalities. In 2010, a patient in the city of Wyoming sued to overturn the city's medical cannabis ban. He lost in local court but later won in the Michigan Court of Appeals. In April 2013, the Michigan

Supreme Court granted Wyoming's request to appeal. In October 2013, the Michigan Supreme Court heard what is considered to be a landmark case that will determine whether Michigan communities can bar medical marijuana. At issue is whether federal marijuana prohibition supersedes state Medical Use law. The American Civil Liberties Union argued in favor of affirming patient's rights to Medical Use. Pending the outcome of this case, Michigan's dispensaries are hanging in the balance.
In December 2013, HB 4271 was approved by the House Judiciary Committee, opening the possibility of allowing individual municipalities to decide whether to allow dispensaries. If enough backers support the measure, the bill may be signed into law in 2014.

Another challenge to Medical Use patients has come in the form of a decision by the Michigan Court of Appeals (State v. Carruthers), in which the court decided that cannabis-infused products and concentrates are not protected by the Michigan Medical Marihuana Act. The absence of infused products both reduces potential market value and deprives some patients of an important medicinal marijuana product alternative. However, the House Judiciary Committee has approved a HB 5104 in December 2013, which would allow multiple parts of the plant to be ingested in edible formats. It remains to be seen if there will be enough support for the bill to be signed into law.

Consumer Access: Moderate

In view of the current legal challenges and restrictions, Medical Use patients' access to cannabis is currently moderate. This determination is based on the numbers of dispensaries in operation in certain cities. The ability of patients to acquire medical cannabis from dispensaries with just a registry application also bolsters access. The state also recognizes out-of-state patients with Medical Use card authorizations.

Although access is currently considered moderate, the legal challenges highlighted above may diminish that standing. Pending the State Supreme Court's ruling, cities may be allowed to proceed with bans that trump the state law.

Competition: Weak

The large number of patients and-low saturation rate imply that the Michigan medical marijuana market is weak. As mentioned, a significant portion of patient purchases is likely from illicit sources.

The absence of state laws regarding legal marijuana businesses coupled with legal challenges to dispensaries in some cities reduce the number of potential competitors in the

Michigan Medical Use market. These conditions may improve—or worsen—substantially as a result of the outcome of the current State Supreme Court case cited above.

Trends & Analysis

- Modest Growth Outlook – legal uncertainties hang over businesses in the Michigan market, hindering growth. ArcView Market Research foresees 10% growth in 2014 over the 2013 market, which implies a 2014 market value of nearly $66 million. Growth may be substantially affected by the outcome of legal challenges currently in the court system.
- Low Dispensary Market Share – primary research indicates that 84 Michigan dispensaries are now serving approximately 33,000 patients. Given a registered patient population of 128,000, dispensaries are therefore serving around 27% of the registered patient market.
- Big, but Questionable, Market Potential – Michigan has the fourth-highest patient population of all of the legal marijuana states and a low 10% saturation rate. An affirmation of state marijuana laws in court could unleash substantial market potential, but some question the likelihood of a ruling that will favor legal marijuana businesses.
- Key Primary Caregiver Role – there are approximately 26,000 registered primary caregivers, each of who may serve a maximum of five patients. Given the low market saturation rate and the difficult political environment for dispensaries, caregivers play an especially important role in the Michigan market. This role may become even more significant to the market if current legal challenges force significant numbers of dispensaries to shut down.

Survey Responses

1 Regulations

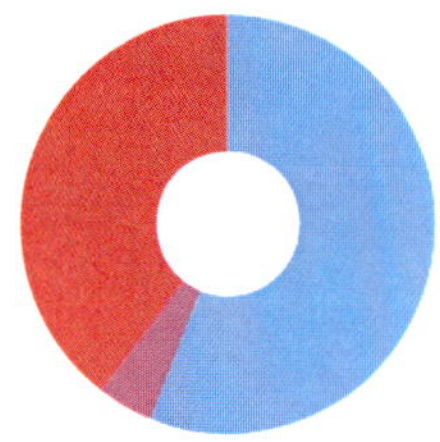

As a business operator, how do you feel about the medical marijuana **regulations** in your state?

- 50.0% Too complex
- 0.0% Too lenient
- 5.0% About right
- 45.0% Are harmful

2 Patient Access

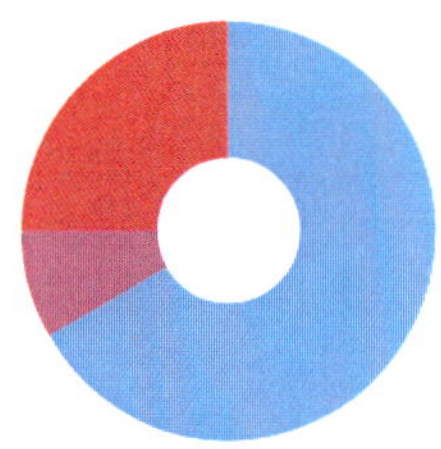

How do you feel about the **patient access** in your state?

- 66.7% It is too hard for patients
- 0.0% It is too easy for patients
- 8.3% It is about right
- 25.0% There should be no patient restrictions

3 Local Competition

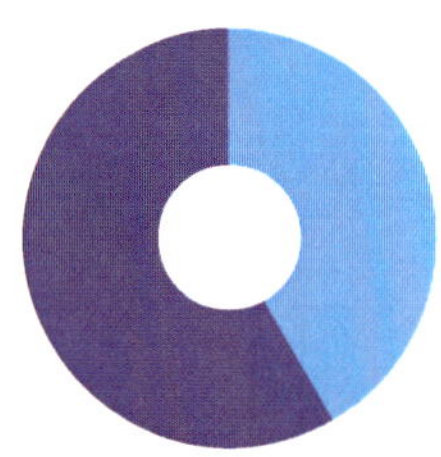

How would you describe your **local competition**?

- 41.7% Very competitive
- 58.3% Not competitive

4 Competitive Environment

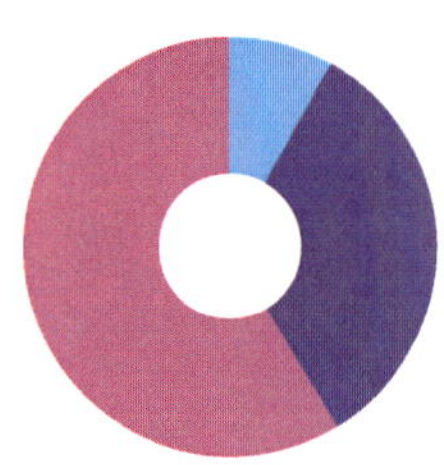

Over the past year, how would you describe your **competitive environment**?

- 8.3% Competition has gotten stiffer
- 33.3% Competition has reduced
- 58.3% No change in competition

5 Local Law Enforcement

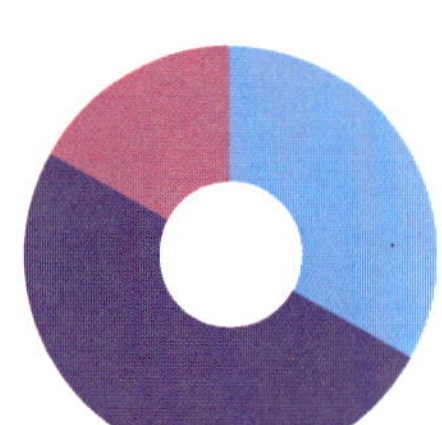

How concerned are you about state or **local law enforcement being a threat** to your business?

- 33.3% Very Concerned
- 50.0% Somewhat concerned
- 16.7% Not concerned
- 0.0% Local law enforcement is helpful to my business

6 Federal Law Enforcement

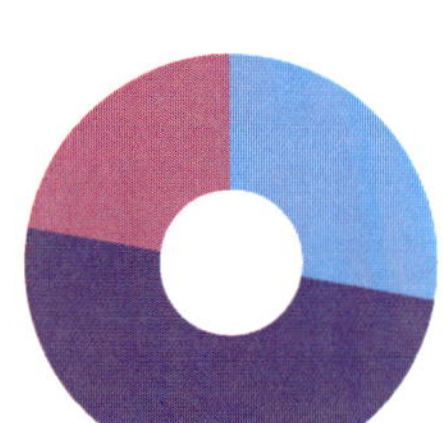

How concerned are you about **Federal law enforcement being a threat** to your business?

- 28.0% Very Concerned
- 50.0% Somewhat concerned
- 22.0% Not concerned
- 0.0% Federal law enforcement is helpful to my business

8

Product Sales Percentage

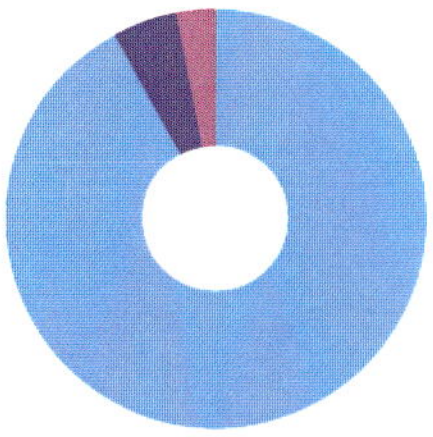

Please estimate what is the **percentage of total sales** for the following products?

- 92.0% Cannabis flowers
- 5.0% Concentrate
- 3.0% Infused Product

9

Retail Price Changes

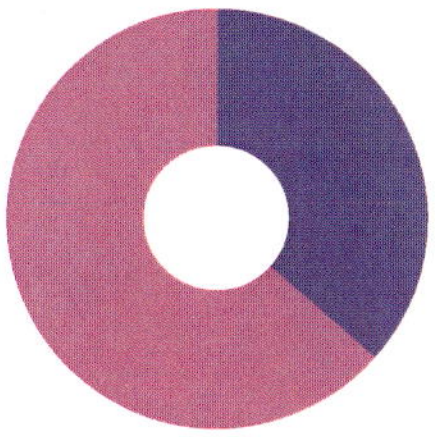

Over the past year, what changes have you seen in **retail prices** for customers?

- 0.0% Prices have gone up
- 36.4% Prices have done down
- 63.6% Prices have stayed the same

10

Previous Retail Experience

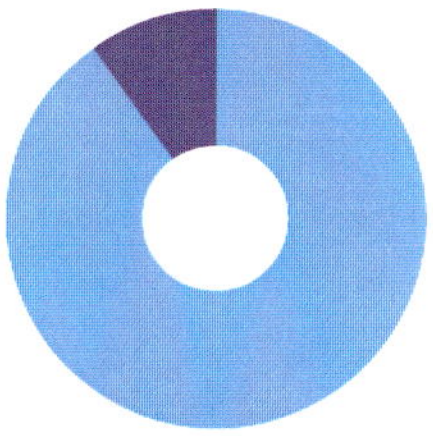

Have you had **previous experience** in the retail industry?

- 90.0% Yes
- 10.0% No

11

Previous Entrepreneurial Experience

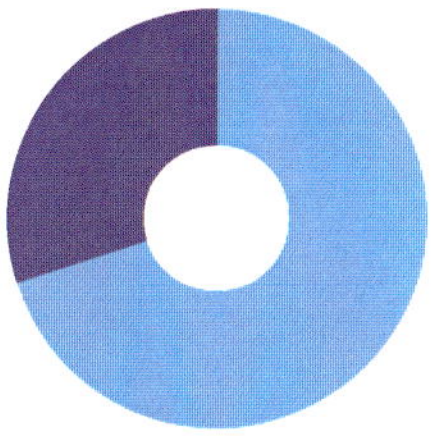

Have you had previous **entrepreneurial experience**?

- 70.0% Yes
- 30.0% No

12

Initial Start-up Costs

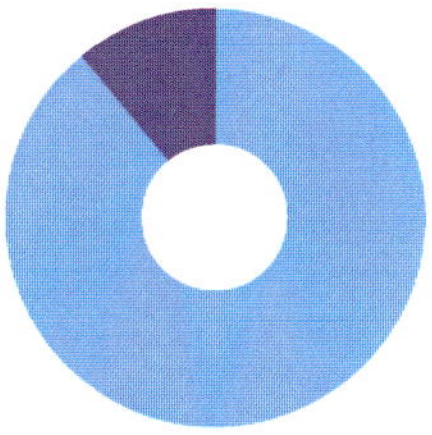

How did you fund your businesses **initial start-up costs**?

- 88.9% Self-financed
- 11.1% Family and friends investment
- 0.0% Angel investment
- 0.0% Institutional investment
- 0.0% Bank loan

Nevada

Nevada's Medical Use regulations are getting a major tune-up, with the first licensed dispensaries to open for business in 2014. This will propel the state market value much higher, which also helps set the stage for the possibility of an Adult Use ballot initiative in the 2016 election cycle.

		Rank
2013 Market Size	$ 3 million	# 8
Customers	1,232	# 8
Saturation Rate	4%	# 9
2013 vs. 2014 Growth Rate	225%	# 3

Overview: Strong

13 years after Nevadan's passed medical marijuana, cannabis businesses will be licensed and create a major boost for the state industry beginning in 2014. The introduction of permitted dispensaries, coupled with a low saturation rate and nonresident patient reciprocity, imply substantial growth potential. ArcView Market Research foresees a greater than two-fold annual increase in Nevada state market value in 2014.

Nevada is also one of eights states ArcView Market Research anticipates will have an Adult Use measure on the ballot in 2016. Prospects for passage appear favorable, which would result in substantial business revenue growth derived from both resident and tourist populations (particularly in Clark and Washoe counties).

Regulatory Status: Strong

In November 2000, 65% of voters approved Question 9, which allows the use, possession and cultivation of marijuana for registered patients who receive written documentation from their physician recommending cannabis to treat a fairly broad set of qualifying conditions. Question 9 allowed patients or their primary caregivers to posess up to one ounce of marijuana, and may cultivate up to seven plants, including a maximum of three mature plants. Patients must register with the Nevada Medical Marijuana Program within the Department of Health and Human Services. No provisions were made for commercial cultivation, processing, or distribution.

Nearly thirteen years later, Governor Brian Sandoval signed Senate Bill 374, thereby amending state regulations to authorize the licensing of medical marijuana businesses including dispensaries, production, and infused product companies. Up to 66 dispensaries may be permitted, and there are limits regarding how many can operate in the various counties as a function of population size. SB 374 also calls for testing for potency, molds, fungus, and other aspects. Patient possession limits were increased to allow for the purchase of two and one half ounces over a 14-day period, though home cultivation is prohibited except for patients living more than 25 miles away from a dispensary. Another home cultivation exception is granted to patients who were growing prior to July 2013, who are able to continue cultivation until March 2014.

The Subcommittee on the Medical Use of Marijuana Commission will craft recommendations for the final details and rules of implementation, which should be completed in early 2014, with license applications beginning in April. However, the cities of Las Vegas and Reno have enacted temporary bans through spring, preventing license applications for those cities. These could be extended for additional time periods such that the first dispensaries may not open until late in the year or early 2015. Business-

es can be formed as for-profit enterprises, and nonresidents may be both license holders and investors in those businesses. There are also provisions for reciprocity of medical marijuana patients with valid certification from other states, and these nonresident patients may purchase cannabis at Nevada dispensaries subject to the same rules as apply to state residents. Commercial cultivation may be done indoors or outdoors in enclosed, locked greenhouse facilities. All businesses must use electronic patient verification and inventory control systems, as well as security measures. In addition to state retail sales taxes, a 2% excise tax on wholesale transfers of marijuana products, and a 2% excise tax on retail sales is to be assessed.

Advocates are planning for introduction of an Adult Use ballot initiative in 2016, which would clearly increase the state market value potential. A poll of state voters conducted by the Retail Association of Nevada in October 2013 found that 54% would support full adult legalization if tax revenues were used for educational funding.

Patient Access: Moderate

Patient access in Nevada is in a state of flux. The existence of delivery services (primarily in Las Vegas) and home cultivation privileges help offset the current absence of licensed dispensaries. As dispensaries begin to come online in 2014, patient access to commercial distribution will improve greatly, even as allowance for home cultivation diminishes.

Competition: Moderate

Commercial competition is now limited to delivery services, especially in Las Vegas. These businesses also compete with home cultivation. Commercial competition will increase from late 2014 and going forward as marijuana businesses are licensed and open for shop. The longer-term prospect for Adult Use retailers after 2016 would greatly increase the overall competitive landscape.

Trends & Analysis

Big Growth in 2014 – The introduction of licensed dispensaries, coupled with the potential for increased patient registrations and tourists exercising reciprocity rights, bodes well for Nevada state market growth. ArcView Market Research projects Nevada will be the third fastest growing market in 2014, with the state market value increasing by225% to nearly $2.8 million in 2014.

- Delivery Services Transition – Dispensaries have opened in Nevada in the past prior to laws permitting these businesses, only to be shut down by authorities. As a result, the commercial market presently is dominated by delivery services, which are more elusive to enforcement efforts. As opportunities for licensing emerge in 2014, many of these dispensaries are expected to apply for permits, and all will face greater competition from storefronts. These dynamics are likely to shrink the delivery service population.
- Nonresident Green Rush – Many out-of-state investors and would be entrepreneurs are currently weighing opportunities to obtain Nevada marijuana business licenses. In addition to near-term Medical Use market opportunities, the prospect of Adult Use legalization on the horizon present significant enticements.
- Potential Adult Use Vote in 2016 – Policy analysts and advocacy groups foresee a good chance for a 2016 full legalization ballot initiative. Nevada tends to lean toward liberal values, particularly in the matters related to commerce. ArcView Market Research anticipates a 2016 Adult Use campaign will prove to be successful.

ARCVIEW MARKET RESEARCH

Oregon

Oregon was the first US state to decriminalize possession of small amounts of marijuana. Yet, as with other states that were part of the first wave of medical marijuana legalization, Oregon's regulatory structure is outdated as compared with current standards. Popular support for cannabis has led to recent efforts to modernize Medical Use laws governing the supply chain. The result is a substantial projected increase in the state market value.

		Rank
2013 Market Size	$ 30 million	# 5
Customers	18,989	# 5
Saturation Rate	9%	# 7
2013 vs. 2014 Growth Rate	25%	# 7 (tied)

Overview: Strong

Big shifts are underway for Oregon's medicinal cannabis regulations. Although Medical Use has been legal for over 15 years, the authorized supply chain has centered on personal cultivation and designated caregivers. Dispensaries have been technically illegal, but many have been operating under essentially nonexistent oversight. Absent any sustained enforcement, the number of dispensary operators has increased rapidly, as has the size of the state market.

During the summer of 2013, state congress approved a bill that authorizes and regulates dispensaries. Implementation may cause some turmoil for dispensaries that will now have to comply with strict guidelines. In spite of a potential shakeout of marginal operators, strong regulation will legitimize dispensaries and increase market growth. This should help increase the state's currently low saturation rate.

Regulatory Status: Moderate

The Oregon Medical Use regulatory model is about to be significantly updated and upgraded. The prevailing system is weak, but a strong system for regulating dispensaries will be implemented in 2014. Accordingly, ArcView Market Research is characterizing this transitional period as "Moderate" in terms of current regulatory status.

In 1998, voters approved Oregon Ballot Measure 67, with the split registering 55% yes and 45% no. The measure permitted Medical Use for patients with a signed physician recommendation, by the patient's primary doctor, for a fairly broad set of conditions.

State registration is mandatory for patients, and the registration process is operated under the Oregon Medical Marijuana Program and implemented by the state Public Health Division, Oregon Health Authority. Laws for licensing dispensaries and cultivators were not addressed. This created a large reliance on the caregiver model, which is how the majority of patients currently obtain marijuana. Caregivers may be reimbursed only for the cost of supplies and utilities used to provide cannabis to patients.

Measure 74, which was put to voters in 2010 and would have created a regulated dispensary system, failed to pass (58% opposed, 42 percent in favor). In spite of this loss, dispensary numbers in the state continued to increase.

However, in the summer of 2013, the state congress passed House Bill 3460, which is aimed at creating a not-for-profit legal distribution system for medicinal cannabis by licensing dispensaries. Under the legislation, the Oregon Health Authority will begin accepting dispensary license applications on March 1, 2014. Dispensary owners must be

Oregon residents, and investment in dispensary businesses is not explicitly addressed. A 13-member committee is overseeing rulemaking for HB3460 and is working to finalize laws by February 1, 2014. Under the law localities may not ban dispensaries but some cities such as Medford and Myrtle Creek have already begun to push back against the new laws, seeking to block dispensaries within their city limits.

Interestingly, the new law does not regulate the cultivation of cannabis. Permissible cultivation is left to the existing system where patients designate caregivers who are allowed to grow for up to 4 patients (up to one and one half pounds per patient). Caregivers are allowed to band together to collectively cultivate at a common address. Dispensaries are forbidden from being cultivators. Under HB3460, caregivers can be compensated not only for supplies and utilities used to produce cannabis for patients, but also for "normal and customary" costs. This compensation model increases the scope of allowable payments to caregiver/cultivators, and should help migrate more growers away from the illicit market and into legal cultivation within the Medical Use system.

There is no explicit tax on Medical Use cannabis under HB3460, and Oregon has no general sales tax. The lack of medical marijuana taxation should help the retail price of legal cannabis be competitive with pricing in the illicit market.

Part of the intention of the new rules is to cull marginal operators and to create standards for quality. Suspicion of some dispensaries' diversion of cannabis to illicit markets has prompted raids by local police and county sheriffs in some regions. Dispensary oversight under the new regulations should filter out questionable operators. Many existing dispensaries are expected to apply for licenses under the new regulatory system. In addition to paying annual licensing fees and adhering to state oversight, dispensaries will also be required to test cannabis for potency, mold, mildew, and pesticides. After operating for years without regulatory oversight, some existing "legitimate" dispensaries may no longer be viable under new compliance and fee requirements. Given the lack of experience operating under tight regulations and professional standards, there may ultimately be substantial attrition of newly licensed dispensary operators over time.

There are also well-funded efforts to bring Adult Use regulations to Oregon in 2014, either through legislative process or by putting the issue on the ballot. Advocacy groups and politicians are now attempting to put "recreational" marijuana laws up for vote during the 2014 election cycle.

Consumer Access: Strong

Oregon has fairly broad allowances for the patient medical conditions that qualify for medical marijuana, which enables relatively easy access to Medical Use. The rapid increase in the number of Oregon dispensaries has substantially increased consumer access. This increase is in addition to Oregon's well-developed caregiver system, which is deeply rooted in the marijuana community. Under the new law localities may not ban dispensaries. This will increase access. However, the number of dispensaries may decline somewhat in the first half of 2014 as new regulations are put in place. However, new operators are likely to more than compensate for any losses, and overall dispensaries will be stronger businesses with improved product offerings.

Competition: Moderate

Continued growth in the number of dispensaries has increased market competition in Oregon over the past two years. This trend is likely to persist in 2014 as storefronts come under supervised regulation and overtly compete on the basis of price and quality. The legal market also has to compete with a well-developed illicit state market in Oregon, where there is a history of production in southern rural areas that are well suited to cannabis cultivation.

Trends & Analysis

- Substantial Growth Outlook – ArcView Market Research projects that the strengthened regulatory system will substantially increase the size of the Oregon legal marijuana market. The market's low saturation rate is also supportive of the state's growth potential in a well-regulated market. An annual growth rate of 25% is foreseen in 2014, thus increasing the value of the Oregon state market to $37 million.

- Caregiver & Personal Cultivation Competition – in addition to competing with each other, dispensaries also have substantial competition from caregivers and from home cultivation. This is especially prevalent in the Oregon's southern regions, which are favorable for outdoor cultivation. A substantial, but unknown, number of delivery services also represent significant competition.

- Caregiver to Dispensary Conversion – in part due to Oregon's history of unregulated cannabis cultivation and distribution, the large majority of Medical Use patients acquire cannabis from sources other than dispensaries (particularly caregivers). Under the new state regulatory regime that will begin in 2014, dispensaries will have the opportunity to generate a substantial number of new customers by winning converts from both illicit and caregiver sources.

- Smoothing of the Dispensary Footprint – Oregon dispensaries are far more prevalent in some counties than in others. Raids by county police in some counties have shrunk local dispensary numbers. Kings County, in contrast, deprioritized marijuana enforcement and as a result has a high concentration of Oregon dispensaries. In 2014, new laws governing dispensaries will reduce enforcement risk and are expected to increase dispensary numbers in other counties and to reduce regional concentrations.

- Portland Enforcement "Safe Harbor" – Approximately one-third of Oregon dispensaries are now located in Portland. This is due both to the city's concentrated patient population, as well as to the occurrence of fewer law enforcement actions in Portland. Dispensary raids in Portland have been far less intensive compared with enforcement in cities situated in other counties. As a result, Portland has become somewhat of a safe haven for dispensaries. This is particularly true compared with Southern Oregon cities such as Medford, where both enforcement actions and pushback from local communities have resulted in a much less friendly operating environment compared with Portland.

- Adult Use Legalization Prospects - Oregon Senate Judiciary Chairman Floyd Proznaski (D-Eugene) has presented draft legislation that would put full legalization up for vote in 2014. Advocacy group New Approach Oregon has filed an initiative with the secretary of state to push for a 2014 ballot measure. A 2013 poll by Greenberg Quinlan Rosner showed that 57% of likely Oregon voters would support a proposal to tax, regulate, and legalize marijuana for recreational use. ArcView Market Research expects an Adult Use measure will be put up for vote in the 2014 election cycle, and projects the measure is likely to succeed.

Oregon

Survey Responses

1
Regulations

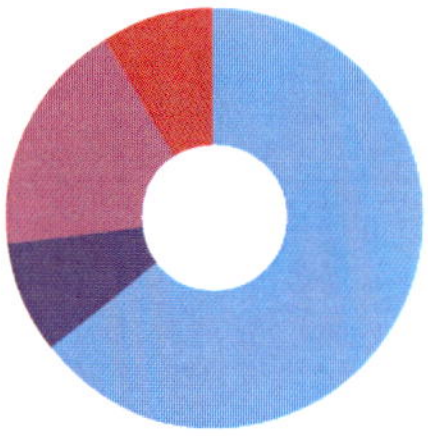

As a business operator, how do you feel about the medical marijuana **regulations** in your state?

- 64.6% Too complex
- 8.7% Too lenient
- 18.0% About right
- 8.7% Are harmful

2
Patient Access

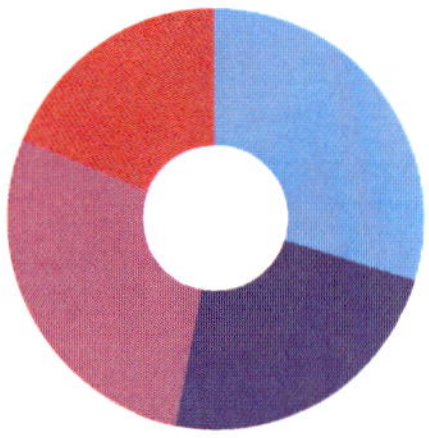

How do you feel about the **patient access** in your state?

- 34.8% It is too hard for patients
- 21.7% It is too easy for patients
- 26.1% It is about right
- 17.4% There should be no patient restrictions

3
Local Competition

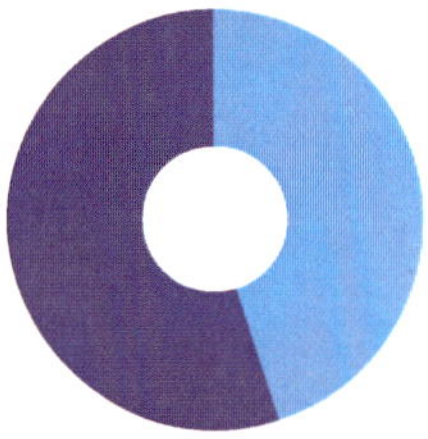

How would you describe your **local competition**?

- 44.0% Very competitive
- 56.0% Not competitive

4
Competitive Environment

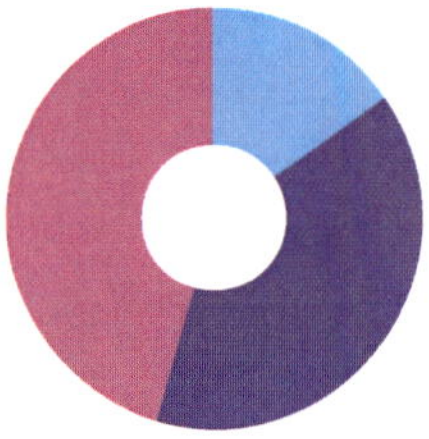

Over the past year, how would you describe your **competitive environment**?

- 15.4% Competition has gotten stiffer
- 39.1% Competition has reduced
- 45.5% No change in competition

5
Local Law Enforcement

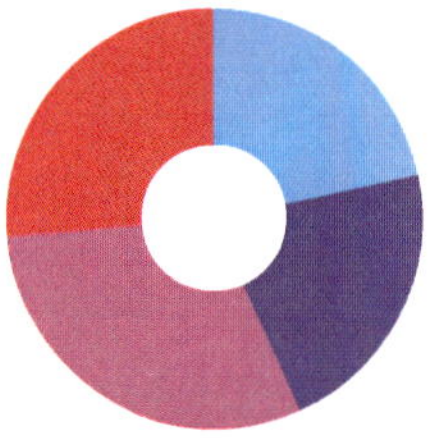

How concerned are you about state or **local law enforcement being a threat** to your business?

- 21.7% Very Concerned
- 21.7% Somewhat concerned
- 30.4% Not concerned
- 26.1% Local law enforcement is helpful to my business

6
Federal Law Enforcement

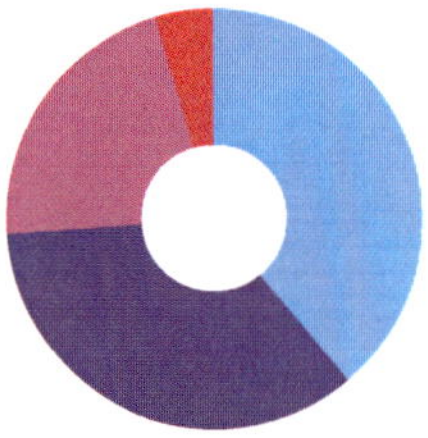

How concerned are you about **Federal law enforcement being a threat** to your business?

- 39.1% Very Concerned
- 34.8% Somewhat concerned
- 21.8% Not concerned
- 4.3% Federal law enforcement is helpful to my business

8

Product Sales Percentage

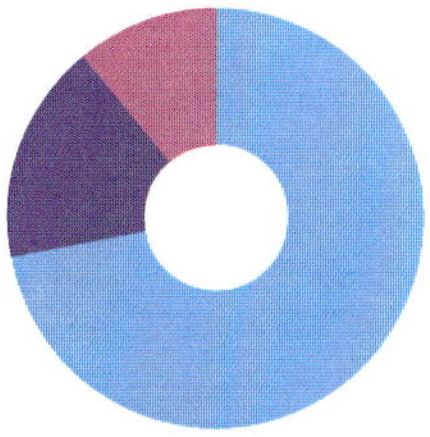

Please estimate what is the **percentage of total sales** for the following products?

- 72.0% Cannabis flowers
- 17.0% Concentrate
- 11.0% Infused Product

9

Retail Price Changes

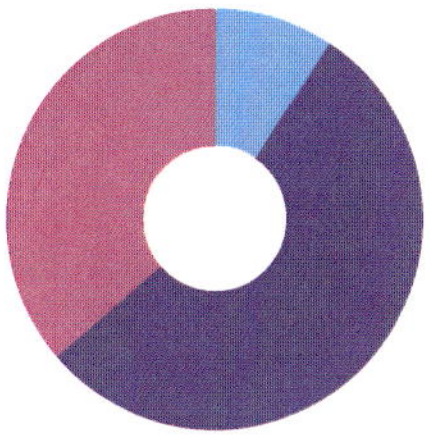

Over the past year, what changes have you seen in **retail prices** for customers?

- 9.2% Prices have gone up
- 54.5% Prices have done down
- 36.3% Prices have stayed the same

10

Previous Retail Experience

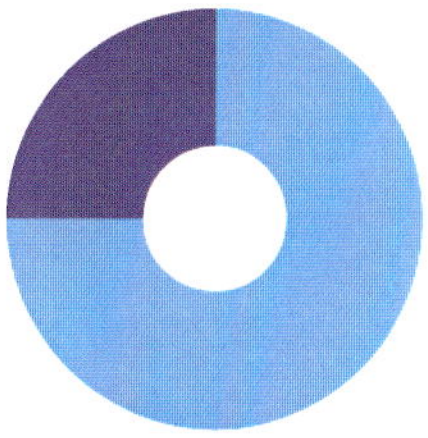

Have you had **previous experience** in the retail industry?

- 75.0% Yes
- 25.0% No

11

Previous Entrepreneurial Experience

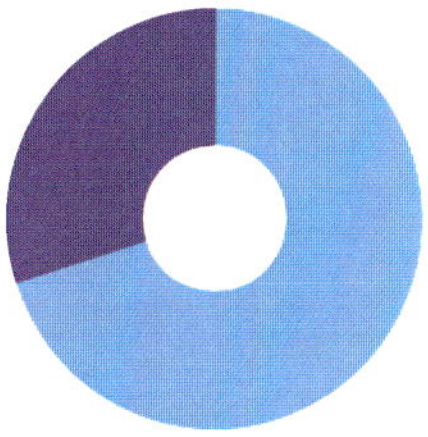

Have you had previous **entrepreneurial experience**?

- 70.0% Yes
- 30.0% No

12

Initial Start-up Costs

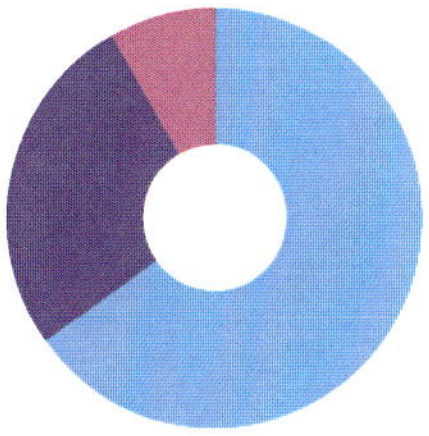

How did you fund your businesses **initial start-up costs**?

- 65.2% Self-financed
- 26.7% Family and friends investment
- 8.1% Angel investment
- 0.0% Institutional investment
- 0.0% Bank loan

Washington DC

The District of Columbia's tiny Medical Use market has endured a very slow start and the smallest customer base of any US legal marijuana market. Dispensaries are reporting very few customer transactions. As more potential customers learn to navigate the state patient registry, the DC market will post a significant growth rate.

While the DC market may be very small, it is symbolically important given that its location is also the seat of federal government. It is notable that members of Congress from states that do not have medical cannabis laws can now drive past and even visit a working cannabis dispensary. That could have significant political implications for initiatives in new state markets. Also, DC does not have the same legal rights as states since it is ultimately controlled by Congress. There is a measure of political significance that legal cannabis is being sold in an area that Congress has control over in a way that it does not for individual states.

		Rank
2013 Market Size	$ 77 thousand	# 12
Customers	89	# 12
Saturation Rate	2%	# 11
2013 vs. 2014 Growth Rate	214%	# 4

Overview: Weak

About 15 years after DC voters approved medical marijuana, the first dispensaries finally opened shop in mid 2013. Qualifying conditions are restrictive, and the patient registration process is cumbersome. Dispensaries have become proactive in helping guide patients registration, so customer counts are on the rise. Physicians are reportedly reluctant to write recommendations based on fears of legal repercussions. Even as challenges persist, ArcView Market Research anticipates the DC market value will more than double in 2014, though remain the smallest US market by a substantial margin.

Regulatory Status: Strong

In 1998, not long after the first Medical Use states approved legal marijuana regulations, 69% of DC voters passed the Legalization of Marijuana for Medical Treatment Initiative, a municipal ballot measure. It was as liberal as California's law in terms who could qualify for medical cannabis and went even further by establishing provisions for retail distribution. In 1998, this allowance was very revolutionary. However, a congressional ban prevented implementation of the measure until the ban was lifted in 2009. In 2010, DC council members gutted the original ballot language and enacted very restrictive legislation which authorized the establishment and regulation of dispensaries. Under the law, the Department of Health issues separate licenses for dispensary and cultivation businesses. The city government may approve up to six cultivation centers and four dispensaries. Businesses can be either for-profit or not-for-profit enterprises. Licensees are limited to cultivating a maximum of 95 plants at any one time. Cultivation must be done in an enclosed facility which is not visible to the public. Given the size, density, and urban makeup of DC outdoor cultivation is largely unfeasible.

Patients are not allowed to grow marijuana, and can only legally possess marijuana obtained from a dispensary. All patients must choose one dispensary as a source for cannabis. Patients may work with a registered caregiver, who is limited to working with one patient. Two ounces of cannabis is the legal limit for patient possession. There is no reciprocity provision for out-of-state patients.

Patient Access: Moderate

Patients are required to acquire cannabis through a dispensary, and must select one dispensary as a source for their medical marijuana. As of December 2013, three dispensaries were in operation, and report having ample inventory for customer transactions.

Competition: Moderate

In the current environment of the nascent market and small numbers of patient transactions, the DC active competition amongst dispensaries has yet to be established. The three dispensaries in operation as of December 2013 appear adequate to meet current customer demand, though limited overall transactions implies minimally competitive environment. As more patients come online in 2014, competitive dynamics will likely increase.

Trends & Analysis

Substantial Growth of the Smallest Legal US Market – Based on increased patient registrations, and a full year of operations, ArcView Market Research projects the DC market will register and increase of over 200% in 2014 to a value of $241,000.

Physician Trepidation – there are a limited number of DC doctors willing to recommend medical marijuana for patient recommendations. This reticence is reportedly based on fears that current laws do not protect them from potential prosecution. Overcoming this perception will be key to increasing patient counts and building market value.

Expanded Qualifying Conditions Sought – In response to figures released at a October 2013 DC city council meeting, which reflected a trickle of patient activity in dispensaries, advocates are asking officials to take measures to increase market participation. This includes a request to broaden qualifying conditions, and improve physician education regarding medical marijuana recommendations. Council member Yvette Alexander voiced concern about the potential for expanding qualifying conditions when a only small fraction of the thousands of individuals which represent the current potential customer population – suffering from conditions like HIV and cancer – are choosing to become Medical Use patients.

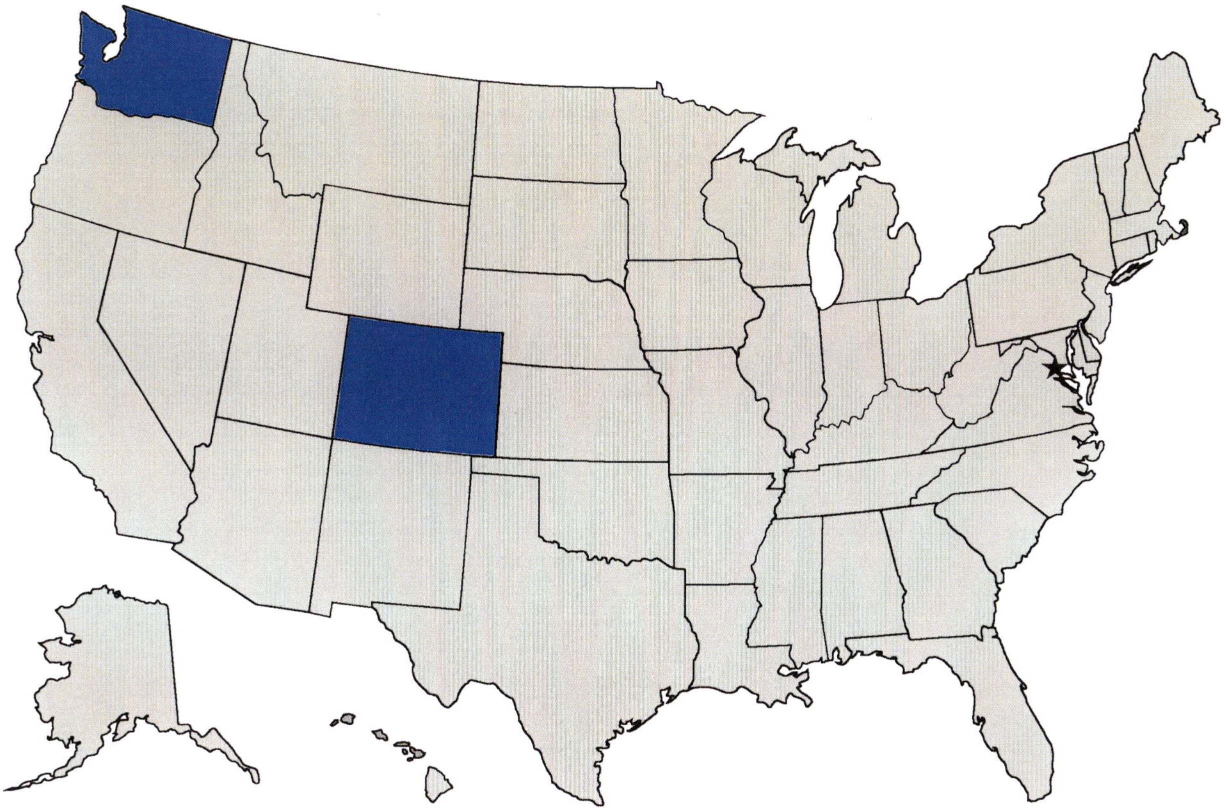

New Jersey

It's been a slow start for the New Jersey legal marijuana market. Legislation was approved in 2010, but impediments have delayed the opening of the first dispensary for nearly three years. More dispensaries are being added, albeit slowly, and paving the way for growth.

		Rank
2013 Market Size	$ 444 thousand	# 11
Customers	740	# 11
Saturation Rate	1%	# 12
2013 vs. 2014 Growth Rate	202%	# 5

Overview: Weak

New Jersey legal cannabis market value was the second smallest of all legal states in 2013. Slow administrative license processing and business location challenges have stalled patient registration and dispensary licensing. The first dispensary opened in December 2012, but was flooded with patients and had to shut down months later just to replenish inventory.

Growth prospects, however, are brightening. Three dispensaries are now operating, with the potential for three more to be added in 2014. As a result, the New Jersey market value is projected to register an annual two-fold increase for 2014, albeit to a level that would still make it one of the smallest legal marijuana market states.

Regulatory Status: Moderate

The New Jersey Compassionate Use Medical Marijuana Act became law in January 2010. The law allows for registered patients to possess and use medical marijuana obtained from a licensed "alternative treatment center" (i.e., dispensary). Regulatory oversight is administered by the New Jersey Department of Health under the Medicinal Marijuana Program. The Department of Health opened the registry to patients in August 2012, who must receive a recommendation from a physician who must also be registered under the Program. The list of qualifying conditions is less expansive than for some other Medical Use states. Patients are allowed possession of up to two ounces of marijuana per month. No personal cultivation is allowed, and there is no patient reciprocity with other states.

Under current laws, the state allows for up to six dispensaries. Licensing of new dispensaries has been impeded by long administrative processes, and in some instances, community opposition over approvals of business locations based on zoning rules. A total of three dispensaries will be operating by the end of 2013, with the potential for three more in 2014. Vertical integration is mandatory, as dispensaries are required to cultivate their own medical marijuana inventory. The first two dispensaries were required to be not-for-profit companies, though subsequent dispensaries may elect for-profit status. There is no special statewide tax on medical marijuana, though sales are subject to 7% state retail sales tax.

Patient Access: Weak

In addition to the inability to grow their own legal marijuana, patients have complained of long registration processing times. New Jersey Medical Use customers now only have three dispensaries serving the state market. This is a marked improvement compared with recent times when one sole dispensary was being overwhelmed by demand from patients located throughout the state. That first dispensary, which opened in December 2012, was asking patients to limit purchase transactions to less than the two ounce legal maximum, is reportedly currently open just one day a month.

The opening of additional dispensaries in 2014 should alleviate some of the access constraints. There is also an effort to allow New Jersey patients to travel to other states to acquire medical marijuana.

Competition: Weak

With only three dispensaries currently in operation, all with vertically integrated cultivation, competition amongst legal marijuana businesses is minimal in New Jersey. Prices are reportedly higher than illicit markets. Unlike dispensaries in well-developed markets, New Jersey dispensaries do not advertise cannabis menus and pricing online.

Trends & Analysis

- High Prices – Good quality legal cannabis in New Jersey dispensaries is reportedly selling for a little over $500 per ounce, which is said to be the illicit market price, and at the top of legal marijuana prices in the US. Good quality medical marijuana in Colorado, at the other end of the price spectrum, is now being sold for around $250 per ounce.

- Diminished Potential Patient Out-of-State Access – A bill introduced by Assemblywoman Linda Stender (D-Union) calls for allowing New Jersey patients to bring home cannabis purchased in other legal states. If successful, implementation of the law would likely require establishing reciprocity provisions in the state marijuana regulations. While improving patient access channels, this measure would also increase competition for New Jersey dispensaries and potentially reduce state market revenues. Passage of the bill faces important hurdles, including opposition by Governor Chris Christie, who views it as a back door approach to full legalization. Christie has voiced strong opposition to Adult Use regulations in New Jersey.

MOVE IN TODAY

Maine

Like DC's, Maine's small qualifying Medical Use patient population constrains legal market demand. However, big changes could be on the horizon. In November 2013, voters of the city of Portland approved a measure eliminating penalties for possessing small amounts of marijuana. That could well prove to be a dress rehearsal for statewide legalization in 2016.

		Rank
2013 Market Size	$ 1.5 million	# 10
Customers	947	# 9
Saturation Rate	15%	# 4
2013 vs. 2014 Growth Rate	25%	# 7 (tied)

Overview: Weak

Maine's restrictive Medical Use regulations limit patient access and market size. The narrow list of qualifying medical conditions for medicinal marijuana makes Maine's existing and potential patient population the smallest of any Medical Use state in the US.

In spite of current limitations, the initiative Question 1, passed by voters in Portland in November 2013, is considered a bellwether by marijuana advocates as to whether East Coast states are ready to follow Colorado and Washington State's lead in approving Adult Use laws.

Regulatory Status: Strong

Ballot Question 2, an initiative that provided for Medical Use, was passed by voters in 1999. Question 2 allows for the use of medicinal cannabis by patients who obtain an oral or written recommendation from their physician. It also allows for possession and personal cultivation. State law was amended several times, most recently in 2011 by Legislative Document 126. Though originally mandatory, patient registration is now optional.

The list of Medical Use qualifying conditions is limited to severe disorders like glaucoma, MS, and nausea from AIDS or chemotherapy. Conditions were expanded to include chronic pain in 2009, though only if patients haven't responded to other treatments for six months. Patients or their primary caregivers may possess two and a half ounces of useable marijuana and six mature plants. A 2010 bill authorized up to eight nonprofit dispensaries, and as of January 2011, patients can obtain a card through the state registry operated by the Division of Licensing and Regulatory Services. Dispensaries are licensed and regulated by the Department of Health and Human Services.

Maine law permits patient reciprocity with other Medical Use states. It allows nonresident visiting patients to possession and use medical cannabis if they have a valid registry identification card or the equivalent. This reciprocity provision, however, does not allow nonresidents to purchase cannabis in Maine.

In the city of Portland, voters approved Question 1 in November 2013, which allows for Adult Use and possession of up to two and one half ounces by adult 21 years and older. Passage of Question 1 doesn't increase the Maine legal marijuana market since it doesn't address distribution and is superseded by state law. Having passed with over two-thirds support, however, it is seen as a positive indicator of success for a potential statewide ballot measure in 2016.

Consumer Access: Weak

Maine's relatively narrow list of qualifying conditions limits consumer patient counts. With a saturation rate of 15%, a minority of the potential patient population are accessing marijuana through dispensaries. Additional access opportunities are available through personal cultivation or designation of a caregiver. Though Portland voters passed Question 1, it does not increase legal marijuana distribution.

Competition: Weak

Maine regulations impose a maximum of eight dispensaries in the state, spread among geographic boundaries. ArcView Market Research was able to verify that six dispensaries are in operation. Dispensaries compete with several delivery services, as well as with caregivers and personal cultivation, which is limited to the indoor format, given the state's weather patterns.

Trends & Analysis

- Solid Near-Term Growth Outlook – ArcView Market Research foresees annual growth of 25% in 2014, for a state market value of $1.8 million. The growth is derived primarily from increased counts of patient accessing cannabis through dispensaries.
- Strong Longer-Term Outlook – With full legalization support for Question 1, ArcView Market Research anticipates passage of full legalization in Maine during the 2016 election cycle. Particularly in light of narrow qualifying conditions for Medical Use, the addition of Adult Use laws will greatly expand the state's market value.
- Dispensary Numbers Appear Below Regulatory Cap – Although Maine regulations allow for up to eight dispensaries, ArcView Market Research could only verify that six are presently in operation. On that basis, additional market growth might be driven by two more dispensaries coming online.

Rhode Island

Rhode Island has had Medical Use marijuana laws on the books for years, though dispensaries were only opened beginning in 2013. While the medical marijuana market is now positioned for growth, the near-term prospect of the passage of Adult Use laws greatly enhance the state's market potential.

		Rank
2013 Market Size	$ 1.6 million	# 9
Customers	843	# 10
Saturation Rate	3%	# 10
2013 vs. 2014 Growth Rate	25%	# 7 (tied)

ARCVIEW MARKET RESEARCH

Overview: Weak

With dispensary sales commencing in 2013, the Rhode Island legal marijuana market is just getting started. While the state has a small number of customers, the low saturation rate and broad set of qualifying conditions positions Rhode Island's Medical Use market for growth in the near-term. Given the potential for a 2014 bill to legalize Adult Use, the state's market value growth may accelerate quickly in the medium-term.

Regulatory Status: Strong

Rhode Island's Edward O. Hawkins and Thomas C. Slater Medical Marijuana Act took effect in early 2006. The Act allows for registered patients with written physician certification to use, possess, and cultivate cannabis. Registration is mandatory for patients and caregivers with the Department of Health's Medical Marijuana Program.

Certifications may be provided by licensed physicians from Rhode Island, Massachusetts, or Connecticut. The list of qualifying conditions is fairly broad, and includes chronic pain. The subject of production and dispensing marijuana businesses was not addressed in the Act. Patients and caregivers may legally possess up to two and one half ounces of cannabis and/or 12 mature plants. Cultivation must be indoors in an enclosed and locked facility. In 2009, legislation was passed authorizing three not-for-profit compassion centers (i.e., dispensaries) under the Department of Heath's oversight. Dispensaries are allowed to cultivate up to 51 immature plants and 99 mature plants, and to possess up to 1,500 ounces of cannabis at any one time. Dispensaries are also allowed to purchase cannabis from registered patients and caregivers, but not from other dispensaries. Business owners must be Rhode Island residents, though no residency requirements are specified for investors. There is no special statewide tax on dispensary sales, though sales are subject to the state sales tax of 7%.

Adult Use regulations may be on the horizon for Rhode Island. A bill has been introduced in 2013 for full legalization. The Marijuana Regulation, Control, and Taxation Act was sponsored by Judiciary Chari Representative Edith Ajello, House Minority Leader Brian Newberry and others. The 2013 legislative session was adjourned without a vote on the bill. However, the prospects for the passage of an Adult Use bill in 2014 look favorable.

Patient Access: Strong

Rhode Island patients are able to both cultivate their own marijuana as well as purchase cannabis from a dispensary now that storefronts have been opened. While the state only has three dispensaries, these are likely able to effectively serve Rhode Island's relatively small number of customers at current low saturation rates. As more potential consumers become patients and customers, a greater number of dispensaries will be needed to maintain good access to cannabis.

Competition: Strong

The small state of Rhode Island is limited to three dispensaries, though this number likely suffices to meet the relatively small number of patients. Online dispensary menu pricing in the $250-$300 ounce range for high quality marijuana suggests pricing which is competitive with more mature state markets. If saturation rates rise over time, more dispensaries will be needed to assure solid competition.

Trends & Analysis

- Solid Near-Term Growth – Rhode Island's three dispensaries were not operating for the entirety of 2013. With all three operating for the full year in 2014, coupled with increased patient registrations, the state market value is projected to grow by an annual increase 25% to $1.9 million.
- Potential for Adult Use Market on the Horizon – State senators and house members have considered legislation for Adult Use legalization, though without a vote in 2013. Based on conversations with leaders at drug policy reform groups, ArcView Market Research expects likely passage of full adult legalization bill in 2014, which will pave the way for substantial Rhode Island market value growth in 2015 and beyond.

New Mexico

Supply chain constraints in New Mexico are limiting patient access and curtailing cannabis purchases at dispensaries. Resolving production limits is the key to unleashing the state's market value potential.

		Rank
2013 Market Size	$ 5 million	# 7
Customers	4,438	# 7
Saturation Rate	13%	# 5
2013 vs. 2014 Growth Rate	15%	# 8 (tied)

Overview: Weak

New Mexico has the distinction of being the first Medical Use state to license cannabis businesses. However, the imposition of production caps is resulting in supply shortages relative to fast-growing patient demand. The state's market growth potential centers on solving inventory shortages and relatively low saturation rates.

Regulatory Status: Moderate

With the April 2007 passage of Senate Bill 523, the Lynn and Erin Compassionate Use Act, New Mexico allowed the use, possession and cultivation of cannabis by registered patients with qualifying physician recommendations. The law was amended in 2009 based on rules determined by the New Mexico Department of Health governing the production, distribution, and use of medical cannabis. Qualifying patient conditions are less expansive than some other Medical Use states, though include severe chronic pain. There are no reciprocity provisions for out-of-state patients. The patient possession limit if six ounces are higher than that of most other legal marijuana states. Patients are also allowed to cultivate up to four mature plants and twelve seedlings. Dispensaries are required to be state-licensed, not-for-profit enterprises. Licenses are awarded based on the merits of applicants, who must be state residents. Vertical integration is mandatory, with distributors required to produce the cannabis they sell. Production caps dictate a mandatory limit of 150 plants (increased from an initial cap of 95 plants), and allow licensed producers to obtain seeds, plants, and useable cannabis from other producers. According to the Marijuana Policy Project, there were 23 licensed producers in New Mexico as of August 2013. Outdoor cultivation is permitted in facilities that have security systems including locks and alarms.

Patient Access: Weak

Even with a relatively low saturation rate of 13%, dispensaries struggle to meet patient demand. Growth in the number of registered patients, which grew by over 10% in 2013 has increased demand. Many complain about the lack of access, as evidenced by a survey commissioned by the Department of Health and conducted in August and September 2013. The survey findings included dispensaries quickly running out of inventory, rationing the amounts sold to individual patients, and sometimes turning patients away. The survey concluded that given the number of registered patients, the state medical market requires annual production of 11,000 pounds to meet demand (versus approximately 2,200 pounds currently produced). Many patients reported having to purchase cannabis from illicit sources.

Competition: Weak

The state sanctioned production caps and resulting scarcity of legal medical marijuana constrains competition amongst retailers. Price competition is limited, with distributors often quickly selling out of cannabis products, and limiting purchase quantities for individual transactions. Some patients report that medical-grade cannabis is more readily available from illicit sources than from dispensaries.

Trends & Analysis

- Moderate Growth Outlook – Increased New Mexico customer counts is the primary driver of the state market growth outlook. Growth is likely to continue to be hampered by supply constraints. ArcView Market Research projects a 15% annual state market growth rate in 2014, resulting in a market value of close to $6 million for the year.
- Supply Constraints Relief? – The New Mexico Department of Health is analyzing the results of the 2013 medical marijuana program survey, including how to contend with supply shortages. Proposed solutions have not yet been formulated, but officials commented that the supply problem is being taken seriously with a view towards determination of the "best next steps."

Arizona

Having overcome significant political headwinds, Arizona is poised for the fastest growth of any legal marijuana state market in 2014. Dispensary operations and patient registrations are quickly ramping up, which will propel Arizona to be amongst the biggest markets in the country.

		Rank
2013 Market Size	$ 27 million	# 6
Customers	15,254	# 6
Saturation Rate	7%	# 8
2013 vs. 2014 Growth Rate	400%	# 1

Overview: Moderate

In spite of staunch opposition from some state political leaders, the first Arizona dispensary opened in late 2012, followed by dozens more in 2013. Even after a Superior Court ruling which ordered implementation of laws for Arizona's successful 2010 Medical Use ballot initiative, political efforts to impede the market have persisted.

Attempts to thwart the market notwithstanding, the Arizona legal marijuana market is strengthening, with over 44,000 registered patients so far in 2013, and a four-fold annual increase in market value projected for 2014.

Regulatory Status: Strong

In November 2010, voters passed the Arizona Medical Marijuana Act, or Proposition 203 (funded and lead primarily by the Marijuana Policy Project), by the narrow margin of 50.13%. Prop 203 allows for the use and possession of cannabis by patients with written physician certification for a set of qualifying medical conditions, including chronic pain. Patients must use the certification to obtain a registry identification card through the Arizona Department of Health Services (ADHS). Patients may obtain marijuana from licensed not-for-profit dispensaries which are permitted to produce and dispense cannabis. Independent cultivation business operations (i.e., not operated by a dispensary) are not allowed.

Patients are allowed to purchase a total of up to two and one half ounces of marijuana from a licensed dispensary within a 14-day period. A patient, or their designated caregiver, may cultivate cannabis only if the patient lives more than 25 miles away from the nearest dispensary. In such cases, up to 12 plants may be grown, including outdoor cultivation, as long as cultivation occurs within a locked facility. Since the majority of registered patients live within the 25 mile limit, most are not allowed to grow marijuana. This provision significantly strengthens dispensary sales and the Arizona state legal cannabis market value. Arizona law includes reciprocity with patients who have out-of-state ID cards. Qualifying out-of-state patients may possess up to two and one half ounces of marijuana, but cannot purchase cannabis from Arizona dispensaries.

Dispensaries are licensed by the ADHS via a lottery system. The state is divided into 126 geographic locations, with one dispensary license awarded for each location. Dozens of licenses were granted 2013, and were required to begin selling marijuana by August 7 or be faced with the loss of their licenses. Some did not open by the deadline, but have been granted the opportunity to appeal for an extension. This necessitates a rewriting of certain rules by the ADHS, which serves to delay the opening of some dispensaries.

Other challenges for dispensaries include efforts by some local officials to change zoning laws in order to prevent dispensaries operations in certain municipalities, but these efforts have been largely unsuccessful.

There has been substantial pushback from some state government officials against provisions of the Medical Marijuana Act. Governor Jan Brewer was a vocal opponent of the ballot initiative, and attempted to overturn key provisions of the law soon after its passage. She contended that federal law preempts state issuance of dispensary permits on the grounds that state employees might face prosecution under the Controlled Substances Act. The governor filed a lawsuit against the Justice Department demanding the federal government clarify its stance on medical marijuana laws, freezing the dispensary licensing process for a period of time. A US District Court judge dismissed the lawsuit in January 2012, clearing the path for the first wave of dispensary permits. In April 2012, Brewer signed a bill into law that bans medical marijuana from being used on campuses of state universities and community colleges. In 2013, Representative John Kavanagh (R-Fountain Hills) filed a resolution to refer Medical Marijuana Act back to the ballot in 2014, but the resolution failed to gain sufficient support for a new ballot initiative.

Another legal challenge has been in the area of cannabis extraction and infused products (see Alternative Ingestion Methods and Extraction Products sections). Some Arizona officials, including Maricopa County Attorney William Montgomery, have argued that cannabis-infused products such as edibles cannot be made with marijuana oil extraction since they are not covered under the definition of "useable marijuana" in the Medical Marijuana Act. The American Civil Liberties Union has filed a lawsuit in October 2013 to protect the parents of an epileptic five-year-old boy who provided their child with extracted oil to treat his condition. If successful, oil extraction-based products will be able to be sold by dispensaries and used by patients. While the case is pending, however, Arizona dispensaries are avoiding the sale of concentrates, and are offering edibles made only with raw cannabis and not extracted marijuana oil.

Patient Access: Moderate

Arizona patient access in 2013 has been limited by the numbers of dispensaries open in the state. There have been delays in the opening of dispensaries in certain locations, limiting access to legal marijuana. However, the market has been building up throughout year as the number of dispensaries coming online increased over the course of the year. Patients' access has concurrently increased, and will strengthen further in 2014 when the full number of dispensaries allowed is in operation. Even at full strength, there will be only one dispensary per each of the 126 permitted geographic location, though patients may purchase cannabis at any of these locations.

Competition: Moderate

Competition amongst dispensaries is increasing as their numbers build. 2014 will be more competitive environment as dispensary numbers reach full strength. However, even at full strength, the 126 dispensary cap, and geographic dispersion in terms of permitted locations, restricts competition. Competition with patient and caregiver cultivation is lessened by the requirement that patients living within 25 miles of a dispensary are not allowed to grow marijuana.

Trends & Analysis

- Huge 2014 Growth – The Arizona market will grow more quickly than any other state in 2014 as dispensary numbers reach full strength and serve a large customer population. ArcView Market Research projects the state market will be worth $135 million in 2014, which is an annual increase of 400% over the 2013 market value.

- Servicing Pent-up Patient Demand – An estimated 6,934 customers were served in 2013 as dispensary operations and patient counts ramped up throughout the year. Given that there are now over 44,000 registered patients in Arizona that will have access to the full number of dispensaries in 2014, customer transactions will increase sharply and fuel market growth as the state's Medical Use demand can be served by vendors.

- Potential for Increased Product Offerings and Dispensary Revenue – Arizona dispensaries are not currently offering cannabis extraction products, including oil-based concentrates and infused products. If the lawsuit brought by the American Civil Liberties Union to allow these products proves successful, dispensaries can increase product offerings. Infused products, in particular, cater to different customer segments, and can result in a significant increase in dispensary sales. Oil extraction products are also increasingly important to legal marijuana sales, and have become important revenue drivers. The result of including these extraction products at Arizona dispensaries would result in additional state market value gains.

Arizona

Survey Responses

1
Regulations

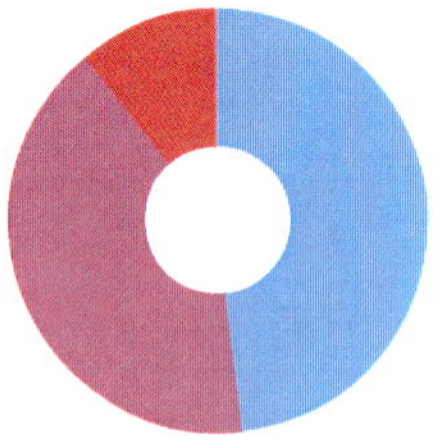

As a business operator, how do you feel about the medical marijuana **regulations** in your state?

- 48.3% Too complex
- 0.0% Too lenient
- 40.6% About right
- 11.1% Are harmful

2
Patient Access

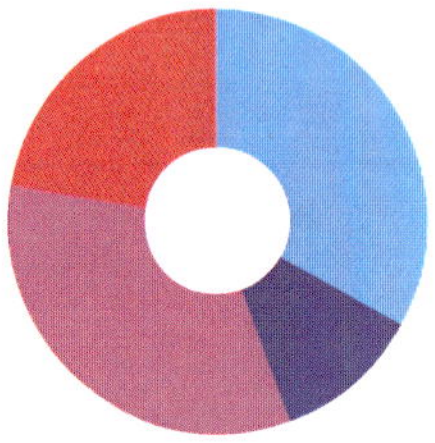

How do you feel about the **patient access** in your state?

- 33.3% It is too hard for patients
- 11.1% It is too easy for patients
- 33.3% It is about right
- 22.2% There should be no patient restrictions

3
Local Competition

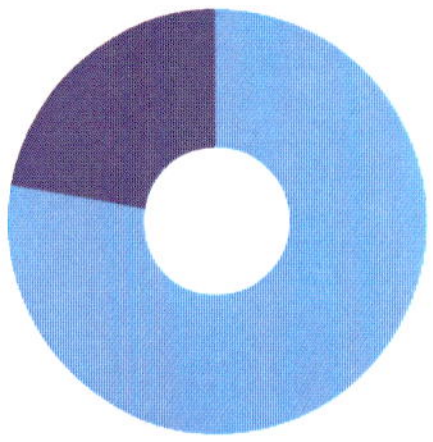

How would you describe your **local competition**?

- 77.8% Very competitive
- 22.2% Not competitive

6
Federal Law Enforcement

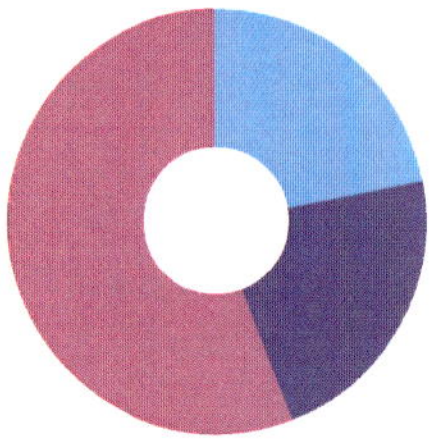

How concerned are you about **Federal law enforcement being a threat** to your business?

- 22.2% Very Concerned
- 22.2% Somewhat concerned
- 55.6% Not concerned
- 0.0% Federal law enforcement is helpful to my business

10
Previous Retail Experience

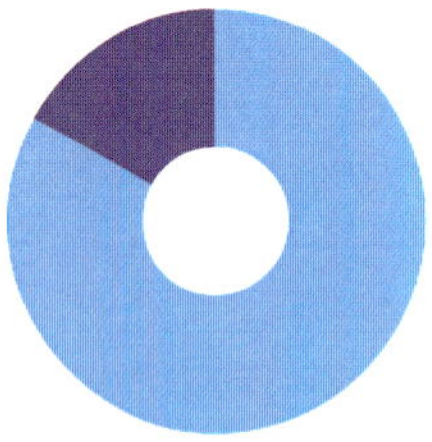

Have you had **previous experience** in the retail industry?

- 83.3% Yes
- 16.7% No

11

Previous Entrepreneurial Experience

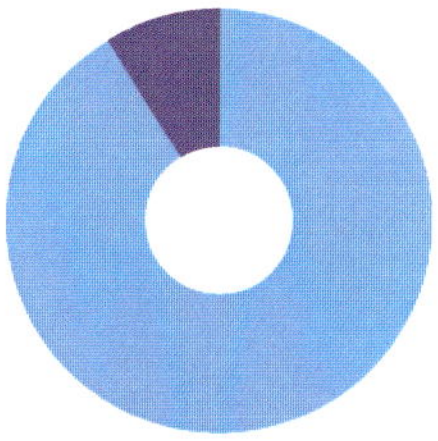

Have you had previous **entrepreneurial experience**?

- 91.2% Yes
- 8.8% No

12

Initial Start-up Costs

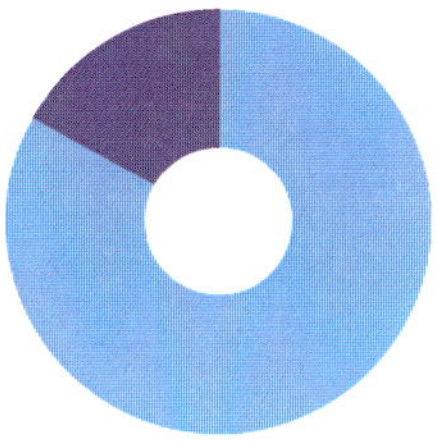

How did you fund your businesses **initial start-up costs**?

- 83.3% Self-financed
- 16.7% Family and friends investment
- 0.0% Angel investment
- 0.0% Institutional investment
- 0.0% Bank loan

Massachusetts

Based on newly implemented Medical Use laws, Massachusetts opens for business in 2014. The state is projected to rank as the sixth largest legal marijuana state market in the US in its first year of operation, even though there likely won't be dispensary sales until mid-year. Strong regulations and solid business operators figure to create the largest East Coast market in the industry next year.

Overview: Moderate

The formation of the Massachusetts legal marijuana market is well underway. Hundreds of applicants have lined up to compete for just 35 dispensary licenses that will be permitted under new state laws. Even though ArcView Market Research expects that these dispensaries won't be able to sell products until June 2014, the state market value is expected to be worth nearly $56 million for the year.

Regulatory demands on dispensaries include the need for very deep pockets, and many well-backed and capable would-be operators are seeking a license. The ratio of potential patients to available dispensaries will be quite high. While this will result in difficulty for the many patients to become customers, it will result in the Massachusetts dispensaries becoming some of the largest in the country. Accordingly, ArcView Market Research foresees that these will become strong operations doing high sales volumes.

Regulatory Status: Strong

Massachusetts became the 18th state to legalize Medical Use in November 2012 with 63% voting approval for the Massachusetts Medical Marijuana Initiative which was funded and lead primarily by the Marijuana Policy Project. In May 2013, the Department of Health, which oversees the industry, created the regulations that govern standards for Medical Use and the supply chain.

Medical marijuana patients must obtain a recommendation from a physician for medical conditions including serious illnesses and debilitating medical conditions that a physician attests could be helped by cannabis. Patient registration with the Department of Health is mandatory, and there is no reciprocity for visiting patients with cards from other states. Patients are allowed to possess 10 ounces of useable cannabis (a 60-day supply). There is also an allowance for a home cultivation permit for patients able to demonstrate financial hardship. Caregiver appointments are allowed, although each caregiver can only serve one patient.

There were about six times as many applicants as available Massachusetts dispensary licenses allowed under the ballot initiative. The application process will be merit based. Each applicant for a nonprofit dispensary license who made it through the first round of vetting may proceed with submitting a final application for a license, along with a nonrefundable $30,000 fee, through November 21, 2013. Among the application requirements is demonstrating the availability of $500,000 in liquid assets. Applicants may be from out of state, as may be the source of funding. Those who succeed in obtaining a license will become Registered Marijuana Dispensaries overseen by the Department of Health. The state must certify dispensaries by January 31, 2014.

A key challenge for dispensary contenders is proving to be location. State law requires at least one dispensary in every county. However, around one third of Massachusetts cities have imposed moratoria on dispensaries, with more considering a similar move. The inability to find a suitable location may take some applicants out of the pool of potential operators.

Seed-to-sale vertical integration is mandatory. Dispensaries will be required to cultivate their own cannabis, although some limited wholesale distribution among dispensaries will also be allowed.

Consumer Access: Moderate

Massachusetts will initially have relatively few dispensaries compared with potential state demand. This is partially mitigated by patients' ability to designate a caregiver, although caregivers are restricted from serving more than one patient. While the list of qualifying conditions is large, the lack of access to storefronts will result in many turning to the illicit market especially in counties that have banned dispensaries.

Competition: Weak

Only 35 dispensaries will be permitted during the first year of market operation, and these will be distributed throughout the state. Yet Massachusetts will have a potential patient population that rivals that of Colorado, where there are hundreds of dispensaries in operation.

Trends & Analysis

- Substantial Growth Outlook – even though operating for only half of the year in 2014, Massachusetts is projected to become the sixth largest legal marijuana state at a value of $56 million. Even without any organic growth (i.e., population increase), the state market could double and be worth at least $112 million in 2015.
- Adult Use on the Horizon – Representative Ellen Story introduced House Bill 1632 in January 2013, a bill that would allow adults 21 years and older to possess and cultivate cannabis. ArcView Market Research anticipates that Massachusetts will pass Adult Use regulations via ballot initiative in 2016.

Illinois

In 2013, Illinois became the twentieth state to legalize medical marijuana by legislative act. There are some pronounced differences in the regulatory framework compared with other states. Medical Use law, for example, is provisional in that it is cast as a pilot program. Multiple state agencies are involved in regulatory oversight. Even with these nuances, and restrictive qualifying conditions for patients, there appears to be strong entrepreneur interest for launching businesses in 2014.

ARCVIEW MARKET RESEARCH

Overview: Moderate

Illinois legal marijuana regulations reflect political compromise. The relatively narrow list of qualifying conditions limits the size of the potential customer based for marijuana businesses. The law is cast a 4-year pilot program, so the Medical Use market could cease in 2018 if not approved for extension. Regulatory oversight is assigned to three different state agencies, which could prove to be a complicating factor for market participants.

Final Illinois regulations are scheduled to be completed by the end of April 2014, with business applications and permitting to follow. Based on a functioning market for a portion of the year, ArcView Market Research projects the 2014 Illinois state market value at $2.7 million.

Regulatory Status: Strong

House Bill 01 was signed into law by Governor Pat Quinn in August 2013, authorizing qualified patients to possess and use cannabis based on physician recommendation for treatment of qualifying conditions. The law goes into effect on January 1, 2014, and the state has through April of that year to finalize rules. Acceptable conditions cover severe ailments, and do not include chronic pain. Patients must be under the recommending doctor's care for the qualifying condition. Regulatory oversight is split among three agencies. The Department of Agriculture oversees cultivation centers. The Department of Financial and Professional Regulation controls dispensing centers. The Department of Health is commissioned with overseeing patient registry and the issuance of patient cards.

Business licenses will be awarded on the basis of merit. There will be a maximum of 22 cultivation centers permitted, with no more than one per each state police district. Cultivation is limited to enclosed, locked facilities. Up to 60 dispensaries may be approved, and will be distributed across the state. Businesses can be formed as for-profit or not-for-profit entities. Cannabis products must be tested for potency and safety.

Home cultivation by patients or their caregivers is not allowed. Patients may obtain up to two and one half ounces of cannabis every two weeks, which can only be purchased from a dispensary the patient specifies during the registry application process. No children can become patients. Some adults are precluded from becoming patients, including anyone with a felony drug conviction or who work in certain professions (e.g., law enforcement, firefighters, commercial drivers). There is no patient reciprocity with other states.

Consumer Access: Moderate

There will eventually be up to 60 dispensaries to serve one of the most populous legal marijuana states, though only a small percentage of the state population will qualify for medical cannabis. As the rules are currently framed, for each qualifying patient who obtains a Medical Use registration card, one dispensary is to be designated for purchases. If these rules are upheld in the final regulations, patient access will be limited to a certain extent.

Competition: Moderate

Fewer than the 60 dispensaries and 22 cultivation centers allowed by law may be operational in 2014. Those that are will be serving a relatively low per capita potential customer population. It appears at this point that competition amongst businesses in the near-term will be moderate.

Trends & Analysis

- 2014 Assessment and Ranking – ArcView Market Research projects an Illinois legal marijuana market of $2.7 million for 2014. Relative to other legal state markets, Illinois will rank as the tenth largest.
- Relatively Small Market in a Relatively Big State - In spite of being the fifth most populous state in the US, Illinois' potential customer population is relatively small based primarily on the restrictive list of qualifying conditions. The state population is nearly twice the size of Massachusetts, yet will have less than 40% of the potential customer base given the comparative qualifying conditions for medical marijuana treatment.
- More Regulatory Details Clarity by Spring 2014 – While there is a regulatory framework for Medical Use businesses, there could be changes once Illinois finalizes rules by April 2014. As an example, there is currently no residency requirement for business owners or investors. However, that provision, along with some others, could change once laws are finalized. Accordingly, some prospective applicants and investors are taking a "wait-and-see" approach to pursuing potential opportunities in the state market.

Connecticut

Connecticut's nascent medical marijuana market will commence operations in 2014, and will be the second smallest in the US.

Overview: Weak

Connecticut lawmakers have created a restrictive legal marijuana regulatory system that will limit the state market size. Limitations on the number of businesses, coupled with narrow qualifying patient conditions, are projected to result in a market value just over $2 million in 2014. Following the award of licenses early in the year, Connecticut marijuana businesses are expected to be open by summer.

A remarkable feature of the new state law is that medical marijuana must be dispensed by a licensed pharmacist. One upside of that approach is it will potentially strengthen empirical systems to study the patient experience.

Regulatory Status: Strong

An Act Concerning the Palliative Use, or Public Act No.12-55, was signed into law by Connecticut governor Dan Malloy in June 2012 which permits Medical Use by registered patients. Qualifying conditions are some of the most restrictive of any legal marijuana state, which cover serious illnesses and does not include chronic or severe pain. Patients may possess up to two and one half ounces of cannabis, and personal cultivation is not allowed. The Department of Consumer Protection is commissioned with regulatory oversight, registration, and permitting. Over thirteen hundred people have registered as medical marijuana patients as of November 2013, even though legal distribution will not likely commence until summer 2014.

All medical marijuana sales will be subject to state sales taxes, currently 6.35%.

Marijuana businesses may be formed as for-profit or not-for profit enterprises. There are separate licenses for production and dispensary operations, and businesses can apply for one or both types of licenses. Three producer licenses, and between three to five dispensary license, will likely be awarded in early 2014. License holders can be Connecticut residents or from out-of-state.

Following the November 2013 deadline for license applications, sixteen groups applied for dispensary licenses and 21 applied for producer licenses. One applicant is from New York, while all others are from Connecticut. License awards will be merit-based. The relatively costly application process is intended to ensure licensees will have sound financial resources. Producer and dispensary applicants have to pay a nonrefundable fee of $25,000 and $1,000, respectively. If successful, producers will each have to pay $75,000 to obtain the license, while dispensary owners will have to pay $5,000. Operators must also post a $2 million bond or insurance policy in favor of the state to substantiate financial resources.

As often happens when new legal marijuana laws are introduced, several Connecticut cities, including West Hartford, have enacted moratoria on medical marijuana businesses. Two other cities have been more welcoming, including Middletown and West Haven, which have approved plans for cannabis businesses.

Patient Access: Weak

Connecticut patients are prohibited from personal cultivation, and will only be able to legally source cannabis from dispensaries when they open in 2014. In the foreseeable future, only three to five dispensaries will be available to patients, and only in cities that have not banned marijuana businesses.

Competition: Weak

The limited number of dispensary and producer licenses implies relatively weak competition for Connecticut legal marijuana businesses. The high costs for licenses, coupled with surety bond provisions, may also entail relatively expensive retail pricing.

Trends & Analysis

Cannabis Cultivation Under the Government's Roof – The city of Middleton has not only approved a cannabis company to operate in the city, but also to grow marijuana in a city-owned building. Greenbelt Management, an applicant for a Connecticut producer license, will lease a cultivation space from the local government in a multiuse building.

Opportunities for Medical Marijuana Study – Some feel the requirement for medical cannabis to be dispensed by a certified pharmacist will open new research channels for cannabis. Patients may be able to report their experiences of using specific cannabis strains to treat their illnesses. This information could potentially be shared with physicians, and would represent a new frontier for US medical marijuana study.

Vermont

With a small potential patient population that is determined by a narrow list of qualifying medical conditions and with just four dispensaries in the state, Vermont is the smallest legal marijuana market in the US.

Overview: Moderate

Although Medical Use regulations in Vermont have been on the books for over eight years, dispensaries have only recently been allowed to open for business. With dispensaries just beginning operations in mid-2013, the Vermont Medical Use customer market has been negligible. The state limits the number of dispensaries to four, all of which should be up in running in 2014, and ArcView Market Research projects the state market value at $852,000.

Regulatory Status: Moderate

In July 2004, Senate Bill 76 went into effect with very narrow qualifying medical conditions for patients. In 2007 the definition of qualifying conditions was expanded by Senate Bill 7 to include chronic pain. The medical marijuana program is overseen by the Vermont Department of Public Safety. No allowance for dispensaries was made until Senate Bill 17 was signed into law in 2011, which allowed for up to four dispensaries. Vertical integration is required of Vermont dispensaries, which must grow all of the cannabis they sell. Dispensary implementation was slow, and it took two years for the first two dispensaries to open in 2013. Also in 2013, possession of small amounts of marijuana was decriminalized.

Patients may possess up to two ounces of useable marijuana and are allowed to cultivate up to two mature plants and seven immature plants. Appointment of a caregiver is also permitted, although only one caregiver is allowed per patient. A patient who designates a dispensary may neither grow marijuana nor designate a caregiver.

Consumer Access: Weak

Dispensaries in Vermont have only recently opened. Only three are currently active, although four dispensaries—the state maximum—are expected to be open in 2014. Patients who elect to purchase cannabis from dispensaries are required to forgo personal cultivation and working with a caregiver.

Competition: Weak

Although there are not many current patients available as dispensary customers in Vermont, there are only three distributors currently in business. Competition will improve somewhat in 2014 as one more dispensary joins the market. Only two dispensaries will operate in cities with relatively sizeable populations (Burlington and Montpelier).

Trends & Analysis

- Dispensary Designation Constraints – Vermont patients are required to select one dispensary from which they may purchase cannabis. The Department of Safety recently reported that 468 out of 869 registered patients have designated a dispensary. Vermont law only allows 1,000 patients to designate a dispensary; this limit significantly curtails the potential medical market growth. There are efforts by advocacy groups, such as the Marijuana Policy Project, to get the patient dispensary designation cap amended or eliminated in 2014.
- Qualifying Conditions Expansion – An effort to add PTSD to the state's narrow list of qualifying medical conditions is foreseen in 2014. If this effort is successful, the number of Medical Use patients could dramatically increase.
- Adult Use Adoption – ArcView Market Research projects that Vermont will pass a legislative measure to fully legalize marijuana for adults in 2015. If successful, the state market would expand substantially on the medium-term horizon beyond the limits of Medical Use.

MARKET TRENDS

Alternative Ingestion Methods

Although smoking cannabis is the traditional form of consumption, it is increasingly giving way to other ingestion formats. Many cannabis consumers, particularly more recent adopters, consider smoking an unhealthy way to ingest marijuana. New technologies provide consumers with several alternative ingestion methods. There are several nonsmoking consumption formats such as vaporization (see Extraction Products section), edibles, and other oral formats including tablets, tinctures, and topical treatments. Innovative marijuana processors and consumption device manufacturers are bringing these alternative ingestion formats to market, which is transforming the way cannabis is consumed. Readers can learn more about this key market trend in the upcoming additional feature to be provided following release of this report.

Multistate Expansion

ArcView Market Research foresees the day when national cannabis companies will dominate much of the industry, post federal legalization. Branded companies with efficient cost of goods from scale economies and managing vast distribution networks will sell mainstay marijuana products in every state. Some companies will build large national market shares based on utilizing particular natural resource advantages. For example, companies in states with ample sunshine and long growing seasons will provide for large shares of regional and national marijuana demand, much as the farming breadbasket in the Central Valley of California serves national produce needs. Today, however, there are no true national cannabis companies. Business operators in many cases must be state residents, interstate commerce in actual cannabis is illegal, and each state market operates under unique regulatory regimes.

Yet the precursors to national companies are emerging. Through creative business strategies and partnerships, a handful of companies have managed to transcend the confines of their local state markets and derive income from

sales in other states. As with mainstream industries, cannabis companies with strong product development, branding, and other intellectual property are best positioned to propagate into territories beyond the limits of their home states.

The licensing agreement is a key vehicle for business expansion beyond one legal marijuana state market into others. Business operators in one state may not be able to own a marijuana business in another state or sell cannabis products to parties in other states, but they can earn fees from licensing intellectual property to other state businesses. Although licensing shares similarities with the franchising business model, franchising may not be currently viable for legal marijuana businesses, since franchises require federal disclosures and are regulated by the Federal Trade Commission.

Licensing agreements will become more common in legal marijuana states as the most successful branded businesses look to expand into new states. Some states implementing new marijuana laws have even built specific provisions for licensing agreements into state regulations that are based on the recognition that local operators may lack specialized industry expertise. These states include Nevada, Massachusetts, and Washington.

Today's legal marijuana multistate licensors are infusion and extraction product companies that have succeeded on three fronts: 1) development of consistent product formulations using cannabis extraction oil, 2) creation of popular branding, and 3) formation of distribution networks.

Delivering product consistency is a key pillar to licensing success. Unlike varying cannabinoid content present in raw marijuana flowers, the use of oil extraction allows producers to make relatively uniform doses in each product unit. The resulting reliable experience for the patient/customer in terms of product quality facilitates branding and the development of a customer following, which in turn builds distribution power. Those cannabis companies that have built recurring revenue streams within state markets on the basis of consistent product formulation and branded intellectual property can look to leverage that success through replication in other legal marijuana states.

Examples of companies using multistate licensing agreements includes Dixie Elixirs & Edibles (see Tripp Keber profile), Cheeba Chews, and Organa Labs (O. pen Vape) (See Ralph Morgan profile). These pioneering companies have developed valuable intellectual property and businesses in their home states, and then have contracted independent licensees operating in other states with marijuana regulations. Licensees contract to use the know-how, trade secrets, branding, and sales support of the licensors in exchange for financial consideration. Compensation is often structured on the basis of fees for packaging or for sales and marketing support, as opposed to profit sharing, so that licensors are not construed as out-of-state business owners.

The exchange of marijuana is usually not part of licensing terms for legal reasons. While licensees may be trained in areas like cannabis oil extraction and product formulations as part of the license, they otherwise have to provision the cannabis by sourcing within their own states for making oil or other marijuana products. Licensees are contractually required to comply with their own state cannabis laws, and to fully shoulder their own compliance requirements and legal risk.

Expansion into new states via licensing entails risks that are often different from the licensors' home-state markets. Local consumer acceptance is one example. There may be consumer preference for "homegrown" businesses rather than ones originating from other states. This is particularly true in seasoned legal marijuana states where local businesses may have already built a following in the region. Some consumers may simply be averse to products offered under a large-scale brand derived from another state. In contrast, consumers in new legal marijuana states without seasoned businesses may offer licensors less resistance.

Licensor risks may also include a licensee's failure to uphold product, branding and other contract standards, which may damage carefully developed intellectual property or new market traction. Other challenges for licensors can include operating in less familiar regulatory environments, including ones more exposed to federal enforcement actions.

Want to optimize performance?
Don't get complacent . . .

Get Busy.

Risks aside, potential licensing advantages are huge. Increased distribution power becomes an asset unto itself, by delivering benefits for licensors beyond earning fees on existing product lines. Those licensors who succeed at building significant market share in multiple states can then attract and incorporate products of other companies into their distribution channels, via partnership agreements or outright acquisition, to increase revenue streams.

Licensing can also be a strategy to position for roll ups or buyouts, particularly upon federal legalization. In that scenario, licensors may be able to convert licenses to franchises or purchase licensee businesses outright. Franchising or roll ups can quickly create a national company with scale economies and become an attractive candidate for a public listing, merger, or acquisition by a large national or multinational concern seeking to enter the marijuana industry.

Although this is a controversial topic within the industry today, large pharmaceutical, tobacco, and alcoholic beverage companies are most often cited as the likely acquirers of valuable multistate marijuana businesses in the federal legalization scenario. The controversy centers on the fact that many in the marijuana industry see themselves as the antithesis of the pharmaceutical, tobacco and alcohol industries. These other industries are viewed as long-standing opponents and not part of the traditional "counter-culture" or ethos represented by many companies and consumers in marijuana markets. Viewpoints aside, non-US pharmaceutical companies already make and distribute cannabinoid products, as discussed in the International Markets section.

INDUSTRY LEADER PROFILES

Tripp Keber / Dixie Elixir & Edibles

Colorado has been a great place to build a scalable branded cannabis business for Tripp Keber, CEO of Denver-based Dixie Elixirs & Edibles. It's a very seasoned state market with a strong regulatory foundation, discerning customers, and plenty of competition.

As a state-licensed Medical Infused Products Company, or MIPS, Dixie is an innovator of cannabis products that has capitalized on the trend towards alternative ingestion methods (i.e., nonsmoking forms of cannabis consumption).

Dixie's biggest selling signature product, THC-infused Dixie Elixirs sodas, is sold at dispensaries in two strengths and in multiple flavors throughout Colorado. The company's distinctive logo is possibly the most recognized marijuana brand in the state. An affiliated company, Red Dice Holdings, houses Dixie's intellectual property assets and also features non-THC products that are distributed nationally under the Dixie Botanicals line of CBD products.

How did Dixie evolve and position to be a multistate licensor? Keber describes the company's evolution as follows:

Dixie 1.0 was a one-product-line, two-person operation making "pot soda" out of a 400 square foot apartment, sold in a bottle prominently featuring a big marijuana leaf.

Dixie 2.0 was the company evolution based on extensive research of delivery systems, sophisticated product branding that didn't need to be hidden from public view, and expansion to 85 products featuring medical cannabis sold in Colorado.

Dixie 3.0 is focused on developing Dixie to be among the dominant brands in the industry through expansion into Adult Use sales in Colorado and through product sales in other legal states via licensing agreements. Arizona is the first new state where Dixie is contracting a licensing deal.

Prioritizing which states to target for licensing is a function of both each state's medical marijuana patient population as well as the state's likelihood to adopt Adult Use laws in the foreseeable future. Keber names Washington, California,

Nevada, Illinois, Massachusetts and Connecticut as priority states in which prospective licensee candidates are being evaluated and will be included in the first wave of Dixie licenses.

Weighing risks of markets in new states is also central to Dixie's licensing expansion strategy. Seasoned states where marijuana laws have already been implemented have different risk profiles, as compared with states that are newly implementing marijuana regulations. Seasoned Medical Use businesses in states such as Oregon and Washington offer attractive consumer populations but have operated in regulatory grey areas according to Keber. "Many of the businesses in these states have developed bad habits since regulatory protocols are lax or even nonexistent," he said. "Since Dixie is passionate about compliance, there can be a real mismatch in management styles between us and potential licensees in those states."

New legal marijuana states, in contrast, are unseasoned but have tight regulatory systems that only award business licenses to applicants who prove solid business backgrounds and financial resources. "The bar is set really high for applicants by regulators in new states like Connecticut, which helps streamline our vetting of potential licensees," Keber explains. "We used to have to interview dozens of licensing candidates in every state, now we only have to talk to eight or nine in newer states since weaker candidates have already been filtered out."

From a product labeling perspective, Dixie's competitive strategy is to adhere to packaging consistent with Food and Drug Administration standards, meaning that ingredient statements, nutritional facts, dosing, and regulatory warnings are all included on tamper-proof packaging. From a product quality continuity perspective, Dixie's strategy is to deliver to consumers the same experience whether in Portland, Oregon or Portland, Maine.

Longer-term, possibilities of a Dixie acquisition are not lost on Keber. He notes, "We already know major pharmaceutical, alcohol, and tobacco companies are closely watching our every move."

Extraction Products

Cannabis concentrate products made though marijuana oil extraction are popular, profitable, and poised to continue impressive market-share growth. ArcView Market Research foresees increased extraction sector investment in both oil product companies and ancillary equipment producers as demand for concentrate products continues to rise.

Background:

The marijuana plant contains dozens of cannabinoid compounds, including the chemicals that deliver the desired effects that consumers and patients seek in cannabis. These ingredients can be extracted from plant material through processing methods to create forms of concentrated essential oil that are made into an array of products.

The market for concentrates underwent a dramatic change beginning in the 1990s when new techniques were applied to the extraction of potent resinous materials from the cannabis plant in order to create intensified smoking materials. The ability to derive strong concentrates from lower-potency leaves, including those trimmed off the flowers when the flowers are prepared for market, greatly increased the total value of the plant beyond the sale of the higher-potency flowers. Before the widespread use of new extraction technology, the plant leaves were often disposed of as waste material. Now, leaf "trim" is in high demand by marijuana processors that use extraction methods to create valuable concentrate products. Trim previously had no commercial value. Now, it can be worth as much as a plant's flowers when sold as feedstock for oil concentrate extraction to make cannabis derivative products.

The growing popularity of cannabis extraction reflects the rapid increase in recent years of consumer product offerings beyond the plant flowers for smoking.

These options include refined concentrated extraction formats for smoking or vaporizing, as well as oral capsules, tablets, and food and beverage products made with marijuana oil concentrates. Consumers now have a multitude of cannabis ingestion formats as a result of advances in concentrate extraction.

Two important categories of cannabis extraction products are solid and liquid oil concentrates.

Solid Oil Concentrates – Solid concentrated cannabis formats have been made for centuries in the form of hashish. These concentrates condense the active ingredients in marijuana into compact resinous forms, which have much higher potency per unit compared with the original plant matter from which they are made.

Concentrate products have the advantages of portability and intensified potency. They are typically ingested through smoking or vaporization, and require fewer inhalations by consumers to achieve the desired effects, as compared with marijuana flowers, due to the intensified cannabinoid content.

Advances in the technology of extraction have resulted in the creation of new forms of concentrate products based on refined cannabis oil. The leading processes entail forcing solvents through the plant matter to pull out the essential oils. These high-potency extractions can test at THC levels exceeding 80%, which may be five to eight times higher than high-quality marijuana flowers. Some of these extracted oil solids are known as "wax," "budder," and "shatter" concentrate products, and are a major and growing segment of dispensary sales.

- Liquid Oil Concentrates – The trend toward alternative ingestion formats has spurred strong growth in demand for extracted liquid cannabis oil. Formulations based on the essential viscous oils drawn from the plant can be smoked, but are also used in a wide variety of alternative formats. One of the most popular formats is vaporization, especially with portable vaporizer "vape pens," which is a technology borrowed from e-cigarettes. These pen-shaped devices carry heating elements for warming extraction oil to the point that a vapor is released, which is then inhaled. The oil is typically housed in a cartridge fitted into the pen that can either be replaced or refilled. The immense popularity of consuming oil with vape pens is based on convenience, portability, and discretion (it's fairly odorless).

Another fast-growing category of extraction-based oil products is infused products. Infused products offer consumers alternatives to smoking or vaporization. These products include infused foods and beverages made with cannabis oil, as well as capsules, tablets, lozenges, mints and other formats that are either swallowed or absorbed in the mouth. Topicals, salves, and lip balms are also made from oil.

One major advantage of liquid cannabis oil is the ability to provide uniform dosing in product formulations. A fairly precise measure of cannabinoid content can be delivered in a metered volume of liquid oil. This precision allows for continuity of dosage, so that consumers can obtain a more predictable amount of cannabis effect per unit consumed, whether in a tablet or in one section of an infused chocolate bar. This is a major advancement for marijuana products that are eaten, which historically could be very unpredictable and caused many to limit their intake or refrain altogether. Similarly, it is easier to gauge dosing from vape pen inhalation than from smoking a marijuana flower joint. Liquid cannabis oil has therefore advanced product standardization, which has important implications for large-scale production and branding.

Two primary methods of cannabis oil extraction are butane extraction and CO_2 extraction.

- Butane Extraction – Butane Hash Oil ("BHO") is made by forcing butane through plant material, a process known as "blasting." A primary advantage of making BHO is a relatively low cost of production. A small-scale extractor can get started by spending around $20 for the necessary equipment at Home Depot. While some sophisticated BHO systems exist, it can also be made through rudimentary means with basic tubes, filters, and butane. Low costs aside, there are important drawbacks to butane extraction. The production process can be hazardous, and there have been increasing instances of injuries and even fatalities from explosions caused by BHO extraction. Another concern of BHO is potential chemical residuals that may be left in the oil concentrate. A further concern in the California Medical Use market is that BHO production is prohibited, ostensibly due to the risks of making oil through this method. Ironically, selling and possessing BHO in California are allowed.

- CO_2 Extraction – CO_2 oil is made with supercritical fluid extraction machines using carbon dioxide (CO_2) as a solvent. CO_2 extraction is used in a variety of industries to strip out or separate botanical elements. To make cannabis oil, CO_2 is forced through plant materials to isolate the essential oils. Advantages of CO_2 extraction include the use of organic solvents that don't leave residues and efficient isolation of cannabinoids. A primary drawback of CO_2 extraction is cost. Entry level CO_2 extraction machines cost can cost upwards of $80,000. Machine maintenance can also be costly. For this reason, CO_2 extraction is limited to large-scale production operations.

Market Players & Dynamics

The oil extraction concentrate product market comprises cultivators who provide trim feedstock, processors who make the oil, and retailers who sell concentrate solids, liquid oils, and products based on oil formulations, such as vape pens, food, beverages, and capsules. In some cases, these operations are unified under common ownership.

Oil processors tend to be either smaller BHO operations that wholesale to a set of dispensaries, or larger CO_2 processors that sell to retailers throughout a state market. The large processors are concentrated primarily in the Colorado market, and some also have branched into other states via licensing agreements (see Multistate Expansion section).

A primary challenge in the oil processor market is access to trim feedstock. Demand for oil concentrate products has increased more rapidly than has the available supply. Product shortages occur at dispensaries, particularly for oil used in vape pens. The price of trim has escalated as a result, having been considered worthless before extraction technologies improved to now selling for around $400 per pound in some states. Cultivators can plan for a significant revenue contribution from trim sales in addition to the revenue from marijuana flowers.

The consistent dosage properties of liquid cannabis oil have enabled some companies to build branded products based on extraction (see Ralph Morgan, O.pen Vape profile). The ability to make product formulations that deliver reliable measured doses is essential to building a scalable product brand. In addition to creating customer loyalty, these brands can then be introduced into other state markets under licensing agreements.

CO_2 equipment manufacturers have enjoyed brisk sales of extraction machines as concentrates have become a key component of legal marijuana markets. While manufacturers like Apex Supercritical and Eden Labs LLC don't publicly report sales figures, anecdotal evidence suggests growing revenues from sales to legal marijuana processors.

Not every state market is ideal for concentrates. In Michigan, oil concentrate products are illegal. The Court of Appeals cited the "heightened potency of THC extract" of infused concentrates as making them outside the definition of useable medical marijuana. Note, however, that products made from unprocessed dried marijuana are allowed in legal Michigan patient formulations.

Manufacturers and distributors of consumption devices that are used to ingest concentrate extractions have also benefitted from the increasing popularity of these products. Though relatively rare several years ago, a large number of vape pens have been introduced to market to capture demand for oil consumption. Sales of glassware and devices used to consume concentrate solids have also been on the rise. Smoking concentrates through glassware and specialty pipes outfitted with titanium plates is sometimes referred to as "dabbing," and the popularity of this format has soared recently, much to the benefit of producers and sellers of pipes and related devices.

Key Trends Outlook

- Rising Trim Prices – Continued growth in vaporization and other alternative ingestion formats is expected to continue. Oil demand may outpace new supply, particularly in 2014 in the states of Washington and Colorado, given the implementation of Adult Use. Multistate expansion via extraction product licensing in other states may also put upward pressure on trim prices because of increased processor demand.

- Concentrate Market Share Gains – Product sales of extraction-based products will likely continue to increase as a percentage of total cannabis sales. Some dispensaries have reported seeing extraction products rise from 5% of total sales in recent years to now in excess of 25%. This impressive growth has also been limited by the availability of trim supplies. Once plant and trim production increase, market share gains of extraction products are likely to increase further.

- Growing CO_2 Equipment Demand – Oil concentrate sales generate strong margins for processors and retailers. The high cost of acquiring CO_2 extraction equipment is amply compensated for by large-scale production and distribution. Demand for CO_2 extraction equipment is likely to increase in both existing and new legal state markets. Since oil cannot be transported across state lines, equipment is needed in every legal state market where concentrate products are offered.

- Increased Investment in Processor & Equipment Manufacturers – Based on increased demand for profitable oil concentrate products, ArcView Market Research anticipates growth in oil processor and extraction equipment manufacturing operations. The largest, most efficient oil processor operators will develop advantages in cost of goods and distribution, thus potentially edging out smaller producers. The substantial capital costs to build operational scale necessitate investment, and investors are already being pitched for private deals in this sector.

INDUSTRY LEADER PROFILES

Ralph Morgan / Organa Labs

Ralph Morgan, Organa Labs CEO, came to the legal marijuana industry as an outsider in 2010. A veteran of the medical device industry, he wanted to create cannabis products that are well-suited to the needs of Medical Use patients. His research and development created products that have been popular with medicinal cannabis users and that have strong crossover appeal to the Adult Use markets.

Morgan set about learning the legal marijuana business from the ground up. He co-founded the Denver dispensary Evergreen Apothecary in 2010, which gave him a front row seat to the legal marijuana cultivation, distribution, and the patient experience. He observed that patients needed access to products that adhere to safe standards, measured medicinal doses, and ease of administration, as well as repeatable, reliable effects.

"Medical marijuana patients often didn't want to adopt a smoking habit in order to ingest their medicine," observed Morgan. "However, if they bought a pot brownie to eat, they had to worry whether the second half of the brownie would deliver the same effect as the first. They also had to wonder if the next brownie would be comparable to the last."

"Morgan sought feedback from cancer patients, asking if they found the available cannabis medicines to be safe, organic, and suited to medicalneeds. He found there simply wasn't any product available that really met these needs. This discovery prompted an investigation into what technologies were available for alternative ingestion methods.

Oil extraction concentrate seemed to have the best potential for regulating dosage into a repeatable experience, and it could be formulated into different preparations. Morgan wasn't encouraged by butane and other extraction technologies, so he turned to CO_2. He knew that CO_2 extraction was used in the food and flavor industries and that it used an organic solvent that didn't leave residuals. The investment in a CO_2 extractor would be very substantial, but the potential benefits seemed even greater.

He co-founded Organa Labs to use CO_2 extraction to create cannabis medicines in alternative ingestion formats. His first product formulation was CannaTabs, a compressed tablet that uses CO_2 oil. It provides patients with measured doses delivered in a sublingual format that is highly bio-available, as compared with pills that are swallowed. Patient reception has been very favorable.

Recognizing the soaring popularity of portable vaporizers, Morgan then turned his attention to developing a vape pen. After some experimentation, he believed the e-cigarette format would be an excellent delivery mechanism, and he went to China and found a vaporizer pen manufacturer with a suitable product. With that he launched the popular O.penVape pen product.

The O.penVape product has been a hit in Colorado. In the past year sales through October 2013 have grown 1,600%. The business follows the Gillette business model: make the razor handle inexpensive to position for repeating sales of replacement cartridges. The vape pen was offered at a low price point—around $25—compared with those of other portable vaporizers, which can cost hundreds of dollars. The CO_2 oil cartridges were further distinguished by being strain specific, rather than using generic cannabis oil. The consistent dosage of the cartridges, coupled with the strain-specific pedigree, made the O.pen product well-suited to branding. Emphasizing the quality of the CO_2 oil, the Organa Labs tagline is "It's what's inside that counts." Further underscoring that principal, O.pen oil cartridges were the first in Colorado to put testing results on the package.

Access to trim supply can limit production capacity. To overcome the challenge of sourcing trim feedstock, Organa Labs required Colorado retailers (who are vertically integrated and grow most or all of their medicine) to provide trim in exchange for the right to carry the product line.

Organa Labs's growth strategy centers on licensing its brand and technology in other legal marijuana states. O.penVape products are now also sold in California and Washington State, with new potential state licensees coming online in 2014.

As testament to the rising popularity of the vape pen product line, Morgan cites how quickly extraction products have risen in terms of total sales at dispensaries. "Cartridges used to almost be a novelty item and accounted for around 5% of total sales. Now they can be 25%–40% of sales, and we expect it may hit 50% in some locations for 2014."In terms of the future for oil extraction, Morgan sees the potential for more concentrate devices to be sold under the O.pen name and for the development of CBD and other targeted-strain oil products. Ultimately, he foresees the potential for CBD products to crossover into the mainstream consumer market. "One day," he posits, "you'll be able to find hemp CBD extraction nutraceutical products at your local Whole Foods."

Large Scale Production

As legal marijuana markets have grown, so too has the size of cultivation operations. The trend towards larger scale grows is driven both by economic and regulatory factors. Large-scale grows benefit from scale economies, and those operating in open air and greenhouse outdoor cultivation sites also profit from energy savings. Regulators in state such as Massachusetts and Connecticut also limit the number of business licenses, meaning average production operation sizes must be larger in scale in order to meet consumer demand. The days of small 3,000 square feet home grows are numbered. Some cultivators are planning for 30,000 square feet and larger grow sites. In an upcoming feature, ArcView Market Research examines the trend and implications of large-scale cultivation sites.

Pricing Dynamics

Marijuana pricing dynamics vary from state to state, and are affected by multiple factors impacting supply and demand. Pricing in some states has declined sharply in in recent years, though has remained stable in other states. Key pricing drivers include factors such as regulatory environment, seasonality, and competition. New technology is also transforming how the plant is used and priced. These factors are examined in detail in a forthcoming feature on cannabis pricing dynamics and trends.

Cultivation Operations. How long did it take to reach profitability?

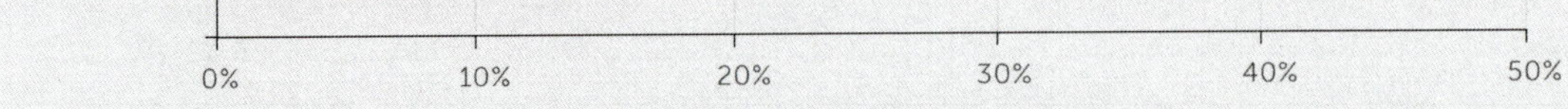

Cannabidiol (CBD)

CBD is one of the many chemical compounds found in the marijuana plant that is demonstrating significant therapeutic properties. CBD is nonpsychoactive —it does not provide the euphoric effects of a "high" when consumed. It does, however, deliver important medicinal qualities that are in great demand. Cultivators are developing CBD-rich strains, and pharmaceutical companies are undertaking intensive research of CBD with the goal of developing new pharmaceuticals to bring to market. CBD is in short supply compared with surging demand, resulting in elevated pricing. Many market participants are working to solve the CBD resourcing puzzle in order to capitalize on opportunities to meet demand. Details of this important trend in cannabis products will be provided to purchasers of this report in an upcoming special feature.

Cannabinoid Chart:

THC	CBD	CBG	CBN	CBC	THCv	CBGa	CGCa	CBCa	THCa	CBDa	
●	●		●	●		●					Relieves Pain *Analgesic*
					●						Suppresses appetite/Helps with weight loss *Anoretic*
	●	●						●			Kills or slows bacteria growth *Antibacterial*
	●										Reduces blood sugar levels *Anti-diabetic*
●	●										Reduces vomiting and nausea *Anti-emitic*
	●				●						Reduces seizures and convultion *Anti-epileptic*
								●			Treats fungal infection *Antifungal*
	●	●		●		●	●		●	●	Reduces inflammation *Anti-inflammatory*
			●								Aids sleep *Anti-insomnia*
	●										Reduces risk of artey blockage *Anti-ischemic*
	●	●		●					●	●	Inhibits cell growth in tumors/cancer cells *Anti-proliferative*
	●										Treats psoriasis *Anti-psoriatic*
	●										Tranquilizing, used to manage psychosis *Antipsychotic*
●	●		●						●		Supresses muscle spasms *Antispasmodic*
	●										Relieves Anxiety *Anxiolitic*
●											Stimulates apetite *Appetite Stimulant*
	●	●		●	●						Promotes bone growth *Bone Stimulant*
	●										Reduces function in the immune system *Immunosuppressive*
	●										Reduces contractions in the small intestines *Intestinal Anti-prokinetic*
	●										Protects nervous system degeneration *Neuroprotective*

Diversity

At present, the legal cannabis industry does not look like America in terms of race and gender. There are notable exceptions, but the leaders and managers of organizations tend to be white males. It is quite common to see women and people of color working as budtenders at dispensaries or trimmers at cultivation centers, but it is more unusual to find them at the ownership or managerial levels.

The frequent lack of diversity in the upper ranks of marijuana organizations is ironic given that cannabis users have historically been socially diverse, and collectively a type of "social minority" unto themselves. The cannabis advocacy movement also shares a strong link to the gay rights movement. Why, then, does the leadership of cannabis organizations generally not mirror the social diversity from which they emerged?

The answer likely reflects a variety of factors, all stemming from traditional roles within the cultural landscape. These factors include the following:

- Risk Tolerance – Marijuana can be risky business. For reasons sociologists study, men generally tend to be more comfortable with higher-risk business endeavors. The personal risk of trading in cannabis was even greater before some states began to reform marijuana laws, although it is still very much in effect today. While there can be substantial rewards from dealing with marijuana, the downside can be severe. Primary risks entail arrest and incarceration, as well as the potential for violence when dealing with a valuable product that is often traded on a cash basis. White males face different marijuana risk/reward prospects compared with women and people of color.

  Many hundreds of thousands are still arrested for marijuana every year, according to FBI statistics. Tens of thousands are incarcerated. Women, traditionally more risk averse and as pillars of the family unit as well as less financially secure, tend to be less inclined to gamble their freedom and family

responsibilities for the potential benefits of cannabis commerce. Over 50% more men try marijuana than do women, according to a July 2013 Gallup poll. Minorities face a very different risk/reward tradeoff with marijuana compared with white people. Nationally, blacks are arrested at a rate over three times greater than whites are, according to a June 2013 American Civil Liberties Union report.

- Stigma – Women and minorities may have more reasons to avoid marijuana stereotypes than do white males. While perceptions are changing with increased marijuana acceptance, cannabis consumers have often been regarded in a negative light by mainstream society. Attributions such as outlaws, stoners, slackers and other stereotypes are common, and are often theatricalized in media. Because of white male privilege, white men may be most prepared to endure, or even enjoy, those perceptions. An informal survey of female marijuana consumers, however, demonstrated that there is a greater tendency to feel uncomfortable disclosing their cannabis use in public (or even to acquaintances). Minorities constantly have to contend with negative stereotypes of many kinds, and disclosing involvement with cannabis may seem particularly burdensome.

- Conventional Industry Migration – Some of the prevalence of white males at the upper levels of marijuana industry may simply reflect the transfer of executives from conventional businesses – which are white male-dominated – to cannabis businesses. White men have tended to have higher education levels and rates, as well as economic resources, compared with women and minorities. As marijuana businesses professionalize, the draw of managers from noncannabis businesses also imports a lack of diversity present in the more traditional industries.

- Sexism – Most cannabis magazines and trade shows prominently feature half-naked women promoting products. An informal survey of women demonstrated that some feel that popular cannabis culture and advertising tends to be very sexist toward women. That may translate to women feeling like the cannabis industry isn't for them.

Potential for Greater Diversity?

There are reasons to expect that cannabis organizations would, and perhaps will, be more diverse than their more traditional counterparts.

- Marijuana proponents are a diverse group. A major driver of cannabis advocacy came from the gay rights movement of the 1970s; medical marijuana was crucial in treating AIDS patients' symptoms. Gay rights advocate Harvey Milk was also a proponent of medical marijuana in support of his community and human rights. Leaders in advocacy sometimes also become leaders in commerce (see Steve DeAngelo Industry Leader Profile).

- Cannabis consumption rates are comparable among white and nonwhite communities. According to Gallup, American whites and nonwhites try marijuana at 38 percent and 39 percent of their overall respective populations. Six percent of whites, and eight percent of nonwhites reportedly count themselves as cannabis consumers. The diversity of consumer groups may eventually translate to diversity in organizational leadership.

- Many women are attuned to the benefits of medical cannabis. There are many examples of female dispensary owners. Some ascribe that fact to women's key roles in healthcare and the healing arts.

- Marijuana can engender a quality of open-mindedness and acceptance of others. Not all cannabis business professionals consume marijuana, though many do. This disposition may allow for more acceptance and upward mobility of women and minorities in organizations.

- As both the potential for social stigma and the uneven criminal consequences for cannabis diminish with increased legalization, the risk assessment for people of color may change in a way that leads more to seek opportunities in the legal cannabis industry.

Though less common with people of color, there are notable examples of women leaders in cannabis industry organizations. Prominent female business and political heads are breaking through barriers, shaping marijuana commerce and advocacy landscapes.

See the Industry Leader Profiles of Betty Yee, Jessica Billingsley, Dale Sky Jones, and Amy Poinsett in this report.

INDUSTRY LEADER PROFILES

Jessica Billingsley / MJ Freeway

As co-founder and Chief Operating Officer of information technology company MJ Freeway, Jessica Billingsley is in a business leadership role that defies stereotypes on multiple levels.

"Traditionally, you haven't seen the majority of women as leaders in business, technology, or marijuana," notes Billingsley. "In that sense, I've broken through a trifecta of stereotypes and expectations."

Billingsley has been breaking the mold of traditional gender roles from early on. Her sport of choice is rock climbing. Her parents were entrepreneurs who became successful executives of companies they founded. They taught their daughter to be comfortable assessing risk/reward tradeoffs, and to wholeheartedly pursue the best of opportunities. In addition to her parents, she was also mentored by several successful business women. These experiences gave Billingsley the fortitude and knowledge that led to her co-founding of one of the most prominent ancillary companies in the legal marijuana industry. MJ Freeway has hundreds of dispensary and cultivator clients who use software services to track hundreds of millions of dollars in commercial cannabis transactions.

Her perspective on why much of the marijuana industry is dominated by males is that "Women are more risk averse than men in are general, and cannabis has been and remains a very risky industry." She also noted the difference in attitudes toward the use of substances. "Men drink more, smoke more, and have historically been greater consumers of illegal drugs."

As for roles at MJ Freeway, Billingsley describes the company as "gender neutral." MJ Freeway is an equal opportunity employer as a corporate policy. "We simply want the best person for the job," she stated. Interestingly, all of MJ Freeway's software developers are women, a fact Billingsley attributes to the flexibility of working from home. "That format is especially appealing to women raising children."

Is it a disadvantage to be a woman working in the legal cannabis industry? Billingsley cites both plusses and minuses and characterizes the dynamic as "net even." "On the one hand, women are excluded from being part of 'the boy's club'," she noted. Further, some clients seem to want to speak with a man, particularly about technical issues. On the other hand, woman professionals in the industry seem to stand out more than their male counterparts. "As the exception, we can be more memorable," she explains.

One of the more uncomfortable experiences for professional women working in the marijuana industry, accordingly to Billingsley, is attending most of the cannabis trade shows. "You're essentially surrounded by women dressed in lingerie promoting products to a predominately male audience."

Still, Billingsley is fairly optimistic about opportunities for diversity in the industry. With more states legalizing marijuana, risk is declining. She reasons that as cannabis becomes more mainstream, it's more inviting to women and minorities. While encouraged, however, she still anticipates that cannabis organizations will continue to be dominated by white men.

"They've been the early players, by and large, and have had a long head start compared to women," said Billingsley. "As a result, they'll likely occupy the upper ranks for a long time to come."

Cannatourism

The emergence of the first Adult Use states has given rise to a whole new vertical within the cannabis industry: Cannatourism. For the first time in history, adults can travel to Colorado and Washington State and legally purchase marijuana. New businesses are being launched to capitalize on those visiting legal Adult Use states to experience cannabis. From tour operators to "bud and breakfasts" to cannabis lifestyle centers, Cannatourism is a whole new ancillary line of business. In an upcoming additional feature, ArcView Market Research surveys the emerging Cannatoursim sector to help readers understand how this ancillary business fits into the Adult Use markets.

Growth in nontraditional customers

Medical Use has ushered in a change to the makeup of cannabis consumers beyond perceptions of the stereotypical "stoner and hippy" crowd. Many consumers have turned to cannabis to treat both mild and serve medical conditions. Older patient populations seeking therapeutic alternatives to pharmaceutical drugs are a growing segment of cannabis consumers. In certain specialized cases, such as children with epilepsy, some strains of cannabis have proven to be more effective in countering seizures than any other form of medicine.

The implications of growth in nontraditional marijuana consumers are reviewed in an upcoming special feature for purchasers of the report.

ANCILLARY BUSINESSES

OVERVIEW

Ancillary businesses operate in legal marijuana markets without ever touching the plant. Some cater to cannabis cultivators and retailers, while others serve cannabis consumers. Ancillary companies have been described as providing the "picks and shovels" to market participants dealing directly with marijuana.

The first ancillary businesses predate legal state markets, and included primarily consumption device manufacturers, cultivation equipment and supply producers, as well as media companies that publish educational and cultural content in books and magazines. Specialty retailers such as headshops and hydroponic stores were also some of the earliest forms of ancillary businesses.

With the emergence of legal marijuana state markets, new types of ancillary businesses also emerged. Market growth and the professionalization of marijuana businesses increased the need for many ancillary products and services. There are now a large range of ancillary company types.

Some types of ancillary businesses have their counterparts in mainstream industries. Insurance services, IT companies, security companies, and packaging firms are a few examples of company types found in many industries, and which also serve the legal marijuana industry. Professionals from these kinds of mainstream companies have frequently found opportunity by migrating their skills and experience to legal cannabis markets.

It is often the case that cultural differences, lack of understanding of the unique needs of cannabis businesses and consumers, or fears of perceptual or legal risk,

has kept mainstream ancillary providers out of the cannabis market. That dynamic has left cannabis businesses and consumers significantly underserved, which presents substantial opportunities for people with relevant skills who take the time and attention to effectively cater to this underserved market. For many of these ancillary companies, the goal is to eventually be acquired by a mainstream business once cannabis gains more acceptance.

Ancillary businesses enjoy some distinct advantages over marijuana companies. In addition to lower legal risk exposures, many ancillary companies can reach across geographic boundaries and service customers in all states and even internationally. IT companies such as websites for cannabis consumers, for example, can attract visitors in all states and even internationally to build patronage and advertising revenues.

Several ancillary business types are examined in this section.

Advisory Services

The complexity of legal marijuana markets gives rise to the need for consultation from seasoned professionals. As the markets expand, consultants with domain expertise in different aspects of cannabis have found rising demand for their services. Entrepreneurs, investors, and regulators are customers of consultants who provide guidance on a range of topics. As a result, consulting services has developed into significant type of ancillary business within the industry. Consulting opportunities are growing not only in the US, but also in certain international markets where legal cannabis market regulations are being adopted.

A rapidly growing area for consulting services is providing assistance with applications for business licenses in new legal marijuana state markets. Increasingly comprehensive state market regulations require applicants to demonstrate competence and thoroughness in their detailed submissions for being awarded licenses. In states where licenses are granted on the basis of merit, applicants are highly incented to retain consultants to strengthen candidacy. Applicants for licenses are known to spend tens of thousands of dollars in consulting fees to help increase their chances of success for being awarded highly valuable licenses to open state-approved businesses. Some of the more prominent consulting firms focused on guiding new license applicants include Denver Relief Consulting, Vicente Sederberg, and 4Front Advisors (see Kris Krane profile).

Another category of consultancy is for cannabis cultivation expertise. Large scale cultivation operations in particular may hire consultants to optimize production capacity and results. Services can range from guidance on constructing cultivation facilities, to growing and processing techniques. TRiQ and Quantum 9 are two of a group of firms offering cultivation consulting services.

Regulators also are customers of marijuana consulting firms. Regulators in new legal state markets often lack experience with the cannabis industry. The Liquor Control Board of Washington State put out an RFP for consulting groups to bid on a contract to advise the state on implementation of Initiative 502, the successful Adult Use ballot measure approved in 2012. More than 100 proposals were submitted, and the contract was awarded to BOTEC Analysis Corporation. The contract is said to have been worth around $1 million in consulting fees.

Cannabis consulting is likely to continue to grow as new states approve legal marijuana laws. International demand is also likely to rise as countries which adopt legal marijuana laws look to seasoned cannabis consultants with experience in the US market.

Kris Krane / 4Front Advisors

After years of working in advocacy with major drug policy reform groups, Kris Krane came to the realization that the private sector was a key force to catalyze social change. This awareness prompted him to move to private enterprise and work with companies that are at the forefront of legal marijuana markets. Following in-depth experiences with dispensaries, Krane cofounded 4Front Advisors, a consulting firm aimed at helping entrepreneurs launch best-in-class dispensary operations.

"Working in the field of policy reform was all I'd ever done," Krane explained. "The only thing that has changed is my transition from advocacy to industry."

Krane was a founding member and Executive Director of Students for Sensible Drug Policy, and also worked for the National Organization for the Reform of Marijuana Laws in DC. As legal cannabis businesses emerged, he recognized the power of private industry to move political reforms forward. "I saw that public-facing businesses have a huge impact, and decided to channel my energy into businesses rather than lobbying and advocacy," Krane stated. He moved to California and joined CannBe, a consulting group led by Steve DeAngelo of Harborside Health Center. The focus was helping dispensaries in the fledgling legal marijuana markets replicate Harborside's business model and success. CannBe developed a set of operating procedures and best practices for starting and running a dispensary. However, as with many marijuana businesses, CannBe was challenged by the major industry crackdown in 2010, and the group dissolved.

Krane was undeterred. He developed a working relationship with Arizona-based investment company Moral Compass Corporation. Moral Compass was founded by billionaire Dr. John Sperling, who had suffered ailments for which medical cannabis provided symptom relief. Krane formed 4Front Advisors with MC Advisors, an investment advisor to Moral Compass, to professionalize legal marijuana businesses and help shape Arizona Medical Use regulations. 4Front leveraged much of CannBe's intellectual property dispensary "playbook," to serve as the backbone of the new entity's consulting services. In early 2013, Krane, with the other founders of 4Front, led a management buyout of the company.

4Front is primarily focused on helping entrepreneurs applying for dispensary licenses in states implementing new regulations. 4Front's value proposition is to offer consultation to dispensaries based on the most comprehensive and professional operating model in the industry. The consulting firm is selective about client engagements, and will only work with those applying for licenses in states with strong regulatory systems. 4Front also only works with clients who sign up for full-service solutions, meaning those wanting a complete turnkey solution rather than piecemeal advice. As Krane asserted, "compared with other firms, 4Front puts forth more time and resources to provide solutions for prospective dispensary operators. That's what really distinguishes us from the competition."

4Front also only works with a small number of clients to deliver the highest level of service possible. The firm is currently focused on the Massachusetts market, where the new legal marijuana market will open in 2014. The dispensary application process is now underway in a highly competitive process.

Regarding competition, Krane sees more consulting firms entering the market, and believes overall quality has improved. However, he cautions that several firms working in the space are not well-qualified, and are simply exploiting exuberance in the industry. "There are some consulting companies out there that simply run to states which are implementing new marijuana regulations and sell application support materials and advice with a lot of flash but no real substance. They make a lot of money and move on without really helping those who signed up with them."

4Front's strategy going forward is to build a presence in Massachusetts and then leverage its brand into other well-regulated state markets. Nevada is a likely target market, given that the state is revamping marijuana laws and will accept dispensary applications in April 2014. 4Front is also looking for other channels to leverage its intellectual property. Establishing an online platform to monetize the firm's operating procedure templates through digital formats is on the horizon.

As for implications of the new Adult Use markets, 4Front doesn't currently have plans to work in this area. "That may well change in the future," Krane noted. "Based on our work in Massachusetts, and the potential for that state to adopt Adult Use laws in 2016, that occurrence would present a natural extension to our existing business."

Information Technology

Information Technology (IT) firms are amongst the most dynamic ancillary companies in the legal marijuana markets. These firms serve key functions including business management, regulatory compliance, marketing and consumer information. Most of these companies are run by professionals from the mainstream IT industry who have applied similar technologies to the cannabis industry. There are two general categories of cannabis IT companies: consumer-facing and business management.

Consumer-Facing

Consumers seek information about cannabis for a range of topics. Information needs cover a broad scope, such as the effects of specific strains to which dispensaries and retailers carry those strains, to reviews of consumption devices and storefronts. Dozens of web companies have emerged to offer marijuana consumers guidance and education.

Dispensary locator and review sites were some of the earliest cannabis web properties to emerge. WeedMaps has dominated this space, though other entrants have also developed large followings, such as Leafly and StickyGuide. These sites earn advertising fees as well as fees from retailers who subscribe to be listed and promoted. Consumers are able to search for dispensaries by region, and to browse their menus. The sites also have other features such as forums, blogs, and other information. Leafly emphasizes strain information and self-reporting of effects by site visitors.

Other consumer-facing web properties focus on cannabis culture, social networking, cultivation instruction, scientific information, and other topics. MassRoots is a cannabis social networking site based on a mobile application. The Weed Blog and rollitup are popular sites that provide consumers with marijuana news and information resources. Some recent consumer-facing entrants include sites that aim to bring compliance efficiency to dispensaries by pre-verifying patients and ensuring maintenance of valid patient cards, as well as to provide loyalty rewards programs to customers.

Business Management

This category of IT companies focuses on supporting commercial and regulatory processes for managing legal cannabis businesses. In addition to innovating software solutions for increasingly sophisticated operators, these IT companies facilitate critical regulatory compliance and reporting.

Absent strong regulatory oversight, legal marijuana businesses have tended to avoid or limit record keeping and transaction tracking based on fears this information could be used against them in the event of a raid. As marijuana regulations evolve, businesses increasingly are required to provide sales and inventory reporting to licensing authorities to prove compliance with laws.

Prior to the entry of specialized cannabis business software, dispensaries employed rudimentary sales and inventory tracking methods, sometimes based on cryptic notes recorded on paper. Some developed spreadsheets or adapted off-the-shelf software such as QuickBooks. The limits of these early attempts proved cumbersome and ill-equipped to keep pace with increasingly complex product lines and transaction volumes. Software companies today provide businesses with IT solutions that address all facets of operational management and compliance reporting.

The first specialized cannabis business software companies emerged in 2010. The early adopters of cannabis software products tended to be those operating in states with more thorough regulatory requirements, especially in Colorado. Initial software products were primarily focused on point-of-sale and inventory tracking solutions for dispensaries. Software for cultivation operations were subsequently developed, in large measure as a response to vertical integration requirements by the Medical Marijuana Enforcement Division in Colorado. The ability to pair cultivator and dispensary software modules enabled operators to track the entire commercial life of a plant from inception to final retail sale (i.e., "seed-to-sale").

Product offerings in the market now address all aspects of the legal cannabis supply chain. In addition to tailored software solutions, some companies also offer related equipment such as cash drawers, bar code readers, package labeling machines, POS terminals, integrated scales, and other accessories.

There are multiple providers of IT solutions for legal cannabis companies. Some providers specialize in particular aspects of the supply chain; MMJ Menu focuses on dispensaries whereas TRiQsoft focuses on commercial cultivation and processing. Others, such as BioTrackTHC, MJ Freeway, and Agrisoft Development Group, provide solutions from production to retail sale. Agrisoft is also offering an innovative IT product for infused products manufacturers.

Some IT providers employ the SaaS (software as a service) delivery model, hosting software and data centrally and providing client IT access via the cloud. Other providers have systems based on servers located onsite at client facilities. Both delivery models have strengths and weaknesses. One advantage of the SaaS model is that data and records are hosted offsite, which may offer businesses more protection from the risk of enforcement officials seizing potentially incriminating records during a raid. In that occurrence, or other type of loss due to events such as fire or theft, operators can restore IT functionality simply by reconnecting to the internet. Drawbacks of not having servers onsite include downtime if there are problems with internet connection, and potentially slower processing speeds for high transaction volume businesses. Some remote cultivation facilities reportedly also have significant limitations with internet connectivity.

The evolving regulatory framework is also increasing the need for specialized IT systems for the regulatory oversight of marijuana businesses. Colorado requires Adult Use businesses to use the Marijuana Inventory Tracking Solution (MITS) system, a web-based tool coupled with Radio Frequency Identification technology that allows both the MITS user and the regulators to track each cannabis plant from "seed-to-sale". The Liquor Control Board, which oversees Adult Use businesses in Washington State, has awarded software company BioTrackTHC the contract to provide the state's traceability software to track each plant and cannabis product from production to final sale.

IT company product offerings will likely continue to evolve, and increase integration with other types of operating equipment elements of cannabis businesses. The ability to integrate cultivation software with grow site environmental controls (i.e., irrigation, humidity, temperature) can increase operational efficiencies. Integration with processing equipment and security systems are also areas where IT services can combine with other key functions to enhance business controls and operational precision.

ArcView Market Research anticipates there may be future mergers and acquisitions of ancillary cannabis IT companies. Sites focused on cultivation may combine with sites designed to serve retailers. Software companies may combine with equipment providers to offer marijuana businesses turnkey functionality across multiple operational aspects. Web properties may also seek to combine with IT service providers to offer multiple electronic products and services, as occurred when WeedMaps combined with MMJ Menu in 2011.

INDUSTRY LEADER PROFILES

Amy Poinsett / MJ Freeway

Amy Poinsett is co-founder and CEO of MJ Freeway, a SaaS company that provides software solutions to legal marijuana cultivation and distribution businesses. She formerly headed a Colorado-based web development company, and took an interest in the burgeoning medical marijuana industry she saw forming around her.

After discussions with a friend who had invested in a Boulder dispensary, which at the time had no Point of Sale (POS) system, Poinsett and her partners perceived there was a great opportunity to create a software company catering to the unique needs of legal marijuana businesses. These businesses had growing needs to manage sales, inventory, and patient clients. They were also subject to the most comprehensive marijuana laws of any state, and had to adhere to increasingly stringent regulations.

"Dispensaries are certainly amongst the most highly regulated retail businesses, more so than others such as liquor stores," Poinsett observed.

The company initially served Colorado businesses, later leveraging its brand by branching out to other legal states. MJ Freeway currently serves hundreds of clients in 12 states, DC, Canada, and Europe. Hundreds of millions of dollars in cannabis transactions have been conducted using the company's software.

MJ Freeway launched GramTracker, its first software product, in 2010. GramTracker is a POS and inventory management system for dispensaries (and now adapted to Adult Use retail sales). In addition to sales and inventory management, the software also provides dispensaries with tools to manage patient relationships, automating systems to assure that each customer is a valid patient qualified to purchase cannabis as required by state laws. GramTracker also allows dispensaries and retailers to automatically post menus both on their own websites, as well as on marijuana business locator sites such as Leafly, Weedmaps, and THCFinder. This is important for marketing purposes, as well as for apprising customers of changing inventories. It is not uncommon for strains and products to sell out through the course of a business day.

In 2011, MJ Freeway introduced GrowTracker, a software module customized to the needs of cultivation operations. A primary impetus for developing GrowTracker was Colorado regulatory requirement for "seed-to-sale" vertical integration, whereby dispensaries are required to produce the majority of cannabis sold to patients. The two software applications allowed business operators to track cannabis from the beginning of a plant's life through to the moment harvested flowers are sold at the retail counter.

In 2013, MJ Freeway debuted MixTracker, a new software solution designed for marijuana processors and infused marijuana product manufacturers. MixTracker enables companies to precisely control, monitor and log the ingredients used to manufacture marijuana-infused products such as edibles and extracts. Infused products typically include marijuana from multiple batches or lots, each with potentially different yields, so the manufacturing and tracking processes are often complicated and error-prone. MixTracker automates the entire manufacturing process, giving infusers an integrated solution that precisely tracks and controls recipe inventories. It also provides robust batch tracking, cost analysis, compliance reporting and end-user labeling data.

Competition has increased as more software companies have entered the legal marijuana industry. "We know we have to work hard to keep existing customers happy, and to attract new ones," Poinsett said. "We continue to innovate, and do software updates every six weeks to ensure the strength of our product offering". One key challenge for winning new customers is developing software for states that are adopting new legal marijuana regulations. The rules often get finalized only several months before implementation, as is the case in Massachusetts and Nevada.

"The compliance reporting aspect of our system is one of MJ Freeway's biggest selling points," according to Poinsett. "Our software is guaranteed to meet every state's regulatory requirements, which is a great competitive advantage for us." As an example, she cites package label requirements, which are different in each state. "Our system generates product labeling that complies with rules for dispensaries and retailers whether they are located in Arizona, New Jersey, Canada, or any other legal market."

Another way MJ Freeway strives to stay ahead of the competition and strengthen its brand is through customer and prospect education. The company hosts free webinars with featured guest speakers on business topics that are valuable to industry operators. MJ Freeway also launched Daily Dose, a free informative email addressing various topics about legal marijuana markets. MJ Freeway also sponsors events in order to strengthen its competitive advantage. "One of the best ways for us to connect with new prospects is by sponsoring and attending NCIA events held all over the country," Poinsett explained. "It gives us an opportunity to meet with people face-to-face. We also often speak at these events, discussing the role of software and seed-to-sale tracking in legal marijuana businesses."

Regarding the outlook for marijuana business software services, Poinsett highlights systems integration as a key trend. Lab testing is increasingly important based on regulatory requirements. "Application programming interfaces with test labs are going to be critical," she explains. This takes the form of being able to capture a test result from the lab and immediately push that information right through to product labels at the retail counter. MJ Freeway has already partnered with a Denver-based test lab, and testing results from samples sent to that lab automatically display on MJ Freeway's system. Working with other labs is on the horizon. Poinsett also sees that software integration with grow monitoring hardware is going to be essential as larger players need to achieve the full benefits of scale economies.

Insurance Services

Working in legal cannabis business entails no shortage of risk. Operators of cannabis companies, by definition, have to be comfortable with the assumption of more overall risk levels compared with those working in the vast majority of mainstream businesses.

Risks exposures are not only to economic losses, but also to the possibility for loss of personal freedom.

Some of the economic risks can be protected with commercial insurance products. Risk mitigation can also take other forms such as security systems and prudent operating procedures.

For many years, legal marijuana businesses were considered uninsurable. Quantifying risks, given many unknowns, was difficult. The industry was also considered taboo by most insurance providers. Over time, some enterprising insurance agents began to develop a niche in insuring established dispensaries. Policies were usually limited to General Liability coverage.

Eventually, a few insurance companies began to offer cultivators property insurance on plants, as well as protection for business interruptions. As the industry matured, insurance became more accessible to businesses (particularly in states with stronger regulations), coverage options expanded, and the divergence in the pricing of polices narrowed. Massachusetts, which will implement new legal marijuana regulations in 2014, became the first new state to require business license applications show proof of the ability to secure insurance. Applicants must be able to provide $1 million of general liability coverage and $2 million of product liability coverage. Most policies sold are underwritten by Lloyds of London, an international syndicate of around 100 insurance member companies who pool and spread risk.

In addition to General Liability insurance coverage, most legal marijuana businesses may also seek coverage for business income, fire, theft, vandalism, and workers compensation. Cultivation businesses in indoor growing environments are more readily insurable than open air outdoor growers. Grower policies include coverage of living plants, curing plant material, and finished stock (processed) marijuana. Dispensaries, infused products and edibles companies may opt for product liability insurance. Physicians providing medical marijuana recommendations can obtain malpractice insurance.

INDUSTRY LEADER PROFILES

Patrick McManamon / Cannasure Insurance Services

Insurance runs in Patrick McManamon's blood. His family has been in the business since 1946, and McManamon has worked at his father's company where he specialized in professional liability for medical professionals for over a decade. In 2010, he had an epiphany when a friend opened a San Diego dispensary and wanted to purchase insurance. Through working with his friend, McManamon discovered an underserved market which was misunderstood by the insurance industry. He saw that he could apply his experience and expertise to serving legal cannabis businesses.

McManamon partnered with industry pioneers Steve DeAngelo and Troy Dayton of The ArcView Group (which owns ArcView Market Research) to form Cannasure Insurance Services. Cannasure is the only insurance specialty firm that is fully dedicated to the legal marijuana industry. When Cannasure launched, most other insurers seemed to avoid cannabis dispensaries based on the stigma of industry, but McManamon viewed these as similar to a combination of pharmacy, retail, and consumer banking businesses.

Dispensaries typically held substantial amounts of cash, dispensed valuable inventories to patients, and dealt with customers through storefront locations.

Prior to Cannasure, cannabis business risk had never been formally analyzed. In most cases, the pricing of policies were uninformed, and coverages were not well-suited to business needs. Cannasure undertook the first formal risk management evaluation of the exposures faced by marijuana companies. "We wanted to create an insurance company by the industry, for the industry," noted McManamon. The review entailed hundreds of hours interviewing business owners and employees, studying market practices, and performing other due diligence measures with dispensaries and cultivators.

In speaking with business owners, McManamon found they were often not thinking about insurance at all, or were not optimizing protection of true risk exposures. "One area that can be difficult to understand is where does responsibility begin and end for retail cannabis businesses," he said, adding "in some ways, it's similar to a bar, in that a customer may get into an accident after visiting the business." However, he noted, dispensaries don't typically allow on-premises consumption, so the bar analogy is limited. Dispensary customers can be reasonably expected to assume more responsibility for their behaviors than bar patrons. In terms of actual product liability, the history of the dispensary and the jurisdiction in which a case is brought are important factors.

Product liability is clearer in the case of infused and edible products manufacturers. Consumers should be able to rely on food product safety in terms of being free of molds, pesticides, and other contaminants. Outside of those elements, however, the issue of potency and the consumers' response to cannabinoids is a different question that has yet to be fully tested in the courts.

McManamon helps business owners better understand risks and how to protect them. Workers compensation is one area where he finds greater focus is often warranted. "Providing employees with the proper tools and work environment is key," he observed. For example, providing workers in a trim room with well-maintained scissors, good lighting, work tables, and regular breaks are basic things that protect employees and can lower the cost of policies. From an insurance perspective, one area that business owners may place too much emphasis is security systems. "Some people spend tens of thousands of dollars on fancy security systems with special features like Kevlar walls and think this will mean cheaper insurance and that simply is not the case," according to McMananmon. He said insurance companies want to see security systems cover the basics of alarms, cameras, and locks. Any extras aren't going to reduce the price of a policy.

For cultivators, there is often a need to refine thinking about what to cover in terms of protecting crop production. Coverage can be expensive, particularly if risks are excessively insured. Many growers aim to protect one year's worth of inventory, which can be too much coverage according to McManamon. For crop failures at a given location, growers may be able to acquire replacement plants from other sites. When thieves target cultivation sites, it's often the equipment that is the most valuable asset that can be stolen. Most plants are not usually ready for harvest, and won't usually be taken. While many do seek policies covering seedlings, McManamon sees that as unnecessary. "In being thoughtful about the true cultivation risks that need coverage, businesses can reduce policy costs from $2 per $100 loss potential down to something like 45 cents per $1,000 loss potential."

For retailers, the biggest risks are in the parking lot. "Liability for things like customers slipping and falling when they go from and to their cars, rather than what happens once inside the dispensary, represent the greatest the exposure for businesses," according to McManamon.

Cannasure's claims experience has been favorable. There haven't been many claims made under policies, which McManamon characterizes as "few and far between." "We've seen a few theft claims for small amounts, as well as a handful of slip and falls, and a couple of fires."

As more insurance competitors have entered the market, Cannasure strives to gain competitive advantage in several ways.

The amount of industry due diligence performed, coupled with the market experience of its principals, positions Cannasure to give business owners expert guidance on optimizing insurance coverage. The company is very active in supporting the industry. Cannasure has hosted educational events aimed at elevating industry risk management best practices and understanding insurance alternatives. In addition, McManamon and Cannsure regularly donate to groups such as National Cannabis Industry Association, Marijuana Policy Project and Students for Sensible Drug Policy.

In terms of the outlook for marijuana business insurance, McManamon foresees increases in insurance rates in the near-term. He believes the introduction of Adult Use markets will likely cause rate increases as insurers begin to evaluate the implications of new market dynamics. He sees rates for product liability, in particular, rising based on perceived risk of more adults consuming cannabis products. In the medium-term, he feels that rates will most likely decline. "I see more insurers entering the market, and lower policy pricing as more actuarial data on losses becomes available."

Cannabusiness Education

"Higher Education" – the business of cannabis business education is evolving with changing industry demands and student motivations. Students used to take courses to learn how to be patients. Now, students want training on how to serve patients. Previously, both students and school management were often self-styled freedom fighters primarily looking to popularize cultivation and to lobby for social change. Now, schools seek to profit from training programs focused on meeting the demands of those motivated to build successful businesses or to work for them.

Acquiring know-how in the cannabis industry evolved greatly following the introduction of medical cannabis regulations. Cannabis education was once confined to self-teaching through trial and error, and in some cases to being mentored by seasoned operators within illicit circles. Virtually all education used to focus on cultivation. A few publications, including grower's handbooks and marijuana magazines, served as valuable references, but many cultivators tightly guarded their proprietary techniques and information so that access for outsiders was restricted. The scientific basis for education was often quite limited.

With the spread of state cannabis regulations, educational needs for marijuana business people are now multifaceted and encompass all aspects of the supply chain. Beyond cultivation, topics such as dispensary management, bud-tending, and manufacturing of infused products now figure prominently. Legal education is also in demand and touches on areas ranging from compliance and permitting to dealing with law enforcement and navigating the nuances of differing regional regulations.

The number of businesses in cannabis education has increased, offering products which are available through multiple distribution channels. Since the

2007 founding of Oaksterdam University (see section Dale Sky Jones Profile), the first formal cannabis business school, the number of schools has grown to about half a dozen. Most of these schools host seminars in states with medical marijuana regulations and offer online and digital content products. The amount of other educational resources delivered via the internet, particularly for cultivation, has also increased dramatically. Several sites offer premium, fremium, and free cultivation instruction. Even sites such as YouTube and Wikipedia offer open access to cannabis horticulture content. The ArcView Market Research outlook for cannabis business schools weighs both market opportunities and competitive risks. Although business education demands increase with each new state that adopts marijuana regulations, the proliferation of online services and free instructional content gives students increasing options, which in turn limits the pricing power for those offering basic educational products.

To withstand the compression of educational product pricing, cannabis schools must differentiate their products by offering specialized courses from recognized authorities in the field. Coursework must move beyond "Cultivation 101" and cover high-value add topics such as dispensary management, extraction production, advanced marijuana botany, and cost accounting. These topics entail nuances that are best conveyed by experts interacting directly with students. Coursework is further augmented by featuring "hands on" training in school labs or cultivation sites. These types of high-value educational products enable schools to differentiate themselves and to charge a premium.

Another feature that will distinguish schools is job placement. Most students seek technical knowledge in order to start a marijuana business or as an employment qualification. Cannabis business schools that offer a recognized certification program and that place students in desirable jobs can command a premium for their educational products. As the marijuana industry matures, we foresee a trend toward school accreditation. We also expect that the most profitable cannabis education businesses will function as trade schools that succeed by building recognition of their brand equity in the market.

INDUSTRY LEADER PROFILES

Dale Sky Jones / Oaksterdam Univeristy

As Executive Chancellor of Oaksterdam University, America's first cannabis college, Dale Sky Jones has seen cannabis business education change from focusing on patient access to guiding entrepreneurs on how to be successful legal marijuana businesspeople. Drawing on her background in corporate America and then in guiding doctors building their practices with medical marijuana patient recommendations, Jones tailors Oaksterdam's course offerings to evolving market demands.

Like other cannabis businesses, regulatory forces and competition have compelled Oaksterdam University to evolve since its creation in 2007. The school was founded by activists Richard Lee and Jeff Jones and originally was connected to a dispensary, a marijuana museum, and a gift shop. Course pricing was essentially subsidized by the other businesses, with an underlying goal of maximizing access to anyone who wants to learn and to join a "movement."

Everything changed in 2012. Federal enforcement authorities raided the dispensary and its related sites. The school had to disassociate from the dispensary, streamline course offerings, and follow a sustainable profit model by setting prices according to credit-based standards borrowed from the community college model.

Course content delivery also evolved. Recognizing educational needs from two distinct student populations, the school now offers coursework in two formats: weekend seminars catering to students visiting from out-of-state, and semester programs primarily for students living in California. Online course offerings are also planned to expand Oaksterdam University's reach; an online delivery platform is cost-efficient and saves students travel and lodging costs.

Increased competition from other schools and from other educational resources has also forced Oaksterdam University to sharpen its game. Student needs are assessed via surveys, and the results shape new course offerings. An example is the resurgence of interest in outdoor cultivation, which has resulted in a new semester program on outdoor agriculture. The need for business management training is now being served by new workshops in areas such as cost accounting for marijuana businesses.

Brand equity, a competitive advantage that more marijuana businesses are developing, is also central to Oaksterdam University's positioning in the market. Jones explains that both the reputation for top-notch faculty and the depth of course content add to the school's first-to-market advantage and distinguish it from the competition. Around 70% of students come to the school in Oakland, California from out of state to learn from recognized experts such as faculty member Ed Rosenthal. The school also reinforces brand equity with its unique marijuana museum, which provides 'living displays ' of course content covering politics, history, cultivation, hemp and cannabis as medicine.

Oaksterdam University's approach to education is another hallmark of its brand. New students usually have ideas about what they want to learn, yet often don't understand other aspects that are critical to their success. "We first teach what 'not' to do," Jones explains. The school's philosophy is that learning how to not get arrested is even more important than learning how to grow. "People need to understand that they could lose everything, including their freedom, businesses, and families." The school can speak to these topics from direct experience in light of the 2012 raid that precipitated Richard Lee's retirement from the industry.

As Jones puts it, "we're setting you up for success and preparing you for the worst."

Additional Ancillary Businesses

ArcView Market Research is also providing additional featured topics about ancillary businesses. The following featured topics will be sent to purchasers of this report as part of a series of informative topics to keep readers informed about important trends that are shaping the industry.

Cannatourism

The emergence of the first Adult Use states has given rise to a whole new vertical within the cannabis industry: Cannatourism. For the first time in history, adults can travel to Colorado and Washington State and legally purchase marijuana. New businesses are being launched to capitalize on those visiting legal Adult Use states to experience cannabis. From tour operators to "bud and breakfasts" to cannabis lifestyle centers, Cannatourism is a new ancillary line of business which ArcView Market Research surveys to help readers understand.

Security Services

Cannabis businesses need security system solutions not only to protect business assets, but in many cases to also comply with state regulations. Video cameras, door locks, and alarms comprise entry-level security systems. New technologies are also giving rise to more sophisticated options like remote door access controls via mobile apps and integration with cultivation environment controls. In addition to examining this ancillary business sector, ArcView Market Research also profiles Dan Williams, CEO of Canna Security Systems.

Consumption Devices

Devices for consuming cannabis have greatly evolved beyond basic pipes and bongs. New technologies have given rise to an expanded range of devices to consume cannabis products. The number of portable vaporizer products available in the market has surged in recent years, giving consumers important alternatives to smoking as an ingestion format. New types of devices have been developed such as specialized water pipes that cater to the market for "dabbing," which is an intensified method for ingesting cannabis concentrate products. The upcoming additional feature on consumption devices profiles these products and opportunities for the ancillary businesses that manufacture these devices to serve cannabis consumers.

INVESTMENT & FINANCE

Overview

There is a palpable excitement in market sentiment among investors and companies in the legal marijuana industry. With the promise of the new Adult Use markets, paired with the perception of reduced exposure to federal intervention, risk/reward tradeoffs seem to be more inviting now than at any previous time. Yet recent history teaches that caution is also warranted, and substantial market challenges remain.

Positive developments at the state and federal levels have the potential both to stabilize the business environment and to accelerate market growth. The breakthrough to full legalization in Colorado and Washington State, the shift in federal enforcement policy in legal marijuana states portrayed in the most recent Department of Justice memo, and the recent Senate judiciary hearing about legal marijuana businesses' access to banking services are all pointing toward opportunity and growth.

Despite the improved business outlook, seekers and providers of capital face a complex investment and finance landscape in the legal marijuana markets. While opportunities for both parties have greatly increased during the last two years, casting deals in this industry often entails braving unchartered waters and assuming substantial risks.

A continuing challenge is the inability of most marijuana companies to obtain financial services from banks and many payment processors. Recent developments at the federal level may prove to resolve the financial services issue, but until that occurs businesses are hampered by the lack of basic tools such as bank accounts and efficient payment processing.

Access to capital has been another industry impediment. Capital formation happens at the intersection of businesses finding investors, and vice versa. Until recently, the mechanisms for their meeting have been very limited. However,

capital-raising channels have been rapidly developing, increasing deal prospects for both startups and expansion-stage companies, and for both cannabis and ancillary companies alike. In addition to a group of companies in the public stock markets, investors are also backing companies through private equity deals.

Investment

Investment activity in the legal marijuana markets has increased considerably over the past two years. New business opportunities, as well as greater numbers and types of investors, serve to expand the number of investments taking place in the industry.

Much has changed in terms of investor participation. Initially, loans were the predominant financing vehicles for legal marijuana businesses. Until recently, most legal marijuana entrepreneurs in need of funding were limited to their own finances or to tapping friends and family sources. Funding was often cast as short-term loans, particularly for cultivation operations that can service debt from the strong cash flows generated after incurring startup or expansion costs. These loans were typically structured with short-term maturities (i.e., 6 to 18 months), and could be easily repaid from the proceeds of a few successful harvest cycles. Dispensary and ancillary businesses also were often funded from similar sources of capital.

Loan structures, if not convertible to equity, are in many cases well-suited to financing legal marijuana business opportunities. Loans often match the cash flow characteristics of cannabis businesses, don't run afoul of residency ownership requirements in certain states, are suited to nonprofit businesses' requirements, and may afford the lender less legal risk compared with stake ownership.

However, with the arrival of many new investors in the market, there is increased interest in benefitting from the long-term fortunes of the companies they back. Equity investment or hybrid structures like convertible notes in the private funding arena are better suited to this objective.

The greater numbers of investors and the widening set of investment structure alternatives are expanding the available capital pool for legal marijuana businesses and entrepreneurs. As with the development of businesses in this industry, innovation plays a central role in how investments are being cast to meet business needs and state regulatory requirements.

Key Considerations

Investors in legal marijuana businesses face a host of issues and risks, some of which are common to other industries and some of which are specific to cannabis.

As with all industries, investors must be able to evaluate company management teams, product offerings, value propositions, addressable markets, proprietary assets, competitive environments, investment terms, and other common investment variables.

Specific to the legal cannabis industry, investors need to weigh local, state, and federal risk factors that may support or challenge companies being considered for investment. For some, investing in ancillary companies is a way to mitigate some of the political and legal risk factors inherent in the industry.

In angel and venture investment, cultural fit may be a further consideration. Seasoned investors from outside the marijuana industry who are purely seeking financial returns may or may not be able to relate to entrepreneurs immersed in the popular cannabis culture or who are significantly motivated by political and social change. In contrast, some investors who are also advocates and who are seeking both financial return and social change may not appreciate companies that are solely profit driven with no drive to contribute to the cause.

State residency may also be a consideration. Many states, such as Colorado, require that business owners be state residents, and this requirement prevents nonresidents from buying equity in legal marijuana companies. Loans, however, may be permissible, and some Colorado companies conduct two-tier investor offerings: equity for residents, and loans for nonresidents. An innovative loan investment vehicle for non-Colorado residents looking to capitalize on Adult Use is being offered by Mjardin and is based on a trust structure; investors buy into the trust, which in turn provides leases for capital assets to marijuana businesses.

Adam Denmark Cohen / MJardin

With more than 10 years of management and legal expertise, with specialization in private equity, real estate and hospitality, Adam Cohen recognized a "generational macro trend" in the emerging legal cannabis industry. Being deeply rooted in the private equity world, Cohen was struck by the dearth of traditional investment capital in what was quickly becoming a multi-billion dollar industry. He observed that institutional investors in particular were sidelined and the growth of the industry and the quality of its participants was suppressed due to outmoded federal prohibition and the resulting conflict between federal and state laws. Yet, the industry was quickly gaining legal standing across the U.S. along with unprecedented public support and was poised for explosive growth.

According to Cohen, it is precisely that intersection between current legal uncertainty and what he views as an unstoppable market force that gives rise to this exceptional opportunity for those brave enough to stomach the risks of being an early mover. "What I saw, and what I continue to see, is a window to invest in an emerging industry with extraordinary growth potential at a time of limited competition, both in terms of capital and management. Eventually, the legal barriers, in the form of federal prohibition, will fall. If you wait for that to happen, you will have missed the real opportunity." Based on that insight, Cohen set about applying his legal and private equity experience to build a company dedicated to the legal cannabis industry.

Prior to his involvement in the cannabis industry, Cohen co-founded and served as Chief Operating Officer for Brilla Group, an alternative asset private equity firm focused on the luxury hotel and resort asset class in South Florida, the Caribbean, and South America. The experience of helping to build a company from the ground-up and dealing with complicated operations across multiple jurisdictions as well as private and institutional investors and structures, served Cohen well in this new venture.

Having completed his undergraduate and legal studies at the University of

Colorado, Cohen was quite familiar with the landscape of Colorado, which fortuitously emerged as a leader in the legal, regulated and taxed Medical Use and Adult Use recreational cannabis industry. Turning his full attention back to Colorado, Cohen had to look no further than his longtime friend, John Fritzel, himself a bold entrepreneur and early mover in Colorado's cannabis industry.

Fritzel had a front row seat in the industry as a founding partner of Denver-based Lightshade Labs, a vertically integrated and licensed cultivation and retail medical cannabis business. Fritzel also saw the writing on the wall and the opportunities for explosive growth but recognized that competition would inevitably increase and the best value proposition was to be not just a good retailer but also an expert large-scale cultivator of high-quality cannabis. With that in mind, he had partnered with James Lowe, a professional large-scale cultivator who had been involved with Colorado's medical cannabis industry since its inception as the founder and CEO of Cloud 9 Consulting, which provided professional third-party cultivation services.

Cohen, Fritzel and Lowe found in each other the critical skill sets required to build a scalable professional company and together formed MJardin (which means "garden" in Spanish). Today, MJardin is an integrated investment and management company focused exclusively on the cultivation and sale of premium cannabis, both as an owner of licensed cultivation and retail facilities and as a third party professional operating company serving the emerging and rapidly expanding legal cannabis industry.

"Our vision was to create an integrated ownership and cultivation management company but like the industry in general, our ability to scale quickly was limited by our ability to attract significant investment capital," recalls Cohen. "What we saw initially was that many investors were excited about the opportunities in the space but didn't know how to access opportunities. Investors realized that the closer you get to the business license, i.e., the plant, the greater the potential upside, but there were many barriers to entry, including an onerous residency restriction in Colorado. A non-resident of Colorado is prohibited from being an owner of a licensed cannabis business here." The solution? Cohen and his partners developed an innovative real estate backed trust structure with the goal of providing investors substantial short-term returns while positioning them for potential longer-term participation and gains through a number of structural features. This is a model that MJardin views as replicable in other markets.

"While our focus remains on the core business in Colorado, we are actively evaluating and, where appropriate, pursuing opportunities in other markets," said Cohen. "We have many years of opportunity ahead both in terms of investment and growth of the professional operating company. As more and more markets come online, emerging, as well as existing, businesses will be looking for professional operators. We intend to be there. And while we need to be aggressive in seizing opportunities while they are ripe, we also need to be smart and ensure that we don't get ahead of ourselves. This is where guidance from seasoned capital partners and advisors is critical."

What does MJardin view as being the most important elements for its success? "Compliance, management, scale and timing," according to Cohen. "These are the four legs of the stool. You need rigid adherence to applicable laws and regulations if you have any hope of being a long-term player - this is the sine qua non. You need highly qualified, talented and energetic management in order to build and expand a successful platform. You need scale in order to be competitive in the long run when traditional commodity market forces come into play, which they inevitably will. And you need to move aggressively in the early stage of the industry to position yourself and acquire market share."

And how does MJardin view the federal risk at this point? "You need to view the federal government's position on prohibition holistically and in context," says Cohen. "The latest Justice Department Memo of August 2013 was not intended to signal an 'all clear' but it has in reality cleared some of the risk for potential investors in this space. Participation in the industry is less of a leap of faith now than it is was a year ago. There has seemingly been a realization on the part of the federal government that this genie is not going back in the bottle and that a transition from prohibition to state regulation is sound public policy."

Whether this shift will ultimately take hold will largely depend on how successful states like Colorado and Washington are in implementing and enforcing state regulation with an eye towards the articulated federal enforcement priorities. "We intend to be part of the solution here," says Cohen, "not part of the problem." "Like any other regulated industry in the world, adherence to and enforcement of the regulations is critical to the success of the market. The professionalization of the industry is a critical step in this evolution. We're excited to be part of this generational change," notes Cohen, "and we intend to be here for the long run."

Valuation is another challenge in the legal marijuana markets. In the absence of a solid base of observable peer transaction valuations, it can be difficult to gauge the worth of a company. Appraising companies is further complicated by the multitude of risk factors that can swing the fortunes of businesses in the market. This aspect increases the importance of investor peer networks that collectively can strengthen company valuation assessments by collaborating and sharing information. For ancillary companies, valuation can be informed by referencing metrics of conventional industry counterparts. For example, a commercial cannabis insurance company can borrow valuation multiples from counterparts in conventional non-cannabis businesses and apply those multiples to premiums and insured assets to arrive at valuation appraisals.

Investors have a growing number of alternatives in the legal marijuana markets. The ideal investments are a function of an individual's market strategy, return objectives and risk tolerance. Decision variables include some of the following:

- Cannabis vs. Ancillary – One basic consideration is whether to invest in companies that directly handle cannabis or in companies that cater to companies (or consumers) that do. Some investors want to get as close to the plant as possible, believing that the closer to the plant, the higher the rewards. Investment in cultivation operations may generate returns most quickly on the basis of harvest proceeds compared with startup and operating costs. Dispensary investment returns depend on a host of factors, including whether the store is allowed to operate as a for-profit concern. Marijuana producers, processors, and retailers also carry the most enforcement risk, which can be mitigated among those operating under tight regulatory oversight.

  Alternatively, ancillary companies are further removed from the plant and may have longer runways, but also carry lower risks. A cannabis product packaging or consumption device company may not start generating large excess cash flows six months from investment, but such also carry less enforcement risk. Importantly, less risk doesn't mean risk free. The packaging company may not be raided by the DEA, but it can still lose customers if the DEA raids the dispensaries that the packaging company caters to.

- Ancillary Type – There are many kinds of ancillary companies, so an investor considering opportunities in these businesses needs to evaluate which sectors are most appealing. Is the investment objective to profit from increased demand by dispensaries and cultivators for services from security companies based on the trend in tighter state regulatory requirements? Or does the investment thesis call for backing vaporizer companies that benefit from greater use of alternative ingestion methods?

- Positive Carry vs. Longer-Run Windfall – Some investors prefer deals that produce income quickly – either in the form of loan interest or stock dividends. These investors may be best-suited to cultivation businesses, for-profit retail operations, or other companies that generate excess cash flows on relatively short investment horizons. Other investors are looking primarily for big windfalls in the longer-term, which is more akin to a VC perspective. The goal here is for companies to build value over a multiyear timeframe and then realize a profitable liquidity event via company sale or possibly even a public listing. Companies fitting this profile may be those building brands and eyeing multistate expansion and ancillary companies that can freely transcend state boundaries and build a national presence.

- Loan, Equity, or Hybrid – the choice of which kind of investment structure to use can be a function of investor and company preferences, as well as state regulatory requirements. Nonprofits are generally limited to loan funding. An out-of-state investor looking for an investment play in Colorado Adult Use is limited to loan funding, according to state regulations (see Adam Cohen Industry Leader Profile). In cases where equity investments are permitted, differences of opinion on valuation may complicate deal negotiations. With few comparables to reference in the emerging legal cannabis market, entrepreneurs' lofty opinions on valuation may clash with investors' assessments. In those cases, hybrid convertible note structures may satisfy the need for securing an investment stake in the company while deferring the determination of valuation to a future date when the industry and company are more fully developed.

Angel Investment

High net worth, accredited angel investors, as a source of private capital, are now playing a key role in the financing of legal marijuana companies. Analogous to the early days of high tech and green tech, angels are providing critical capital to seed-, startup-, and expansion-stage companies. As with technology investment, angels are often experienced industry operators with specialized knowledge and networks. They are able to provide both strategic and financial capital to young businesses. For businesses, introductions to vendors, customers and professional service providers can be equally, and sometimes even more, important than the provision of funds. As this market channel matures, angel investors are also coming from outside of the industry, including high net worth individuals who may invest both for financial return objectives as well as to empower the legal marijuana companies that are hastening social change and the end of cannabis prohibition.

One challenge for angels looking to place money in legal marijuana businesses is the limited channels to access deal flow. Industry insiders, by virtue of their business dealings, may have the advantage of already being connected to promising entrepreneurs seeking capital. Other deal flow channels are informal and formal angel networks, whereby colleagues share expertise in the vetting of investment opportunities and may also co-invest to leverage and diversify their financial commitments. The first formal angel investor group, the ArcView Investor Network, was formed in 2011 and hosts quarterly events whereby entrepreneurs pitch to dozens of investors to raise capital. The group has grown from just 20 investor members in November of 2012 to more than 100 members as of November of 2013. The amount and quality of company applicants to the network has also shifted dramatically. One year ago there was very little competition for the pitch slots, but as of November, around 100 applicants were competing for about a dozen pitch slots available at the January 2014 quarterly investor event. While the ArcView Investor Network, which is a member of the Angel Capital Association, includes the kinds of investors who are common in angel groups around the country that

don't specialize in cannabis, there is also something unique happening. People who would do not usually fit the profile of an angel investor like billionaires, CEO's of NASDAQ- traded companies, and representatives of venture funds with millions to invest, are joining ArcView presumably because the knowledge gap that exists in cannabis does not exist in other industries. New York Republican state legislator Steve Katz is also a member.

A group of companies, including cannabis and ancillary firms, have collectively raised over $3 million as a result of their participation in the ArcView Investor Network in 2013. These companies include:

- Apeks Fabrication, which makes equipment for creating cannabis extractions
- Uptoke, which makes a portable vaporizer
- Rodawg, which is a lifestyle and cannabis packaging company
- Medicine Man, which is a cannabis dispensary and cultivation business in Denver that is expanding to meet the demands of the Adult Use market
- Mass Roots, which is a social networking application for cannabis consumers
- Canna Security America, a security services company for cannabis businesses

There are others that have been funded that are not being public about their being funded. (Disclosure note: the ArcView Investor Network is operated by The ArcView Group, which owns ArcView Market Research).

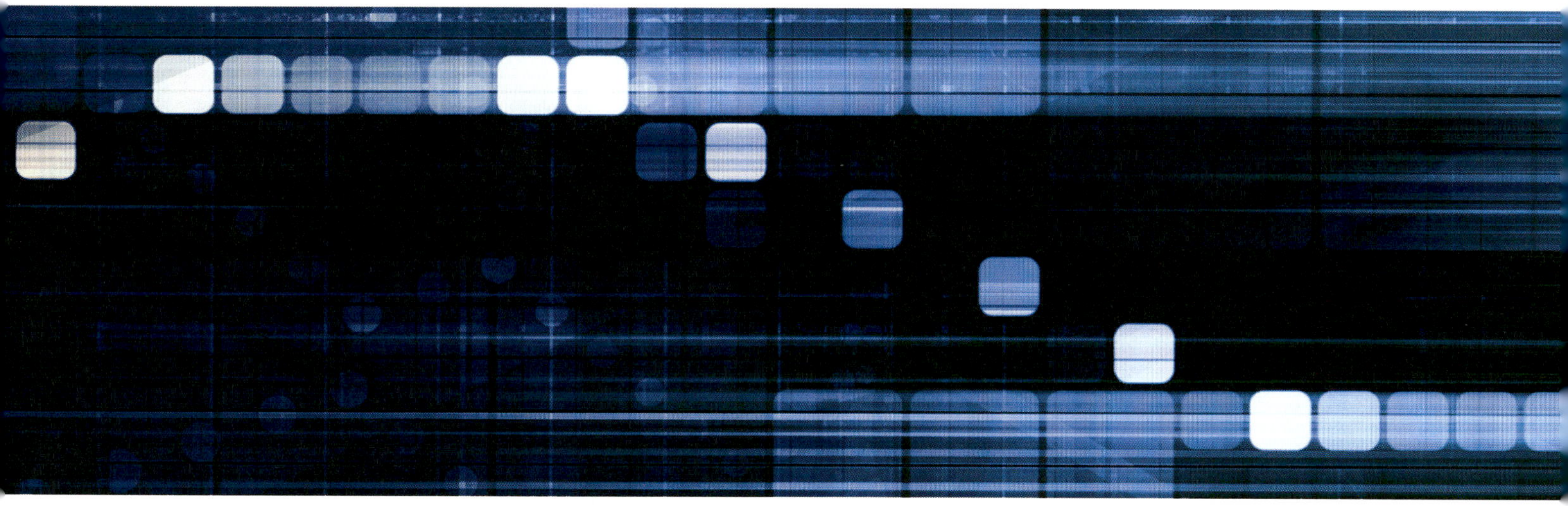

INDUSTRY LEADER PROFILES

Jim Willett

Washington State resident Jim Willett might not fit the profile of what most people would expect of a private investor in the legal marijuana industry. He's a family man who has never tried cannabis. As a former Navy pilot, he used to fly drug interdiction runs for the US government. He voted against Initiative 502 in November 2012, the state ballot measure which legalized Adult Use. As a high net worth accredited investor who once worked as a broker for Merrill Lynch, Willett liked to invest but legal cannabis simply wasn't, as he put it, "on his radar."

Upon the passage of I 502, Willett came to the realization that legal cannabis was a fast-growing industry where investing in the right opportunities had the potential for big returns. "I was reading the papers after I 502 passed, and was surprised to see that a marijuana business investor network was holding events featuring pitches from cannabis entrepreneurs," he said. "I knew there were some public cannabis-related stocks, but I wanted to get an insider's perspective on investing in emerging companies in the industry." Willett joined the ArcView Investor Network and was amazed by the deals he saw being pitched. (Dislosure Note: ArcView Investor Network is operated by The ArcView Group, which owns the publisher of this report, ArcView Market Research.

Willett was inspired to do more research on legal marijuana markets. He went to Denver to tour marijuana businesses and network with industry players. While he recognized investment in cannabis companies such as cultivation operations offered the potential for big returns, he also felt the risks were substantial. He decided ancillary businesses were better-suited to his risk/reward preferences. Likening the industry to the time before the end of alcohol prohibition, "it's similar to investing in bottling plants before prohibition ended."

As with alcohol prohibition, Willett felt there was no question that a large market already existed. He perceived there were great opportunities to invest in a big market that was simply transitioning from underground to above ground. "There's no secret about what this market can become," he said, it's easy to see the demand, potential size, and profits." We're just talking about a shift in the equation in going from illegal to legal," he added.

He evaluated several ancillary company investments, which he felt had the potential for substantial profits with relatively minor risks. He targeted companies that he believed provided essential services to the legal cannabis industry. "My first direct investment was in the security company Canna Security America, which is a deal I saw presented at an ArcView event. I've also invested in a software company. Both companies offer services which dispensaries and cultivators absolutely must have to operate and comply with regulations," he noted.

How does Willet approach investment? "My first rule is diversification, so I'm never the lone investor. I always co-invest along with other investors in the same deals," he explained. "This diversity lowers my risk, and is a source of strength because I don't know everything about the industry and every co-investor brings some perspective to the table."

In terms of his outlook, Willett sees the industry as being in its infancy and only getting better over time. He is positioning for growth in value, and invests strictly in equity for the upside potential. Having invested around one million dollars to date, he sees "no end in sight" for the industry. "Legal cannabis is the growth portion of my overall portfolio," he said, adding "it's just rare to see great opportunities like this being created almost out of thin air."

Venture Capital Investment

Investment participation by venture capitalists and institutional investors in the legal marijuana markets is limited, but growing. Venture capital firms, by definition, look to be early investors in emerging private companies that have high-return potential and that carry significant risks. In that respect, legal marijuana businesses fit VC investment objectives. The potential of this industry has caught the attention of many venture capitalists and has been featured on the cover of Venture Capital Journal, even though most cannot invest in marijuana enterprises because of the reticence of their limited partners. There are presently only two VC firms focused exclusively on legal cannabis investment that ArcView Market Research knows of.

Privateer Holdings, based in Seattle, is the first private equity firm dedicated to venture capital investments in legal marijuana businesses. It targets investments that have strong potential to generate both financial returns and to create opportunities for positive social change. Privateer recently closed a $7 million fund, and is preparing a new one (see Brendan Kennedy Industry Leader Profile). Emerald Ocean Capital, based in Southern California, launched in June 2013. Emerald's cofounders are Doug Francis and Justin Hartfield, both key figures in the highly successful WeedMaps.com, a company that pioneered a cannabis-related search finder and social media site.

Brendan Kennedy / Privateer Holdings

As legal marijuana businesses professionalize, so too do their investors. Fast industry growth means capital requirements are outpacing resources available from friends and family, as well as those from many angel investors. But with institutional investors largely sidelined prior to federal legalization, the market is ripe for venture capital investors.

VC participation is a telling development about early investor perceptions of the upside potential for legalized marijuana commerce. Just as the entry of venture capitalists was a key milestone in the early days of high-tech investing, such is the case with legal cannabis.

With the 2010 formation of Privateer Holdings, a Seattle-based venture capital firm, cannabis investing took a major leap forward. Privateer co-founder Brendan Kennedy saw such vast opportunity in the emerging cannabis markets, he quit his work as a high-tech Silicon Valley venture capitalist with a leading firm to start the first-ever private equity fund dedicated exclusively to legal marijuana businesses.

Kennedy recognized a compelling, yet complex, industry opportunity. "I've seen well over a thousand business plans, and this is the most complicated set of businesses I've ever looked at," said Kennedy. "Legally, politically, socially, medically—this market is among the most difficult to assess." Challenges notwithstanding, he saw great potential rewards.

Absent good data, Kennedy had to evaluate the industry directly from the ground up. He studied the market for months and talked to marijuana cultivators and dispensary operators, as well as to ancillary companies. He began to form a sense of the industry's size, players, opportunities, and risks. Having developed an investment thesis, he raised a seven million dollar fund from a group of 30 domestic and international high net worth investors.
Privateer's first investment was in the ancillary space in the form of online web property Leafly, a strain information, dispensary locator, and cannabis

news website. While there were other popular dispensary locator sites such as WeedMaps and StickyGuide, patient information about cannabis strains and effects was very limited. Leafly bills itself as "the world's largest cannabis strain resource," and it currently has detailed information on nearly 600 strains, including thousands of patient reviews. Another key Leafly distinction is aesthetics. Leafly doesn't match the typical media cannabis clichés. In contrast to other sites, which are often plastered with close-ups of marijuana flowers, Leafly has a clean and professional mainstream appearance. "We want to do really well with 35-year-old soccer moms and seniors," Kennedy explains.

Privateer's investment scope goes beyond the US border, having set up Lafitte Ventures Ltd, a Canadian company formed for legal cannabis investment. Lafitte Ventures is seeking to establish a Health Canada-approved medical marijuana production warehouse at Duke Point in the city of Nanaimo in British Columbia. Lafitte would be making a $1.5 million capital investment in the facility, which would create up to 40 new jobs. The objective is to begin cannabis cultivation by February of 2014 in anticipation of Canada's new Marijuana for Medical Purposes Regulations that commence in April 2014.

Most recently, Privateer has established Arbormain, a Seattle real estate subsidiary company. Arbormain is opening facilities to serve as business hubs for cannabis businesses which are compliant with Adult Use regulations in Washington State. The company will lease individual secure areas to business tenants for cultivation, processing and distribution of legal marijuana products.

How are legal marijuana investors different from investors in other industries? According to Kennedy, most of his investors are looking for a financial return, but all are looking for a "social" return. "Social returns can take the form of advancing civil liberties, human rights, and health care," he explains. While he didn't set out to be an activist, like his fund investors did, Kennedy has become motivated both by financial and social objectives. He speaks of investment in legal marijuana businesses as a catalyst to end prohibition.

Next on the horizon for Privateer is the launch of a second fund raise of at least $25 million, "sooner rather than later," according to Kennedy. Investor interest has risen rapidly in tandem with the expansion of state marijuana laws and business activity. When asked about his longer-term fund formation and investment objectives, Kennedy states: "Raise enough capital to end prohibition." If he hits that goal, both financial and social ROIs could well be substantial.

Public Markets

Angel and venture-capital investment is readily accessed by most investors on the basis of the requirement for Accredited Investor status, as defined by the Security and Exchange Commission. For nonaccredited investors, a number of publicly traded marijuana stocks are listed and available, but these require careful consideration of the potential risks.

420 Stock index

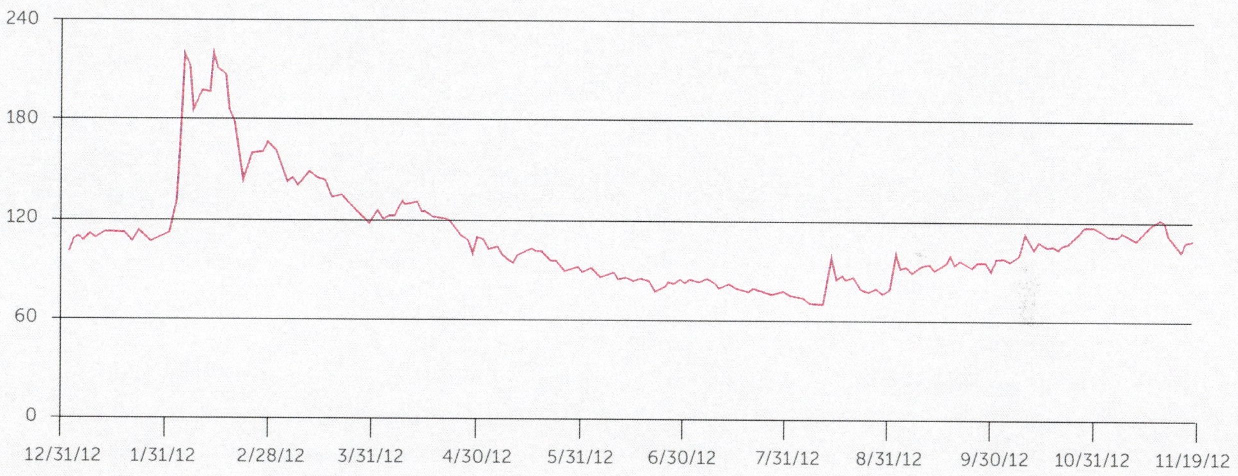

Public marijuana stocks are ancillary companies that cover business types and products ranging from cannabis vending machines to growing equipment to biotech hemp research. The market capitalizations range from hundreds of thousands to hundreds of millions of dollars. Many are penny stocks that trade on the pink sheets, although some trade over the counter, and one trades on the NASDAQ in the US (GW Pharma).

Considering investment in these companies is quite different than for most other public companies. In addition to representing the marijuana and hemp niches, most of the public marijuana companies are not fully reporting and have limited disclosure which constrains the information available to investors. Some of these companies have also provided questionable disclosures and financial information, which is being increasingly scrutinized by professional stock analysts who have begun to follow the sector.

Another consideration for public marijuana stocks has been high volatility. The relatively small market capitalizations, coupled with periodic investor exuberance, make the market vulnerable to manipulation and large price swings.

To shed more light on public marijuana stocks, ArcView Market Research has included a review by Alan Brochstein, principal of AB Analytical Services. Mr. Brochstein is not recommending stocks, nor is he providing investment advice. His review is intended to shed light on the public market for marijuana stocks and to provide a brief summary of each company's background and certain stock characteristics. As of November 2013, Mr. Brochstein does not hold any positions in the stocks he reviews below.

Public Stock Review by Alan Brochstein, CFA

2013 will be remembered as the year cannabis became an investment theme for individual investors. While many thought that the sector would be a quick ticket to riches, the reality didn't match the early-in-the-year hype, and most of the stocks ended up declining to levels below where they began the year or at least underperforming the broad market's rally. The seeds of optimism were actually planted in November 2012, when voters approved legal cannabis in both Colorado (Amendment 64) and Washington State (Initiative 502). Excitement about the prospects for the industry attracted tens of thousands of individuals into the sector, with one company alone reporting 40,000 shareholders early in the year. The flood of investors into a limited universe of potential investments, however, had left the companies with valuations that proved unsustainable. Still, as the year played out, a few players were able to maintain or even extend their gains. More importantly, the public market learned to better differentiate between companies and appears eager to embrace legitimate new entrants.

To see how 2013 has played out, we can look at the 420 Stock Index, which consists of eight stocks equally weighted at the beginning of the year (Cannabis

Sciences, Greengro Technologies, Growlife, GW Pharma, Hemp, Inc., Medbox, Medical Marijuana, Inc., and Terra Tech):

The year began with the sector rallying in line with the overall market but then surging in early February, with the index more than doubling from its year-end level. Of the eight names in the index, three had more than tripled by February. An article by an anonymous self-declared short on the financial portal Seeking Alpha raised questions about one of the leading names in the sector, Medical Marijuana, Inc., and the bubble quickly began to deflate.

By August, the sector had clearly lost its buzz, as investors quickly realized that the reality didn't match the hype, as most of the companies reported strong growth in share count only, rather than in things like sales or cash flow. The 420 Stock Index bottomed out down at nearly 30% when the out-of-the blue reversal by CNN Chief Medical Correspondent Sanjay Gupta of his formerly negative views on medical cannabis brought renewed interest to the group. But a warning by self-regulatory organization Financial Industry Regulatory Authority (FINRA) regarding potential "scams" quickly deflated the sector again.

In late August, clarity from the Department of Justice regarding the implementations of legal cannabis in Colorado and Washington provided impetus for the sector to begin its recovery, and the index moved well into the positive territory but still lagged the overall market. The rally that began in late August was driven by just a few of the index members, those seemingly most tied to the positive developments in August. In fact, of the eight members of the index, only two traded above the closing prices heading into Labor Day, while half of the group traded in late November below the lows in August.

While FINRA was late to the game, its warning from August 20 was quite appropriate. The key points that the organization raised were that investors were subject to deception by the companies themselves as well as from outside promoters looking to take advantage of a relatively unsophisticated investor base. The "Marijuana Stock Scams" alert didn't actually call out names, but it pointed to the behaviors of several companies that left little question about which companies were motivating FINRA's warning.

Investors in the sector need to be aware of the inherent risks in penny stocks. All but one of the stocks trades over -the -counter, and many of them do not even file with the SEC. Ironically, some of the largest and best-known names fall into this category. Even those that do file with the SEC face "going concern" issues. The

supply of companies in the sector is quite limited relative to the demand, and many investors fail to appreciate that the industry is highly fragmented, with the current crop of publicly traded companies representing a tiny fraction of the entire industry. In fact, the odds of success for most of these companies are quite low.

So, as we enter 2014, what should we expect? The good news is that some of the companies in the sector appear to be capable of capitalizing on the growth in recreational and legal cannabis. Additionally, the market will likely see new opportunities as more companies access the capital markets through reverse merger. New listings, whether through reverse merger or through the formation of subsidiaries by existing companies, has been a theme late in 2013, although several of the companies seem to lack substance.

A final observation before a discussion of the names in the sector is that many of the companies provide to accredited investors what appears to be a much lower risk investment. Specifically, high net worth individuals are able to buy either restricted stock or convertible notes with very favorable terms that offer substantial discounts to the market prices of the stocks.

The following descriptions of the larger names in the cannabis sector are intended to give readers an idea of the basic business model, the capital structure, and the level of transparency. The market capitalization, which is based on the price as of November 22, 2013, assumes conversion of all potentially dilutive securities, including preferred stock and convertible debt. The publicly traded universe is actually larger than the list that follows, and additional companies and their corresponding tickers are included at the end.

Here are some other cannabis-focused companies below the $10M market cap threshold:

Alternative Energy Partner (AEGY), Abbattis Bioceuticals (ATTBF), Cannabis Sativa Inc. (CBDS), Crown Marketing (CWNM), Easton Pharmaceuticals (EAPH),

Endocan (ENDO), Enertopia (ENRT), Tranzbyte (ERBB), Creative Edge Nutrition (FITX), GreenGro Technologies (GRNH), ML Capital Group (MLCG), Neutra Corp (NTRR), Rapid Fire Marketing (RFMK), SK3 Group (SKTO), and Vape Holdings (PLPE VAPE)

Alan Brochstein, CFA, has been in the investment industry since 1986. Since 2007, he has been principal at AB Analytical Services, where he offers consulting and investment research to institutional investors and subscription-based research services to individuals. Alan launched 420 Investor (www.420investor.com) in 2013 in order to help individuals capitalize on the Green Rush.

Advanced Cannabis Solutions	(CANN)	$2.60	$39 M Market Cap	
CANN is a late-2013 reverse merger that intends to lease growing space in Colorado.				
AVT, Inc.	(AVTC)	$1.65	$48 M Market Cap	Pink Sheet
AVTC, which was formerly OTC-listed but is behind on its filings, manufactures vending machines and is a supplier to Medbox.				
Cannabis Sciences	(CBIS)	$0.033	$25M Market Cap	OTC
Colorado-based CBIS was the second company in the space to go public (2009) and is focused on medical marijuana research.				
CannaVest	(CANV)	$19.75	$504M Market Cap	OTC
CANV, which manufactures high-CBD hemp oil and health and beauty products, was created in late 2012 through a reverse merger transaction at $0.05 per share, with Medical Marijuana, Inc., contributing hemp oil inventory and intellectual property in exchange for $35M in cash or shares (initially valued at $5, with a collar of $4.50–6.00 governing future installment payments). The share count assumes that $6M in convertible notes issues to the CEO and to a partner ($0.60 per share) will be converted and that the final installment payment will be in shares. Note that the company, which has a very small public float, is in the process of selling up to 10 million restricted shares at $1.				

<table>
<tr><td>Endexx</td><td>(EDXC)</td><td>$0.062</td><td>$12M Market Cap</td><td>Pink Sheet</td></tr>
<tr><td colspan="5">EDXC recently became current in its filings and is a technology provider, offering its M3Hub to dispensaries to help with regulatory compliance, Autospense vending machines and its recently acquired THCFinder.com to help consumers locate dispensaries.</td></tr>
<tr><td>FusionPharm</td><td>(FSPM)</td><td>$0.22</td><td>$32M Market Cap</td><td>Pink Sheet</td></tr>
<tr><td colspan="5">FSPM manufactures PharmPods, container car growing systems. The vast majority of the value of the company is in convertible preferred stock held by insiders.</td></tr>
<tr><td>GrowLife</td><td>(PHOT)</td><td>$0.083</td><td>$72M Market Cap</td><td>OTC</td></tr>
<tr><td colspan="5">PHOT, which has been one of the strongest performers in 2012, operates seven hydroponics stores across the country, after a transformational acquisition earlier this year. The company traditionally sold equipment, such as the Phototron, but it has broadened its offering to include products such as soil and nutrients. PHOT, which announced its GrowLife Infrastructure Funding & Technology (GIFT) program late in the year, has created a joint venture that will give it up to $40M or more in funds to help finance the program and that will allows growers to spread the cost of infrastructure over time. The company also announced a kiosk-based solution (GrowLife Financial) to help dispensaries with payment, cash management, and regulatory compliance. Note that the market cap assumes the conversion of convertible notes and warrants.</td></tr>
<tr><td>GW Pharma</td><td>(GWPH)</td><td>$35.04</td><td>$518M Market Cap</td><td>NASDAQ</td></tr>
<tr><td colspan="5">UK-based biotech GW Pharma listed its ADRs on the NASDAQ in May. GWPRF continues to be an alternative vehicle to invest in the company, which went public in 2001. The company has enjoyed a strong 2013 by capitalizing on increased investor awareness of its current product, Sativex, as well as on its substantial pipeline. GWPH is in two different Phase 3 trials for Sativex, which is approved in 22 other countries, and it is studying Epidiolex for childhood epilepsy. Following the IPO, the company has substantial cash: approximately $60M as of 9/30/13.</td></tr>
<tr><td>Hemp, Inc.</td><td>(HEMP)</td><td>$0.013</td><td>$46M Market Cap</td><td>Pink Sheet</td></tr>
<tr><td colspan="5">HEMP was created in 2011 when Bruce Perlowin left Medical Marijuana, Inc. The company has not had material revenue, and its business model isn't clear. The market cap is inflated by the presence of two separate convertible preferred stocks.</td></tr>
<tr><td>mCig</td><td>(MCIG)</td><td>$0.081</td><td>$41M Market Cap</td><td>OTC</td></tr>
<tr><td colspan="5">MCIG was created when its CEO acquired an existing company rather than pursue a technology licensing arrangement. The company launched a $10 vaporizer in October that is designed to handle both wax and plant material. The market cap takes into account the 23 million preferred shares held by the CEO, which can be converted back into common stock next year.</td></tr>
</table>

<table>
<tr><td>Medbox</td><td>(MDBX)</td><td>$19.51</td><td>$580M Market Cap</td><td>Pink Sheet</td></tr>
<tr><td colspan="5">MDBX is focused on providing automated dispensing systems. The company has filed an S-1 with the SEC and is attempting to sell 3 million shares between $16–20, and other owners, such as the founder and the CEO, also selling some shares. There are 3 million preferred shares convertible into 15 million common shares, and insiders own most of the common shares as well. MDBX has been selling restricted stock at $5 for most of the year. The company announced three acquisitions this year, but two ended in litigation.</td></tr>
<tr><td>Medical Cannabis Payment Solutions</td><td>(REFG)</td><td>$0.21</td><td>$16M Market Cap</td><td>Pink Sheet</td></tr>
<tr><td colspan="5">REFG is a reverse merger from 2013 that announced two software applications aimed at helping dispensary owners, and it is expecting to implement a "seed-to-sale" product as well. At the time of publication, the company had not filed its Q3 disclosure on time.</td></tr>
<tr><td>Medical Marijuana, Inc.</td><td>(MJNA)</td><td>$0.11</td><td>$104M Market Cap</td><td>Pink Sheet</td></tr>
<tr><td colspan="5">The first publicly traded cannabis stock, MJNA has shifted its business model to that of a direct-marketing company focused on CBD-based products offered by its HempMedsPX subsidiary. It also owns the rights to CanChew CBD gum and is pursuing clinical trials for a combination THC/CBD gum. The company is controlled by CannaBank and its affilliates, which own 51% of the stock.</td></tr>
<tr><td>MediSwipe</td><td>(MWIP)</td><td>$0.017</td><td>$11M Market Cap</td><td>OTC</td></tr>
<tr><td colspan="5">MWIP offers hemp-based drinks and a cloud-based patient data service that is HIPAA compliant. The company announced a 10:1 reverse merger that is expected to be effective in late November.</td></tr>
<tr><td>Nuvilex</td><td>(NVLX)</td><td>0.125</td><td>$67 M Market Cap</td><td>OTC</td></tr>
<tr><td colspan="5">NVLX repositioned itself as a biotech company and announced intentions for its subsidiary, Medical Marijuana Sciences, to study marijuana for brain cancer.</td></tr>
<tr><td>Plandia Biotechnology</td><td>(PLPL)</td><td>$0.485</td><td>$52M Market Cap</td><td>OTC</td></tr>
<tr><td colspan="5">PLPL announced its intention in late October for its subsidiary, Cannabis Biosciences, to develop a cannabinoid extract that removes THC.</td></tr>
<tr><td>Puget Technologies</td><td>(PUGE)</td><td>$1.65</td><td>$48M Market Cap</td><td>OTC</td></tr>
<tr><td colspan="5">PUGE was a late-in-the-year reverse merger that has announced several medical marijuana research projects.</td></tr>
<tr><td>Terra Tech</td><td>(TRTC)</td><td>$0.07</td><td>$17M Market Cap</td><td>OTC</td></tr>
<tr><td colspan="5">TRTC has traditionally been an equipment provider, but it is actively attempting to become a grower of hemp or medical marijuana. The company acquired an organic produce company in 2012.</td></tr>
</table>

ARCVIEW INVESTOR NETWORK

Invest in the next great American industry.

ArcView Investor Network Meeting, NYC June 2013

Ross Kirsh of Quark Distribution pitches investors on his cannabis packaging company

AS FEATURED ON:

npr Marketplace
MSNBC
YAHOO! Finance
FORTUNE
The New York Times
THE WALL STREET JOURNAL.
msn Money
MarketWatch
The Seattle Times

"As a serial entrepreneur, angel investor, and advisor for many years, I am always looking to support innovation and change by backing the best entrepreneurs. I'm so impressed by the caliber of the entrepreneurs, as well as the investors at ArcView. I am thrilled to be finding viable investments on the ground floor of a new industry that is also making the world a freer and safer place."

-- Sean Trigony, ArcView investor member

THE ARCVIEW GROUP

The ArcView Investor Network is a project of The ArcView Group. www.arcviewgoup.com

If you are an accredited investor looking to invest 50K+ into early-stage private companies in this sector, or if your company seeks capital, partnerships, and mentorship, please visit ArcViewGroup.com

Finance

Perhaps the preeminent challenge for companies in the legal marijuana industry is access to banking services based on provisions of the Bank Secrecy Act. Banks are regulated by the Federal Reserve Bank systems and by the US Treasury Department. As another layer of federal enforcement actions against legal marijuana businesses, pressure from these sources has in many cases shut out legal marijuana businesses from vital banking and payment-processing services.

Many companies, including ancillary businesses, have suffered from restrictions that the majority of banks place on doing business with the industry. Banks have come under increasing pressure from federal sources to avoid dealing with marijuana companies. Threats of the loss of federal depository insurance or the accusation of dealing with companies in violation of drug laws has compelled most banks to refuse to offer services to legal marijuana companies. The crackdown is so severe that even some ancillary companies have reported account closures due to bank managers seeing the word “canna” in the company name.

Even though they may be in full compliance with state laws, the inability to deposit cash, to process electronic payments, or to obtain loans and cash management services greatly hinders many companies in the industry. These limitations can force them to transact on a cash-only basis, meaning that they may hold large cash balances on company premises. Coupled with potentially maintaining valuable cannabis inventories, the concentration of liquid assets increases the risk of exposure to theft. Limiting transactions to cash payment can also hinder sales and vendor relationships.

Another burden to some dispensaries that have been forced to transact in cash has been the loss of access to armored car services. Some armored car companies

reported receiving instructions from the DEA to cease dealing with dispensaries in California and Colorado. The lack of armored car services has further exacerbated the risks that dispensaries have faced by holding stores of cash.

As identified earlier, even the federal government has recognized this dilemma, which results from the contradiction of state and federal laws, and is looking for resolution. The recent Senate Judiciary hearing revealed that the US Departments of Justice and Treasury are working to find ways to facilitate marijuana business banking.

Some merchant payment services companies have found opportunity in solving legal cannabis business banking problems. They have developed a system outside of the conventional banking circuit to process credit card transactions for both business-to-business and business-to-consumer payments.

Industry Leader Profile: Lance Ott

Lack of access to banking and payment processing services is a key constraint that hampers many legal marijuana businesses. Most banks won't do business with dispensaries, processors, and cultivators due to concerns about the exposure to money laundering charges under the Bank Secrecy Act. As a result, many cannabis companies are forced to transact primarily on a cash basis, which both limits commerce and increases security risks. Some merchant payment processors have developed creative alternatives for processing legal marijuana business payments. Recent activity at the federal level from the Department of Justice and banking regulators indicates that it is likely they will solve this problem in the interest of public safety soon. In an upcoming additional feature, ArcView Market Research profiles Lance Ott of Guardian Data Systems, which helps cannabis companies overcome the limits of cash transactions through the provision of payment processing service.

APPENDICES

Odgen Memo

U.S. Department of Justice

Office of the Deputy Attorney General

The Deputy Attorney General

Washington, D.C. 20530

October 19, 2009

MEMORANDUM FOR SELECTED UNITED STATES ATTORNEYS

FROM: David W. Ogden
Deputy Attorney General

SUBJECT: Investigations and Prosecutions in States
Authorizing the Medical Use of Marijuana

This memorandum provides clarification and guidance to federal prosecutors in States that have enacted laws authorizing the medical use of marijuana. These laws vary in their substantive provisions and in the extent of state regulatory oversight, both among the enacting States and among local jurisdictions within those States. Rather than developing different guidelines for every possible variant of state and local law, this memorandum provides uniform guidance to focus federal investigations and prosecutions in these States on core federal enforcement priorities.

The Department of Justice is committed to the enforcement of the Controlled Substances Act in all States. Congress has determined that marijuana is a dangerous drug, and the illegal distribution and sale of marijuana is a serious crime and provides a significant source of revenue to large-scale criminal enterprises, gangs, and cartels. One timely example underscores the importance of our efforts to prosecute significant marijuana traffickers: marijuana distribution in the United States remains the single largest source of revenue for the Mexican cartels.

The Department is also committed to making efficient and rational use of its limited investigative and prosecutorial resources. In general, United States Attorneys are vested with "plenary authority with regard to federal criminal matters" within their districts. USAM 9-2.001. In exercising this authority, United States Attorneys are "invested by statute and delegation from the Attorney General with the broadest discretion in the exercise of such authority." *Id.* This authority should, of course, be exercised consistent with Department priorities and guidance.

The prosecution of significant traffickers of illegal drugs, including marijuana, and the disruption of illegal drug manufacturing and trafficking networks continues to be a core priority in the Department's efforts against narcotics and dangerous drugs, and the Department's investigative and prosecutorial resources should be directed towards these objectives. As a general matter, pursuit of these priorities should not focus federal resources in your States on individuals whose actions are in clear and unambiguous compliance with existing state laws providing for the medical use of marijuana. For example, prosecution of individuals with cancer or other serious illnesses who use marijuana as part of a recommended treatment regimen consistent with applicable state law, or those caregivers in clear and unambiguous compliance with existing state law who provide such individuals with marijuana, is unlikely to be an efficient use of limited federal resources. On the other hand, prosecution of commercial enterprises that unlawfully market and sell marijuana for profit continues to be an enforcement priority of the Department. To be sure, claims of compliance with state or local law may mask operations inconsistent with the terms, conditions, or purposes of those laws, and federal law enforcement should not be deterred by such assertions when otherwise pursuing the Department's core enforcement priorities.

Typically, when any of the following characteristics is present, the conduct will not be in clear and unambiguous compliance with applicable state law and may indicate illegal drug trafficking activity of potential federal interest:

- unlawful possession or unlawful use of firearms;
- violence;
- sales to minors;
- financial and marketing activities inconsistent with the terms, conditions, or purposes of state law, including evidence of money laundering activity and/or financial gains or excessive amounts of cash inconsistent with purported compliance with state or local law;
- amounts of marijuana inconsistent with purported compliance with state or local law;
- illegal possession or sale of other controlled substances; or
- ties to other criminal enterprises.

Of course, no State can authorize violations of federal law, and the list of factors above is not intended to describe exhaustively when a federal prosecution may be warranted. Accordingly, in prosecutions under the Controlled Substances Act, federal prosecutors are not expected to charge, prove, or otherwise establish any state law violations. Indeed, this memorandum does not alter in any way the Department's authority to enforce federal law, including laws prohibiting the manufacture, production, distribution, possession, or use of marijuana on federal property. This guidance regarding resource allocation does not "legalize" marijuana or provide a legal defense to a violation of federal law, nor is it intended to create any privileges, benefits, or rights, substantive or procedural, enforceable by any individual, party or witness in any administrative, civil, or criminal matter. Nor does clear and unambiguous compliance with state law or the absence of one or all of the above factors create a legal defense to a violation of the Controlled Substances Act. Rather, this memorandum is intended solely as a guide to the exercise of investigative and prosecutorial discretion.

Memorandum for Selected United States Attorneys Page 3
Subject: Investigations and Prosecutions in States Authorizing the Medical Use of Marijuana

Finally, nothing herein precludes investigation or prosecution where there is a reasonable basis to believe that compliance with state law is being invoked as a pretext for the production or distribution of marijuana for purposes not authorized by state law. Nor does this guidance preclude investigation or prosecution, even when there is clear and unambiguous compliance with existing state law, in particular circumstances where investigation or prosecution otherwise serves important federal interests.

Your offices should continue to review marijuana cases for prosecution on a case-by-case basis, consistent with the guidance on resource allocation and federal priorities set forth herein, the consideration of requests for federal assistance from state and local law enforcement authorities, and the Principles of Federal Prosecution.

cc: All United States Attorneys

Lanny A. Breuer
Assistant Attorney General
Criminal Division

B. Todd Jones
United States Attorney
District of Minnesota
Chair, Attorney General's Advisory Committee

Michele M. Leonhart
Acting Administrator
Drug Enforcement Administration

H. Marshall Jarrett
Director
Executive Office for United States Attorneys

Kevin L. Perkins
Assistant Director
Criminal Investigative Division
Federal Bureau of Investigation

Cole Memo

U.S. Department of Justice

Office of the Deputy Attorney General

The Deputy Attorney General

Washington, D.C. 20530

August 29, 2013

MEMORANDUM FOR ALL UNITED STATES ATTORNEYS

FROM: James M. Cole
Deputy Attorney General

SUBJECT: Guidance Regarding Marijuana Enforcement

In October 2009 and June 2011, the Department issued guidance to federal prosecutors concerning marijuana enforcement under the Controlled Substances Act (CSA). This memorandum updates that guidance in light of state ballot initiatives that legalize under state law the possession of small amounts of marijuana and provide for the regulation of marijuana production, processing, and sale. The guidance set forth herein applies to all federal enforcement activity, including civil enforcement and criminal investigations and prosecutions, concerning marijuana in all states.

As the Department noted in its previous guidance, Congress has determined that marijuana is a dangerous drug and that the illegal distribution and sale of marijuana is a serious crime that provides a significant source of revenue to large-scale criminal enterprises, gangs, and cartels. The Department of Justice is committed to enforcement of the CSA consistent with those determinations. The Department is also committed to using its limited investigative and prosecutorial resources to address the most significant threats in the most effective, consistent, and rational way. In furtherance of those objectives, as several states enacted laws relating to the use of marijuana for medical purposes, the Department in recent years has focused its efforts on certain enforcement priorities that are particularly important to the federal government:

- Preventing the distribution of marijuana to minors;
- Preventing revenue from the sale of marijuana from going to criminal enterprises, gangs, and cartels;
- Preventing the diversion of marijuana from states where it is legal under state law in some form to other states;
- Preventing state-authorized marijuana activity from being used as a cover or pretext for the trafficking of other illegal drugs or other illegal activity;

- Preventing violence and the use of firearms in the cultivation and distribution of marijuana;
- Preventing drugged driving and the exacerbation of other adverse public health consequences associated with marijuana use;
- Preventing the growing of marijuana on public lands and the attendant public safety and environmental dangers posed by marijuana production on public lands; and
- Preventing marijuana possession or use on federal property.

These priorities will continue to guide the Department's enforcement of the CSA against marijuana-related conduct. Thus, this memorandum serves as guidance to Department attorneys and law enforcement to focus their enforcement resources and efforts, including prosecution, on persons or organizations whose conduct interferes with any one or more of these priorities, regardless of state law.[1]

Outside of these enforcement priorities, the federal government has traditionally relied on states and local law enforcement agencies to address marijuana activity through enforcement of their own narcotics laws. For example, the Department of Justice has not historically devoted resources to prosecuting individuals whose conduct is limited to possession of small amounts of marijuana for personal use on private property. Instead, the Department has left such lower-level or localized activity to state and local authorities and has stepped in to enforce the CSA only when the use, possession, cultivation, or distribution of marijuana has threatened to cause one of the harms identified above.

The enactment of state laws that endeavor to authorize marijuana production, distribution, and possession by establishing a regulatory scheme for these purposes affects this traditional joint federal-state approach to narcotics enforcement. The Department's guidance in this memorandum rests on its expectation that states and local governments that have enacted laws authorizing marijuana-related conduct will implement strong and effective regulatory and enforcement systems that will address the threat those state laws could pose to public safety, public health, and other law enforcement interests. A system adequate to that task must not only contain robust controls and procedures on paper; it must also be effective in practice. Jurisdictions that have implemented systems that provide for regulation of marijuana activity

---

[1] These enforcement priorities are listed in general terms; each encompasses a variety of conduct that may merit civil or criminal enforcement of the CSA. By way of example only, the Department's interest in preventing the distribution of marijuana to minors would call for enforcement not just when an individual or entity sells or transfers marijuana to a minor, but also when marijuana trafficking takes place near an area associated with minors; when marijuana or marijuana-infused products are marketed in a manner to appeal to minors; or when marijuana is being diverted, directly or indirectly, and purposefully or otherwise, to minors.

must provide the necessary resources and demonstrate the willingness to enforce their laws and regulations in a manner that ensures they do not undermine federal enforcement priorities.

In jurisdictions that have enacted laws legalizing marijuana in some form and that have also implemented strong and effective regulatory and enforcement systems to control the cultivation, distribution, sale, and possession of marijuana, conduct in compliance with those laws and regulations is less likely to threaten the federal priorities set forth above. Indeed, a robust system may affirmatively address those priorities by, for example, implementing effective measures to prevent diversion of marijuana outside of the regulated system and to other states, prohibiting access to marijuana by minors, and replacing an illicit marijuana trade that funds criminal enterprises with a tightly regulated market in which revenues are tracked and accounted for. In those circumstances, consistent with the traditional allocation of federal-state efforts in this area, enforcement of state law by state and local law enforcement and regulatory bodies should remain the primary means of addressing marijuana-related activity. If state enforcement efforts are not sufficiently robust to protect against the harms set forth above, the federal government may seek to challenge the regulatory structure itself in addition to continuing to bring individual enforcement actions, including criminal prosecutions, focused on those harms.

The Department's previous memoranda specifically addressed the exercise of prosecutorial discretion in states with laws authorizing marijuana cultivation and distribution for medical use. In those contexts, the Department advised that it likely was not an efficient use of federal resources to focus enforcement efforts on seriously ill individuals, or on their individual caregivers. In doing so, the previous guidance drew a distinction between the seriously ill and their caregivers, on the one hand, and large-scale, for-profit commercial enterprises, on the other, and advised that the latter continued to be appropriate targets for federal enforcement and prosecution. In drawing this distinction, the Department relied on the common-sense judgment that the size of a marijuana operation was a reasonable proxy for assessing whether marijuana trafficking implicates the federal enforcement priorities set forth above.

As explained above, however, both the existence of a strong and effective state regulatory system, and an operation's compliance with such a system, may allay the threat that an operation's size poses to federal enforcement interests. Accordingly, in exercising prosecutorial discretion, prosecutors should not consider the size or commercial nature of a marijuana operation alone as a proxy for assessing whether marijuana trafficking implicates the Department's enforcement priorities listed above. Rather, prosecutors should continue to review marijuana cases on a case-by-case basis and weigh all available information and evidence, including, but not limited to, whether the operation is demonstrably in compliance with a strong and effective state regulatory system. A marijuana operation's large scale or for-profit nature may be a relevant consideration for assessing the extent to which it undermines a particular federal enforcement priority. The primary question in all cases – and in all jurisdictions – should be whether the conduct at issue implicates one or more of the enforcement priorities listed above.

Memorandum for All United States Attorneys
Subject: Guidance Regarding Marijuana Enforcement

Page 4

As with the Department's previous statements on this subject, this memorandum is intended solely as a guide to the exercise of investigative and prosecutorial discretion. This memorandum does not alter in any way the Department's authority to enforce federal law, including federal laws relating to marijuana, regardless of state law. Neither the guidance herein nor any state or local law provides a legal defense to a violation of federal law, including any civil or criminal violation of the CSA. Even in jurisdictions with strong and effective regulatory systems, evidence that particular conduct threatens federal priorities will subject that person or entity to federal enforcement action, based on the circumstances. This memorandum is not intended to, does not, and may not be relied upon to create any rights, substantive or procedural, enforceable at law by any party in any matter civil or criminal. It applies prospectively to the exercise of prosecutorial discretion in future cases and does not provide defendants or subjects of enforcement action with a basis for reconsideration of any pending civil action or criminal prosecution. Finally, nothing herein precludes investigation or prosecution, even in the absence of any one of the factors listed above, in particular circumstances where investigation and prosecution otherwise serves an important federal interest.

cc: Mythili Raman
Acting Assistant Attorney General, Criminal Division

Loretta E. Lynch
United States Attorney
Eastern District of New York
Chair, Attorney General's Advisory Committee

Michele M. Leonhart
Administrator
Drug Enforcement Administration

H. Marshall Jarrett
Director
Executive Office for United States Attorneys

Ronald T. Hosko
Assistant Director
Criminal Investigative Division
Federal Bureau of Investigation

Cole Testimony to Senate Judiciary Committee

Department of Justice

STATEMENT OF

JAMES M. COLE
DEPUTY ATTORNEY GENERAL

BEFORE THE

COMMITTEE ON THE JUDICIARY
UNITED STATES SENATE

FOR A HEARING ENTITLED

"CONFLICTS BETWEEN STATE AND FEDERAL MARIJUANA LAWS"

PRESENTED ON

SEPTEMBER 10, 2013

Testimony of James M. Cole
Deputy Attorney General
United States Department of Justice
Before the United States Senate Committee on the Judiciary
September 10, 2013

Good afternoon Chairman Leahy, Ranking Member Grassley, and distinguished Members of the Committee. I am pleased to speak with you about the guidance that the Department recently issued to all United States Attorneys regarding marijuana enforcement efforts. That guidance instructs our prosecutors to continue to enforce federal priorities, such as preventing sales of marijuana by criminal enterprises, preventing violence and the use of firearms in the cultivation and distribution of marijuana, preventing distribution to minors, and preventing the cultivation of marijuana on public lands – priorities that we historically have focused on for many years – and also notes that we will continue to rely on state and local authorities to effectively enforce their own drug laws as we work together to protect our communities.

I. Introduction

As you know, the relevant federal statute, the Controlled Substances Act of 1970 (CSA), among other prohibitions, makes it a federal crime to possess, grow, or distribute marijuana, and to open, rent, or maintain a place of business for any of these purposes.

For many years, all 50 states have enacted uniform drug control laws or similar provisions that mirrored the CSA with respect to their treatment of marijuana and made the possession, cultivation, and distribution of marijuana a state criminal offense. With such overlapping statutory authorities, the federal government and the states traditionally worked as partners in the field of drug enforcement. Federal law enforcement historically has targeted sophisticated drug traffickers and organizations, while state and local authorities generally have focused their enforcement efforts, under their state laws, on more localized and lower-level drug activity.

Starting with California in 1996, several states have authorized the cultivation, distribution, possession, and use of marijuana for medical purposes, under state law. Today, twenty-one states and the District of Columbia legalize marijuana use for medical purposes under state law, including six states that enacted medical marijuana legislation in 2013.

Throughout this time period, the Department of Justice has continued to work with its state and local partners, but focused its own efforts and resources on priorities that are particularly important to the federal government. The priorities that have guided our efforts are:

- Preventing the distribution of marijuana to minors;
- Preventing revenue from the sale of marijuana from going to criminal enterprises, gangs, and cartels;
- Preventing the diversion of marijuana from states where it is legal under state law in some form to other states;
- Preventing state-authorized marijuana activity from being used as a cover or pretext for the trafficking of other illegal drugs or other illegal activity;
- Preventing violence and the use of firearms in the cultivation and distribution of marijuana;
- Preventing drugged driving and the exacerbation of other adverse public health consequences associated with marijuana use;
- Preventing the growing of marijuana on public lands and the attendant public safety and environmental dangers posed by marijuana production on public lands; and
- Preventing marijuana possession or use on federal property.

Examples of our efforts have included cases against individuals and organizations who were using the state laws as a pretext to engage in large-scale trafficking of marijuana to other states; enforcement against those who were operating marijuana businesses near schools, parks, and playgrounds; and enforcement against those who were wreaking environmental damage by growing marijuana on our public lands. On the other hand, the Department has not historically devoted our finite resources to prosecuting individuals whose conduct is limited to possession of marijuana for personal use on private property.

II. The Department's Updated Marijuana Enforcement Guidance

In November 2012, voters in Colorado and Washington State passed ballot initiatives that legalized, under state law, the possession of small amounts of marijuana, and made Colorado and Washington the first states to provide for the regulation of marijuana production, processing, and sale for recreational purposes. The Department of Justice has reviewed these ballot initiatives in the context of our enforcement priorities.

On August 29, 2013, the Department notified the Governors of Colorado and Washington that we were not at this time seeking to preempt their states' ballot initiatives. We advised the Governors that we expected their states to implement strong and effective regulatory and enforcement systems to fully protect against the public health and safety harms that are the focus

2

of our marijuana enforcement priorities, and that the Department would continue to investigate and prosecute cases in Colorado and Washington in which the underlying conduct implicated our federal interests. The Department reserved its right to challenge the state laws at a later time, in the event any of the stated harms do materialize – either in spite of a strict regulatory scheme, or because of the lack of one.

That same day, the Department issued a guidance memorandum to all United States Attorneys directing our prosecutors to continue to fully investigate and prosecute marijuana cases that implicate any one of our eight federal enforcement priorities. This memorandum applies to our prosecutors in all 50 states and guides the exercise of prosecutorial discretion against individuals and organizations who violate any of our stated federal interests, no matter where they live or what the laws in their states may permit. Outside of these enforcement priorities, however, the Department will continue to rely on state and local authorities to address marijuana activity through enforcement of their own drug laws. This updated guidance is consistent with our efforts to maximize our investigative and prosecutorial resources during this time of budget challenges, and with the more general message the Attorney General delivered last month to all federal prosecutors, emphasizing the importance of quality priorities for all cases we bring, with an eye toward promoting public safety, deterrence, and fairness.

Our updated guidance also makes one overarching point clear: the Department of Justice expects that states and local governments that have enacted laws authorizing marijuana-related conduct will implement effective regulatory and enforcement systems to protect federal priorities and the health and safety of every citizen. As the guidance explains, a jurisdiction's regulatory scheme must be tough in practice, not just on paper. It must include strong enforcement efforts, backed by adequate funding.

We are emphasizing comprehensive regulation and well-funded state enforcement because such a system will complement the continued enforcement of state drug laws by state and local enforcement officials, in a manner that should allay the threat that a state-sanctioned marijuana operation might otherwise pose to federal enforcement interests. Indeed, a robust system may affirmatively address those federal priorities by, for example, implementing effective measures to prevent diversion of marijuana outside of the regulated system and to other states, prohibiting access to marijuana by minors, and replacing an illicit marijuana trade that funds criminal enterprises with a tightly regulated market in which revenues are tracked and accounted for. In those circumstances, consistent with the traditional allocation of federal-state efforts in this area, enforcement of state law by state and local law enforcement and regulatory bodies should remain a necessary part of addressing marijuana-related activity.

III. Conclusion

The Department of Justice is committed to enforcing the CSA in all states, and we are grateful for the dedicated work of our Drug Enforcement Administration agents, our federal prosecutors, and our state and local partners in protecting our communities from the dangers of illegal drug trafficking. The Administration also remains committed to minimizing the public health and safety consequences of marijuana use, focusing on prevention, treatment, and support for recovery.

As our updated guidance reflects, we are continuing our practice of targeting conduct that implicates federal priorities and causes harm, regardless of state law. We expect our state and local partners to continue to do so as well. In those jurisdictions that have enacted laws that legalize and seek to regulate marijuana for some purposes, this means that strong and effective regulatory and enforcement systems must address the threat those state laws could pose to public safety, public health, and other law enforcement interests.

I look forward to taking your questions.

About the Editor & Lead Researcher

Steve Berg - Editor

Steve Berg, in addition to being ArcView Market Research's editor for the 2nd Edition of The State of Legal Marijuana Markets is also the founder of BRC LLC, a financial consultancy focused on capital formation and business strategy for new and expanding businesses. Steve was instrumental in the creation and development of the ArcView Investor Network, a coalition of investors in the legal cannabis industry.

With over 22 years experience in investment banking, capital markets, and venture finance, Steve works with companies and investors in the legal cannabis industry to optimize business and financial success. Formerly a Managing Director at Wells Fargo Bank's capital markets group, Steve also worked at UBS and Banque Paribas in New York. He was an innovator of structuring funding and investment solutions for key commercial and private bank clients in credit, equity and commodity markets. Steve has an MBA from New York University as well as a B.S. in Finance from San Francisco State University.

Kris Lotlikar - Lead Researcher

Kris Lotlikar was lead researcher for the 2nd Edition of The State of Legal Marijuana Markets. He hired and led a team of experienced researchers to compile the market data and develop the market size estimates and projections. This is Kris' second report on marijuana markets having produced the heralded 1st Edition in 2011 which is the most oft-cited report on the cannabis markets.

Kris has over a decade of experience following marijuana policy and reforms since co-founding and serving as the first executive director of Student for Sensible Drug Policy in 1998. Since then Kris has been a successful entrepreneur and consultant. Kris is founder and President of Renewable Choice Energy, one of the leading renewable energy providers in the country with over 50 Fortune 500 clients. He brings years of experience operating in newly emerging and fast growing markets in the U.S. and is a prominent proponent of sustainable and mission-driven businesses. Kris' unique experience and background makes him one of the top experts in the country on marijuana businesses and markets.

CPSIA information can be obtained
at www.ICGtesting.com
Printed in the USA
LVXC02n0254120314
376988LV00001B/1
9780991366507